Iona and Peter Opie

Children's Games in Street and Playground

Volume 1: Chasing, Catching, Seeking

Floris Books

First published in 1969 by Oxford University Press
This edition, in two volumes, published in 2008 by Floris Books

© Iona and Peter Opie 1969

British Library CIP Data available

ISBN 978-086315-666-3

Printed in Great Britain
By Bell & Bain Ltd, Glasgow

Contents

Foreword 11
Authors' Preface to Original Edition 13
Introduction 19

1. Starting a game 37

The preliminaries to a game can be a sport in themselves

AVOIDANCE OF DISLIKED ROLE. Players take action, when a game is proposed, to exempt themselves from starting in the principal role 38

HE-NAMES. The name of the player who has a certain power in the game is subject to regional variation 40

SELECTION MADE BY CHANCE. Appointment of a player to the disliked role felt to be fairest if made a matter of luck 45

ODD MAN OUT. A method of deciding who is to take the disliked role by flashing fingers 47

DIPPING. The method of determining who shall take the disliked role by counting-out with a verbal formula 50

DIPS. Examples of the formulas — usually nonsense rhymes or phrases — that are used for counting-out 52

CHINESE COUNTING. The use of gibberish rhymes for counting-out 68

COUNTING FISTS OR FEET. Players' fists or feet counted-out, rather than their persons 92

PARTICIPATION DIPS. Formulas in which the players being counted-out themselves affect the number of counts 96

2. Chasing games 103

Games in which a player tries to touch others who are running freely in a prescribed area

TOUCH. The basic game in which a player touched by the chaser becomes chaser in his place 103

THE LANGUAGE OF THE CHASE. Regional variation in the names for touch-chasing 104

PLAYERS RESTRICTED TO PARTICULAR WAY OF MOVING 109

CHASES IN A DIFFICULT ENVIRONMENT 111

Touch Conveyed by Substitute for Hand
BULL. The touch made with the hands but carried in such a way that they
    represent something else (cf. 'Widdy' p. 138f; 'Bully Horn' p. 139) 112
WHACKO. Touch made with twisted scarf (cf. 'Whackem' Vol.2 p. 44) 113
DADDY WHACKER. Touch made with stick or whip 114
BALL HE. Touch made with ball (cf. 'Kingy' p. 140f) 115
THREE LIVES. Ball or other object in effect takes the place of the chaser 116

The Touch having Noxious Effect
FRENCH TOUCH. The part of the body where player was touched has to be
    held until another player has been touched 117
THE DREADED LURGI. The touch alleged to be noxious 118

Immunity from the Touch
TOUCHWOOD. TOUCH IRON. TOUCH COLOUR. COLOURS. Immunity obtained by
    contact with particular substance or quality 120
OFF-GROUND HE. Immunity obtained by being above ground level 124
BUDGE HE. Twos and threes. Immunity obtained transiently by being at par-
    ticular spot 125
TOM TIDDLER'S GROUND. Immunity lost when designated area entered 127
SHADOW TOUCH. Immunity obtained by not having a shadow 129
THREE STOOPS AND RUN FOR EVER. Immunity obtained through posture 130

Proliferation of Chasers
HELP CHASE. Chaser continues chasing throughout game, and those he
    touches become chasers with him 134
CHAIN HE. As 'Help chase', but chasers have to link hands while chasing (cf.
    'Stag' p. 176ff) 134
VESTIGIAL FEATURES IN 'CHAIN HE' VARIANTS. Chasers have to return to base
    when a player is touched 136
KINGY. The touch made with a ball (cf. 'Ball He' p. 115f) 140

Suspense Starts
POISON. Players do not know when chaser will begin chasing 145
CRUSTS AND CRUMBS. Players do not know whether they are to be chasers or
    runners (cf. 'Hesitation Starts' to races Vol.2 p. 22; 'Birds, Beasts, Fishes, or
    Flowers' Vol.2 p. 129) 146
LITTLE BLACK MAN. Start is delayed until those to be chased give the word (cf.
    'Black Peter' p. 178f) 147

WHAT'S THE TIME, MR. WOLF? I'LL FOLLOW MY MOTHER TO MARKET. JOHN BROWN. DEAD MAN ARISE. Players do not know when chaser will begin chasing, and suspense is intensified by dramatics (cf. 'Sheep, Sheep, Come Home' pp. 180f; and Acting Games, Vol.2 p. 157) 148

BOGEY. Players do not know when chaser will begin chasing nor do they know his whereabouts 154

Players being Chased Assist each Other

CROSS TOUCH. Players divert chaser to themselves 156

STUCK IN THE MUD. UNDERGROUND TIG. TUNNEL TOUCH. TICKY LEAPFROG. GLUE-POTS. Players can rescue those who have been touched 156

Chaser at Disadvantage

CAT AND MOUSE. Chaser's way is obstructed (cf. 'Fox and Chickens' in Acting Games, Vol.2 p. 164) 161

FOX AND CHICKENS. Chaser has to hop while rest may run 163

BLIND MAN'S BUFF. JINGLING. Chaser or chasers are unable to see (cf. 'How Far to London?' Vol.2 p. 165) 165

FROG IN THE MIDDLE. Chaser has to remain seated 169

3. Catching games 172

Games in which a player attempts to intercept other players who are obliged to move from one designated place to another (often from one side of a road to another), and who if caught either take the catcher's place or, more often, assist him

RUNNING ACROSS. Players at two different points have to change places simultaneously and try to do so without being caught 172

CHINESE WALL. Players have to cross ground all together when commanded 174

WALL TO WALL. Players have to keep moving between two places but can do so in their own time 175

STAG. Players have to move between two places when commanded, and catcher links hands with anyone caught (cf. 'Chain He' p. 134f) 176

BLACK PETER. SHEEP, SHEEP, COME HOME. Catcher is made out to be fearsome, but players still have to cross when challenged or commanded (cf. 'Little Black Man' p. 147; 'What's the time, Mr Wolf?' pp. 148; 'I'll Follow my Mother to Market' p. 150f) 178

FARMER, FARMER, MAY WE CROSS YOUR GOLDEN RIVER? As 'Black Peter' but players wearing a named colour cross safely (cf. 'Colours' Vol.2 p. 30) 182

BAR THE DOOR. The catcher names a player to attempt the crossing on his own 185

COCKARUSHA. As 'Bar the Door', but everybody hops 186

CIGARETTES. As 'Bar the Door', but catcher does not know whom he is challenging to cross on his own 187

BRITISH BULLDOG (1). The catcher has to use force to stop a player from crossing 188

BRITISH BULLDOG (2). As 'Bar the Door', but catcher has to use force to stop player from crossing 191

WALK THE PLANK OR JOIN THE CREW. As above, but challenged player given the option to submit 192

KINGS, QUEENS, AND JACKS. As 'British Bulldog' (1) but catcher names the type of movement (cf. 'Dance, Fight, or Windmill' Vol.2 p. 58) 193

PRISONERS' BASE. Players from opposing teams try to intercept opponents before they catch or release other players 193

FRENCH AND ENGLISH. Players attempt to catch members of opposing side before they can steal possessions or release prisoners (cf. 'Relievo' p. 225f) 197

4. Seeking games   199

Games in which a player tries to find others, who obtain safety by remaining out of sight or by getting back to the starting place

Dissimilar Number of Players Hiding and Seeking

HIDE-AND-SEEK. Single player looks for the rest 204

ONE MAN PLUS. Single seeker is assisted by those he finds 206

MAN HUNTING. All players seek a single hider 207

SARDINES. All players individually seek a single hider and join him when found 208

I DRAW A SNAKE UPON YOUR BACK. The seeker is chosen by a method embodying guessing (cf. 'Stroke the Baby' Vol.2 p. 145) which gives the hiders an equitable time to hide 208

BLOCK. The seeker has to race anyone he sees back to the starting-place 212

BUZZ OFF. Hiders reaching starting-place safely free those already caught (cf. 'Relievo' p. 225f) 215

COME TO COVENTRY. Hiders are made captive simply by being seen, but can be freed merely by the sight of the rescuer 216

WHIP. Hiders remain where found 216

TIN CAN TOMMY. Hiders can only be caught and kept captive while a tin or other object is in position at the starting place 217

Equal Number of Players Hiding and Seeking

OUTS. One side tries to find and take captive members of the other side 220

KISS CHASE. Seekers have claims on those caught 221

HUNTS. As 'Outs', but hiders attempt to return to starting place 223

HUNT THE KEG. Hiders attempt to smuggle a particular object back to the
    starting place 224

RELIEVO. Hiders try to release captives despite there being a guard on them
    (cf. 'Tin can Tommy' p. 217f) 225

GEE. Hiders when seen chase the seekers 228

Endnotes   229

See volume 2 for Index of Games

Foreword

As an editor of a natural parenting magazine I have gathered from our many contributors that the essential work of childhood is 'play'. Children use play for all sorts of things: to develop skills; as a therapeutic tool, to strengthen their imagination and thus their chances to dream their lives as future adults; to learn to socialize, to enjoy being in the 'now' which is such an essential skill that we adults can find so challenging at times.

I believe that children are different beings, not mini-adults, and that they deserve us to understand who they are and what their needs are. In their classic book *Children's Games in Street and Playground* Iona and Peter Opie took the time to research and document the games that children play when being left to their own devices. The context of their research may have changed but, as Iona expresses in her later, 1984 preface, the essence of the games is the same. These games show what children are about. The richness of the book for me comes mainly, but not only, from the fact that if we as adults can have access to this type of information, we may be able to review our assumptions about who children are. Our resulting behaviours towards them, the environments that we create for them and the policies that influence their lives may change.

Children's Games in Street and Playground is a book written in the early 1960s which presents the results of an extensive research study into the games children play of their own volition, between the ages of 6–12, out of sight of adults and without the aid of 'props' like bat, ball and skipping rope.

The research evidence challenges the presumption that children in the 60s have few diversions of their own, are incapable of self-organization and have become addicted to spectator amusements and will languish if expected to rely on their own initiative. While accepting that 'in the past' parents were reluctant to play an active role in their children's development through play, it also challenges the basis of the progressive notion prevalent in the 60s that an enlightened adult or parent thinks of ideas for the children, provides play materials and spends time playing with them. That is, adults structuring the play environment of our children to strengthen the value of play.

The essence of the research was to find out what children do when left to their own devices in situations where child interacts with child, and learning and play is not factored by the interaction of adults/parents. To find out, the researchers looked where children play without being overlooked, in street and on wasteland, but also as a counterpoint they observed those adult 'protected' areas of the school playground and recreation ground designed to make play safe or certain.

The interesting result of this study was the observation that where children were 'controlled' or protected in, say, a school playground, the play was often violent and aggressive. Alternatively where children were able to get on with their own play, this had a constructively civilizing influence on the interaction between children.

Almost fifty years on from this research, there is much debate about the role of parenting in children's play and the impact of passively engaging experiences like television and computer games. It might also be said that the wastelands have disappeared and the streets have been taken over by cars and the spectre of paedophilia. Are we intervening too much in the important child-to-child area? How much does our natural desire to guide our children's play and protect their play environment at school and home, generate young people with violent and aggressive tendencies? Where does a child go to find other children with whom to relate within their own space? Do we allow children to create environments that respond to their innate nature, or are we reading children as mini-adults and taking away the essential free time and space that they need to flourish? The Opies provide us with valuable research to consider these questions and behave responsibly towards our future generations.

Patricia Patterson-Vanegas
Juno Magazine
August 2008

Authors' Preface to Original Edition

During the past fifty years shelf-loads of books have been written instructing children in the games they ought to play, and some even instructing adults on how to instruct children in the games they ought to play, but few attempts have been made to record the games children in fact play. It seems to be presumed that children today (unlike those in the past) have few diversions of their own, that they are incapable of self-organization, have become addicted to spectator amusements, and will languish if left to rely on their own resources. It is felt that the enlightened adult is one who thinks up ideas for them, provides them with 'play materials', and devotes time to playing with them. Certainly our attitude to the young has changed since the nineteenth century, when Herbert Spencer could complain that men of education felt the rearing of fine animals to be a fitter subject for attention than the bringing up of fine human beings. Yet our vision of childhood continues to be based on the adult-child relationship. Possibly because it is more difficult to find out about, let alone understand, we largely ignore the child-to-child complex, scarcely realizing that however much children may need looking after they are also people going about their own business within their own society, and are fully capable of occupying themselves under the jurisdiction of their own code.

In the present study we are concerned solely with the games that children, aged about 6–12, play of their own accord when out of doors, and usually out of sight. We do not include, except incidentally, party games, scout games, team games, or any sport that requires supervision; and we concentrate for the most part on the rough-and-tumble games which, though they may require energy and sometimes fortitude, do not need even the elementary equipment of bat and ball. We are interested in the simple games for which, as one child put it, 'nothing is needed but the players themselves'. It is intended that the intricacies of ball-bouncing and other ball games, of skipping, marbles, fivestones, hopscotch, tipcat, and gambling, shall be described in a further volume, where they can be treated more fully, together with the singing games.

Our accounts of these games are based on information from more than 10,000 children attending local-authority schools in England, Scotland, and the eastern part of Wales; and this survey in the 1960s has been supplemented by the similar investigation we undertook in the 1950s when preparing *The Lore and Language of Schoolchildren* (1959). It should be remarked, however, that although our survey has extended from the Channel Islands to the Shetland Islands, and takes notice of a number of remote areas, the vast majority of children who have contributed have spent their lives in great cities such as London, Liverpool, Bristol, and Glasgow, and are the children who are ordinarily supposed to be the least satisfied with simple pleasures.

The fact is that there is no town or city known to us where street games do not flourish. Indeed, during twenty years' inquiry, we have not met a child who was unable to tell us something interesting, and who did not unwittingly increase the size of our files. However, the research-worker who is blessed with an unending flow of information can be in as embarrassing a position as he whose sources are limited, when he comes to making his report. Our problem editorially has been to present our findings in a form in which the facts are readily available, yet not so prosaically that the spirit of street play, its zest, variety, contradictions, and disorderliness, is entirely lost. Street play is not a social activity that lends itself to neat analysis and tabulation. The robustness of juvenile society allows of no more than partial agreement on what each game is called, let alone on how it is played. Yet long acquaintance with the games has sometimes shown that the differences between one place and another are more apparent than real. Having the benefit of several hundred descriptions of the more popular games, from perhaps fifty to sixty places, we have, we think, usually been able to understand the basic principle of a game; and have thereafter been able to identify the more significant regional variations and idiosyncrasies. We have then, where necessary, appended a list of its colloquial and dialect names. Thus no matter under what name a game is known to the reader, its whereabouts in the volume should be readily located by reference to the index, which includes every one of the 2,500 names of games appearing in the text.

We have also given thought to the order in which the games appear, arrangement being by the basic motif of the game; and it is hoped that with the aid of the pages of Contents and Analysis (pp. ooo–ooo), it will be possible to find a game even when its name is not known, as when, for instance, the British equivalent is sought to a game played elsewhere in the world. For this reason we have not felt it necessary to record every name of every parallel game played in other countries. Reference is made to a game's counterparts in other languages only when the comparison is significant; or when, as happens not infrequently, the sport was described or depicted at an earlier date on the Continent than in Britain.

It was at first thought that it would be possible to give the histories of only a minority of present-day street games; and that these few, being well-known antiques (e.g. 'Leapfrog', 'Blind Man's Buff', and 'Piggy-back Fighting'), would be so well documented already that an appropriate reference to where the history could be found would suffice. Unhappily the more we examined these histories and checked the original sources, the more unsatisfactory were previous works on children's games found to be. Further, it became increasingly evident that the way a game was played in the past is sometimes highly relevant when an explanation is required of a peculiarity in the way it is played today. The majority of games are therefore accompanied by a historical note, following the sign §, and we hope that the reader who is interested only in the activities of the contemporary schoolchild will not be too dismayed at finding his amusements compared with those in medieval France or ancient Greece.

In saying that we find the previous histories of children's games unsatisfactory it should not be thought that we are ungrateful for them. The pioneer work in Britain, Strutt's *Glig-Gamena Angel Deod, or, The Sports and Pastimes of the People of England*, 1801, is a remarkable undertaking that embodies considerable research, and can scarcely be faulted in what it says, only in what it does not say, for it allows small space to the 'sports of children'. For the past seventy years the standard work has been Alice Bertha Gomme's *Traditional Games of England, Scotland, and Ireland*, 2 vols., 1894–8. Lady Gomme, wife of George Laurence Gomme, a pioneer folklorist and first secretary of the Folk-Lore Society (founded 1878), was attracted to the subject of children's play by the singing games, and these remained her abiding interest.[1] In consequence her work is a vivid reflection of the exciting years towards the end of the Victorian era when English folksong was being discovered, and children, too, were found to be filling the air with unwritten poetry. However, these wonders on the lips of the people, whether milkmaids or mudlarks, were looked upon almost uniformly as relics of antiquity. They were examined as if they were archaeological remains, rather than living organisms which are constantly evolving, adapting to new situations, and renewing themselves or being replaced. Alice Gomme, under the influence of her husband (author of *Folk-lore Relics of Early Village*

Life), was fascinated by the possibility that the games she was collecting were the survivals of primitive custom and belief; and this somewhat romantic attitude, as it now seems, materially affected the quality of her research. Lovers of English folksong will ever be indebted to her for stimulating the collection of children's songs in the nineteenth century, and for inducing several excellent folklorists (notably Addy and Gregor) to contribute their collectings to her pages. But since she thought of change chiefly in terms of decay, she had little interest in working upon historical principles; and she had, apparently, no curiosity to study early or foreign literature. Her literary references are almost without exception taken at second hand, are not always correctly transcribed or understood, and her notes, other than those for the singing games, are seldom the labour of love they appear to be.

A more scholarly and perceptive work to our mind, and attractively written as well, is W. W. Newell's *Games and Songs of American Children*, 1883, augmented 1903. Newell, like everyone else in his time, thought the games were fast disappearing; but he had a sense of history, a good knowledge of languages, and an understanding of the operation of oral tradition. He realized that any game or rite, wherever collected, was likely to be only a local version of a general stock, and with modestly presented references he drew attention over and over again to the European versions of games he was discovering on his side of the Atlantic. In this he has been well supported in recent times by his countryman Paul G. Brewster in *American Nonsinging Games*, 1953; and it has been a pleasure to refer on occasion to both these works as places where additional analogues are to be found.

Many folklorists, however, seem to be magically insulated from literature not strictly within their discipline; and neither Newell, one of the founders of the American Folklore Society, nor Lady Gomme, seems to have been aware of the juvenile books on children's games which had long existed, even in their day, both in Britain and in the United States. This extensive literature has been examined systematically for the present work, apparently for the first time. In addition full use has been made of the signposts, clearly marked for those willing to look for them, that are provided by *The Oxford English Dictionary* and *The English Dialect Dictionary*. And the work has also benefited from a happy twenty years of general reading. Yet our greatest asset as historians has been fortuitous. It has been the knowledge we already happened to possess about the ways in which the games are played today. It is remarkable how much guesswork has been expended on classical, medieval, and Tudor pastimes, simply because the learned commentators in the eighteenth and nineteenth centuries, closeted in their studies, lacked knowledge of the games that their own children were playing in the sunshine outside their windows. And this in itself is an illustration of the gap there always is between the generations. For although some games have disappeared, and many, naturally, have altered over the years, it can still be said that the way to understand the 'wanton sports' of Elizabethan days, and the horseplay of even earlier times, is to watch the contemporary child engrossed in his traditional pursuits on the metalled floor of a twentieth-century city.

Iona and Peter Opie
West Liss, Hampshire, 1959–1969

It is fifteen years since *Children's Games in Street and Playground* was first published, but I believe the picture it gives of children's unofficial games is substantially the same today as it was in 1969. Certainly my weekly visits to Liss playground confirm that the old favourites are still being played — 'Om Pom', 'British Bulldog', 'Egg Bacon and Chips', 'Mr Wolf', 'Queenie, Queenie, Who's Got the Ball?', 'Stick in the Mud', and 'Farmer, Farmer, May We Cross Your Golden River?'; and when a seven-year-old excitedly fetches me to 'Come and see our new game' I am reminded that the games are new to each generation of children, and have no need to be replaced. Playgrounds in other parts of the country, where I have in recent years been recording singing games for a companion volume, *The Singing Game*, have provided further evidence that the competitive games are being played much as before, and even the repertoire of dipping rhymes seems scarcely to have altered. Correspondents have reported variations and elaborations, and occasionally a new local name; but such real innovations as have occurred have been in the daring and pretending games, which are most affected by modern technology, television, and current events. As well as continuing to play 'Last Across' in front of trains and across busy streets, children now ride up and down on top of lifts in tower blocks, and hurl rolls of metal foil at high-voltage electricity cables, holding the end of the foil as long as they dare before the two make contact in a lethal flurry of sparks. Pretending games, though mostly based on family life and wars between unspecified opponents, now often enact episodes from galactic sagas such as

'Star Wars'; and world news, as seen on television, continues to inspire its quota of games — 'Hostages' was in vogue during the siege of the Iranian Embassy in 1980, and 'Falklands War' throughout the summer of 1982.

Iona Opie
West Liss, 1984

Introduction

'And the streets of the city shall be full of boys and girls playing
in the streets thereof.'
Zechariah, viii. 5

When children play in the street they not only avail themselves of one
of the oldest play-places in the world, they engage in some of the oldest
and most interesting of games, for they are games tested and confirmed
by centuries of children, who have played them and passed them on, as
children continue to do, without reference to print, parliament, or adult
propriety. Indeed these street games are probably the most played, least
recorded, most natural games that there are. Certainly they are the most
spontaneous, for the little group of boys under the lamp-post may not
know, until a minute before, whether they are to play 'Bish Bash' or
'Poison' or 'Cockarusha', or even know that they are going to play.

A true game is one that frees the spirit. It allows of no cares but those
fictitious ones engendered by the game itself. When the players commit
themselves to the rhythm and incident of 'Underground Tig' or 'Witches
in the Gluepots' they opt out of the ordinary world, the boundary of their
existence becomes the two pavements this side of a pillar-box, their only
reality the excitement of avoiding the chaser's touch. Yet it is not only
the nature of the game that frees the spirit, it is the circumstances in
which it is played. The true game, as Locke recognized years ago, is the
one that arises from the players themselves.

> Because there can be no Recreation without Delight, which
> depends not alway on Reason, but oftener on Fancy, it must be
> permitted Children not only to divert themselves, but to do it after
> their own Fashion; provided it be innocently, and without Preju-
> dice to their Health.

It may even be argued that the value of a game as recreation depends on
its inconsequence to daily life. In the games which adults organize for
children, or even merely oversee in a playground, the outside world is ever
present. Individual performances tend to become a matter for congratula-
tion or shame; and in a team game, paradoxically, individual responsibility

presses hardest. The player who 'lets down his side' can cheer himself only with the sad reflection that those who speak loudest about the virtues of organized sport are the people who excel in it themselves, never the duffers. He is not likely to have been told that such a man as Robert Louis Stevenson felt that cricket and football were colourless pastimes, scarcely play at all, compared with the romance of Hide and Seek.

The appeal of the games

Play is unrestricted, games have rules. Play may merely be the enactment of a dream, but in each game there is a contest. Yet it will be noticed that when children play a game in the street they are often extraordinarily naïve or, according to viewpoint, highly civilized. They seldom need an umpire, they rarely trouble to keep scores, little significance is attached to who wins or loses, they do not require the stimulus of prizes, it does not seem to worry them if a game is not finished. Indeed children like games in which there is a sizeable element of luck, so that individual abilities cannot be directly compared. They like games which restart almost automatically, so that everybody is given a new chance. They like games which move in stages, in which each stage, the choosing of leaders, the picking-up of sides, the determining of which side shall start, is almost a game in itself. In fact children's games often seem laborious to adults who, if invited to join in, may find themselves becoming impatient, and wanting to speed them up. Adults do not always see, when subjected to lengthy preliminaries, that many of the games, particularly those of young children, are more akin to ceremonies than competitions. In these games children gain the reassurance that comes with repetition, and the feeling of fellowship that comes from doing the same as everyone else. Children may choose a particular game merely because of some petty dialogue which precedes the chase:

> 'Sheep, sheep, come home.'
> 'We're afraid.'
> 'What of?'
> 'The wolf.'
> 'Wolf has gone to Devonshire
> Won't be here for seven years,
> Sheep, sheep, come home.'

As Spencer remarked, it is not only the amount of physical exercise that is taken that gives recreation, 'an agreeable mental excitement has a highly invigorating influence'. Thus children's 'interest' in a game may well be the incident in it that least appeals to the adult: the opportunity it affords to thump a player on the back, as in 'Strokey Back', to behave stupidly and be applauded for the stupidity, as in 'Johnny Green', to say aloud the colour of someone's panties, as in 'Farmer, Farmer, may we cross your Golden River?' And in a number of games, for instance 'Chinese Puzzle', there may be little purpose other than the ridiculousness of the experiment itself:

> Someone as to be on. The one who is on as to turn round while the others hold hands and make a round circul. Then you get in a muddle, one persun could clime over your arms or under your legs or anything ales that you could make a muddle, then when they have finished they say "Chinese Puzzle we are all in a muddle", then the persun turns round and goes up to them and gets them out of the muddle without breaking their hands, and then the persun who was on choose someone ales, and then it goes on like that. It is fun to play Chinese Puzzle.

Here, indeed, is a British game where little attempt is made to establish the superiority of one player over another. In fact the function of such a game is largely social. Just as the shy man reveals himself by his formalities, so does the child disclose his unsureness of his place in the world by welcoming games with set procedures, in which his relationships with his fellows are clearly established. In games a child can exert himself without having to explain himself, he can be a good player without having to think whether he is a popular person, he can find himself being a useful partner to someone of whom he is ordinarily afraid. He can be confident, too, in particular games, that it is his place to issue commands, to inflict pain, to steal people's possessions, to pretend to be dead, to hurl a ball actually at someone, to pounce on someone, or to kiss someone he has caught. In ordinary life either he never knows these experiences or, by attempting them, makes himself an outcast.

It appears to us that when a child plays a game he creates a situation which is under his control, and yet it is one of which he does not know the outcome. In the confines of a game there can be all the excitement and uncertainty of an adventure, yet the young player can comprehend the whole, can recognize his place in the scheme, and, in contrast to the confusion of real life, can tell what is right action. He can, too, extend his environment, or feel that he is doing so, and gain knowledge of sensations beyond ordinary experience. When children are small, writes Bertrand Russell, 'it is biologically natural that they should, in imagination, live through the life of remote savage ancestors'. As long as the action of the game is of a child's own making he is ready, even anxious, to sample the perils of which this world has such plentiful supply. In the security of a game he makes acquaintance with insecurity, he is able to rationalize absurdities, reconcile himself to not getting his own way, 'assimilate reality' (Piaget), act heroically without being in danger. The thrill of a chase is accentuated by viewing the chaser not as a boy in short trousers, but as a bull. It is not a classmate's back he rides upon but a knight's fine charger. It is not a party of other boys his side skirmishes with but Indians, Robbers, 'Men from Mars'. And, always provided that the environment is of his own choosing, he — or she — is even prepared to meet the 'things that happen in the dark', playing games that would seem strange amusement if it was thought they were being taken literally: 'Murder in the Dark', 'Ghosties in the Garret', 'Moonlight, Starlight, Bogey won't come out Tonight'. And yet, within the context of the game, these alarms *are* taken literally.

The age of the players

When generalizing about children's play it is easy to forget that each child's attitude to each game, and his way of playing it, is constantly changing as he himself matures; his preferences moving from the fanciful to the ritualistic, from the ritualistic to the romantic (i.e. the free-ranging games, 'Hide and Seek', 'Cowboys and Indians'), and from the romantic to the severely competitive. The infants, 5–7 years old, may play some of the same games in their playground that the juniors do across the way, but in a more personal, less formalized style. Their chasing game, in which they clutch the railings to be safe, is called, perhaps, 'Naughty Boys'. 'We're playing naughty boys, we've run away from home.' ('Touch Iron' or 'Touch Green' is only emerging from make-believe.) The boys who are moving on hands and feet, stomachs upward, in another part of the playground, say they are being Creatures, 'horrible creatures in the woods'. The juniors, in the next playground, would not play like this, not move about publicly on hands and feet, unless, that is, it was part of a 'proper' game, one in which they were *chasing* each other.

Today, in an increasingly integrated society, children become self-conscious about the games they play on their own more quickly than they used to do. They discard them two, and even three years earlier than they did in the days before the introduction of organized sport. When Lord John Russell, aged 11, started his school-days at Westminster in 1803, he recorded in his diary that 'the boys play at hoops, peg-tops, and peashooters'. At Eton in 1766 the sports in vogue included Hopscotch, Headimy, Peg in the Ring, Conquering Lobs (marbles), Trap-ball, Chuck, Steal Baggage, and Puss in the Corner. At Sedgley Park School in Staffordshire, about 1805, the boys were content with Kites, Marloes (marbles), Peg-tops, Hoops, Backs (leap-frog), Beds (hopscotch), Cat, Rounders, Skipping, and even with 'playing horses'. Today few boys at grammar school would contemplate such sports. The experts are aged eight, nine, and ten. Even girls, who it might be thought would hold out against being organized, now look down upon informal games once they have a chance of taking part in the recognized sports:

> When I was five I played at Beddies. At seven I learned to
> play E.I.O. At nine I played "Alla Baba who's got the ball-a".
> Now I am fourteen I play tennis and netball, not the games
> I used to play when I was smaller.

Indeed, a game which at one time was the breath of life to a child a short while later may be cast aside and become an embarrassment to remember. Thus a 10-year-old's description of 'Queeny' starts as follows:

> My favourite game is a game that lots and lots of children can
> play at once. It is a lovely game, children of two years old can
> play it right up to the age of twelve. It is very enjoyable. It has
> also a rhyme to it. It goes like this:
>
>> Queeny, Queeny, who's got the ball,
>> Is she fat or is she small,
>> Is she big or is she thin,
>> Does she play the violin,
>> Yes or no?

But a 14-year-old girl says of the game:

> When I was smaller I used to play with my friends games
> which seem very silly and babyish to me now ... for
> example Queeny Ball. Now that was babyish! Today I
> would never dream of standing out in the street chanting
> "Queeny ball, ball, ball" but then I simply wallowed in such
> fun as I called it.

Thus one child's attitude to a game may vary from another's to a greater extent than does either of them from that of the adult spectator. In fact when a child enters his teens (earlier if in the 'A' stream) a curious but genuine disability may overtake him. He may, as part of the process of growing up, actually lose his recollection of the sports that used to mean so much to him. As a 13-year-old wrote when describing 'Aunts and Uncles', 'King Ball', 'Kick the Can', 'Hide and Seek', and 'I Draw a Snake':

> All these games are quite common round Glenzier, that is
> how I can remember them. There are other games played
> once in a while but these I cannot remember. The games
> I can remember are a little too young for me to play,
> although I play King Ball sometimes.

Older children can thus be remarkably poor informants about the games. Twelve-year-olds may be heard talking like old men and women ('Our street used to be very lively but children don't play the games like we used to do'). A 15-year-old in Liverpool, where 'Queeny' is popular, was certain the game was no longer known. Fourteen-year-olds, re-met in the street, from whom we wanted further information about a game they had showed us proudly a year before, have listened to our queries with blank incomprehension. Paradoxical as it may appear, a 5-year-old in his first term at school may well be aware of more self-organized games than a 15-year-old about to leave school.

The age of the games

These games that 'children find out for themselves when they meet', as Plato put it, seem to them as new and surprising when they learn them as the jokes in this week's comic. Parties of schoolchildren, at the entrance to the British Museum, secretly playing 'Fivestones' behind one of the columns as they wait to go in, little think that their pursuits may be as great antiquities as the exhibits they have been brought to see. Yet, in their everyday games, when they draw straws to see who shall take a disliked role, they show how Chaucer's Canterbury pilgrims determined which of them should tell the first tale. When they strike at each other's plantains, trying to decapitate them, they play the game a medieval chronicler says King Stephen played with his boy-prisoner William Marshal to humour him. When they jump on a player's back, and make him guess which finger they hold up ('Husky-bum, Finger or Thumb?') they perpetuate an amusement of ancient Rome. When they hit a player from behind, in the game 'Stroke the Baby', and challenge him to name who did it, they unwittingly illuminate a passage in the life of Our Lord. And when they enter the British Museum they can see Eros, clearly depicted on a vase of 400 BC, playing the game they have just been told to abandon.

There was no need for Plato to urge that boys be forbidden to make alterations in their games, lest they be led to disobey the laws of the State in later life. Boys are such sticklers for tradition that after 2,000 years they have not yet given up Epostrakismos ('Ducks and Drakes'), Schoenophilinda ('Whackem'), Apodidraskinda (running-home 'Hide and Seek'), Ostrakinda (a form of 'Crusts and Crumbs'), Chytrinda ('Frog in the Middle'), Strombos ('Whipping top'), Dielkustinda ('Tug of War'), and at least two forms of Muinda ('Blind Man's Buff' and 'How Far to London'). Even the limping witch Empusa seems to have survived to this day in the guise of Limpety Lil.

If a present-day schoolchild was wafted back to any previous century he would probably find himself more at home with the games being played than with any other social custom. If he met his counterparts in the Middle Ages he might enjoy games of Prisoners' Base, Twos and Threes, street-football, Fox and Chickens, Hunt the Hare, Pitch and Toss, and marbles, as well as any of the games from classical times; and judging by the illuminations in the margins of manuscripts, he would be a prince among his fellows if he was good at piggyback fighting.

The Elizabethans played Bowls (one of their most common games), Barley-break, Stoolball, 'King by your Leaue' (a form of running-home Hide and Seek), 'Sunne and Moone' (Tug of War), and 'Crosse and Pile' (Heads and Tails). Shakespeare himself mentions 'All hid, all hid',

'Cherrie-pit', 'Fast and loose', 'Handy-dandy' (see *Oxford Dictionary of Nursery Rhymes*, pp. 197–8), 'Hide Fox and all after', 'Hoodman-blinde', 'Leape-frogge', 'Push-pin' (a game now played with pen-nibs), and 'Span-counter'.

Amongst games 'used by our countrey Boys and Girls', named by the Cheshire antiquary Randle Holme in 1688, were 'Battle-dore or Shuttle cock', 'Bob Apple' (see *Lore and Language of Schoolchildren*, pp. 272–3), 'Chase Fire', 'Drop Glove', 'Hare and Hound', 'Hide and seech', 'Hop skotches', 'Hornes Hornes', 'Fives', 'Jack stones', 'King I am', 'Long Larrance', 'Pi[t]ch and Hussle', and 'Puss in the corner'. And the 'innocent Games that Good Boys and Girls' diverted themselves with in *A Little Pretty Pocket-Book*, 1744, one of the first books to be published for juvenile amusement, included: Cricket, Base-Ball, 'Chuck-Farthing', 'Peg-Farthing', 'Taw' (marbles), 'Knock out and Span', 'Hop-Hat', 'Thread the Needle', 'All the Birds in the Air', and 'I sent a Letter to my Love'.

Even more revealing, perhaps, than the age of the games, is the persistence of certain practices during the games. The custom of turning round a blindfold player *three times* before allowing him to begin chasing seems already to have been standard practice in the seventeenth century. The quaint notion that a player becomes 'warm' when nearing the object he is seeking was doubtless old when Silas Wegg adopted it (*Our Mutual Friend*, III. vi). The stratagem of making players choose one of two objects, such as an 'orange' or a 'lemon', to decide which side they shall take in a pulling match, was almost certainly employed by the Elizabethans. The rule that a special word and finger-sign shall give a player respite in a game appears to be a legacy of the age of chivalry. The convention that the player who does worst in a game shall be punished, rather than that he who does best shall be rewarded, has an almost continuous history stretching from classical antiquity. And the ritual confirmation that a player has been caught, by crowning him or by tapping him three times, prevalent today even in such sophisticated places as Ilford and Enfield, was mentioned by Cromek in his *Remains of Nithsdale and Galloway Song* in 1810 ('If the intruder be caught on the hostile ground he is *taend*, that is, clapped three times on the head, which makes him a prisoner'), and is also the rule — as are other of these conventions — amongst children in France, Germany, Austria, Italy, and the United States.

Variation in the games

If children played their games invariably in the way the previous generation played them, the study of youthful recreation could be a matter merely of antiquarian scholarship. But they do not. Despite the motherly influence of tradition, of which we have seen examples, children's play is like every other social activity, it is subject to continual change. The fact that the games are played slightly differently in different places, and may even vary in name, is itself evidence that mutation takes place. ('Chinese Puzzle', for instance, is also known as 'Chinese Muddle', 'Chinese Puddle', 'Jigsaw Puzzle', 'Chinese Knots', 'French Knots', 'Chain Man', 'Tangle Man', 'Policeman', and 'Cups and Saucers'.) In addition, as is well known, new sports emerge that may or may not in the course of time become traditional. (During the past decade there has been the 'Hula Hoop', 'Scoobeedoo', 'Split the Kipper', 'American Skipping', and 'Ippyop' or 'Belgian Skipping'.) And for reasons that are usually social or environmental, some games become impracticable (e.g. games played with caps are fast disappearing), while others are overlaid or replaced by new versions that are found to be more satisfactory. ('Conkers', played with horse chestnuts, which became possible with the introduction of the horse-chestnut tree, *Aesculus hippocastanum*, has now displaced the centuries-old contest with cobnuts.)

Yet the most fundamental kind of change that takes place is less obvious, although continual. This is the variation that occurs over the years in the relative popularity of individual games. At any one time some games are gaining in popularity; some, presumably, are at their peak; and others are in marked decline; and this variation affects not only the frequency with which each game is played but its actual composition. Thus games that are approaching their peak of popularity are easily recognizable, just as are customs and institutions that are nearing their zenith and about to decay. A game enjoying absolute favour fatally attracts additional rules and formalities; the sport becomes progressively more elaborate, the playing of it demands further finesse, and the length of time required for its completion markedly increases. (In our day 'Statues' was a simple amusement of seeing who, after a sharp pull, could be the best statue; today it is a procedure-ridden pastime incorporating at least four additional operations.) Indeed, as a game grows in popularity its very name may grow. (Thirty years ago in Liss the old game known as 'Stoop' was already being called 'Three Stoops and Run for Your Life'; today, still

more popular, it is 'Three Stoops, Three Pokers, and Run for Your Life'.)
On the other hand, games which are in a decline lose their trimmings;
the players become disdainful of all but the actual contest; the time-taking preliminaries and poetic formulas which gave the game its quality
are discarded; and fragments of the game may even be taken over by
another game that is on the up-grade (part of the introductory formula
of 'Hickety, Bickety', for instance, is now repeated in the seeking game,
'North, South, East, West').

The identification and listing of games that have been declining in
popularity over the past fifty years, and those that have been most notice-
ably gaining in popularity, may help to show the factors that currently
affect children's choice of games (see opposite).

There has been a marked decrease in the playing of games in which
one player is repeatedly buffeted by the rest. (It is apparently not now
felt as amusing as it used to be that one player should remain at a disadvantage indefinitely.) There has been an increase (possibly a corre-
sponding increase) in the playing of games in which children fight each
other on roughly equal terms. Above all, we feel it is no coincidence that
the games whose decline is most pronounced are those which are best
known to adults, and therefore the most often promoted by them; while
the games and amusements that flourish are those that adults find most
difficulty in encouraging (e.g. knife-throwing games and chases in the
dark), or are those sports, such as ball-bouncing and long-rope skipping,
in which adults are ordinarily least able to show proficiency.

Where children play: playing in the street

Where children are is where they play. They are impatient to be started,
the street is no further than their front door, and they are within call
when tea is ready. Indeed the street in front of their home is seemingly
theirs, more theirs sometimes than the family living-room; and of more
significance to them, very often, than any amenity provided by the local
council. When a young black boy from Notting Hill was being given a
week's holiday in a Wiltshire village, and was asked how he liked the
country, he promptly replied, 'I like it — but you can't play in the road
as you can in London.'

Yet, as we know, Zechariah's vision of the new Jerusalem is not as
splendid in practice as he makes it appear. Windows are liable to be bro-

Games diminishing in popularity	Games growing in popularity
Anything under the Sun	Bad Eggs (a ball game)
Baste the Bear (virtually obsolete)	Bar the Door
Blind Man's Buff	Block
Bull in the Ring	British Bulldog
Cat and Mouse	Budge He
Crusts and Crumbs	Donkey (a ball-bouncing game)
Duckstone (an aiming game)	Fairies and Witches
Finger or Thumb?	Farmer, Farmer, may we cross your
Fool, Fool, Come to School	Golden River?
French and English	Film Stars
Hide and Seek (the simple form)	Hi Jimmy Knacker
Honey Pots	I Draw a Snake upon your Back
I Sent My Son John	Jack, Jack, Shine a Light
King of the Castle	Kerb or Wall
Kiss in the Ring	Kingy
Knifie (Mumbletypeg)	Kiss Chase
Leapfrog	May I?
Odd and Even (a gambling game)	Off-Ground He
Old Man in the Well	Peep Behind the Curtain
Prisoners' Base	Poison
Sardines	Queenie (in its new form)
Stag	Relievo
Stroke the Baby (Hot Cockles)	Split the Kipper
Territories	Statues
Tipcat	Stuck in the Mud
Tom Tiddler's Ground	Three Stoops and Run For Ever
Touch Iron and Touchwood	Tin Can Tommy
Tug of War	Touch Colour
Twos and Threes	Truth, Dare, Promise, or Opinion
Warning	What's the time, Mr Wolf?

Table showing games dimishing and growing in popularity.

ken, caretakers appear from blocks of flats telling the children to keep off the grass, obstinate car-drivers insist on making their way down the street, and, nightly, little dramas are enacted between 10-year-olds and the tendentious:

> We were having a lovely game of Relievo when a man
> across the road came out and moved us. My friend Ann
> said, "Oh shut up you're always moaning". Then the man
> said, "I will see your father about this it is going too far.
> Someone is trying to have a sleep." Then my other friend
> said "So is my dad". Then the man shouted for his dog Flash
> and sent him after us.

What is curious about these embroilments is that children always do seem to have been in trouble about the places where they played. In the nineteenth century there were repeated complaints that the pavements of London were made impassable by children's shuttlecock and tipcat.[2] In Stuart times, Richard Steele reported, the vicinity of the Royal Exchange was infested with uninvited sportsmen, and a beadle was employed to whip away the 'unlucky Boys with Toys and Balls'. Even in the Middle Ages, when it might be supposed a meadow was within reach of every Jack and Jill in Britain, the young had a way of gravitating to unsuitable places. In 1332 it was found necessary to prohibit boys and others from playing in the precincts of the Palace at Westminster while Parliament was sitting. In 1385 the Bishop of London was forced to declaim against the ball-play about St Paul's; and in 1447, away in Devonshire, the Bishop of Exeter was complaining of 'yong peple' playing in the cloister, even during divine service, such games as 'the toppe, queke, penny prykke, and most atte tenys, by the which the walles of the saide Cloistre have be defowled and the glas wyndowes all to brost'.

Should such persistent choice of busy and provocative play-places alert us that all is not as appears in the ghettos of childhood? Children's deepest pleasure, as we shall see, is to be away in the wastelands, yet they do not care to separate themselves altogether from the adult world. In some forms of their play (or in certain moods), they seem deliberately to attract attention to themselves, screaming, scribbling on the pavements, smashing milk bottles, banging on doors, and getting in people's way. A single group of children were able to name twenty games they played which involved running across the road. Are children, in some of their games, expressing something more than high spirits, something of which not even they, perhaps, are aware? No section of the community is more rooted to where it lives than the young. When children engage in 'Last Across' in front of a car is it just devilment that prompts the sport, or may it be some impulse of protest in the tribe? Perhaps those people will appreciate this question most who have asked themselves whether the convenience of motorists thrusting through a town or village is really as important as the well-being of the people whose settlement it is, and who are attempting to live their lives in it.

Play in restricted environment

> It is a pleasant sight to see the young play with those of their own age at tick, puss in the corner, hop-scotch, ring-taw, and hot beans ready buttered: and in these boyish amusements much self-denial and good nature may be practised. This, however, is not always the case ...
>
> *The Boy's Week-Day Book, 1834*

The places specially made for children's play are also the places where children can most easily be watched playing: the asphalt expanses of school playgrounds, the cage-like enclosures filled with junk by a local authority, the corners of recreation grounds stocked with swings and slides. In a playground children are, or are not, allowed to make chalk diagrams on the ground for hopscotch, to bounce balls against a wall, to bring marbles or skipping ropes, to play 'Conkers', 'Split the Kipper', 'Hi Jimmy Knacker'. Children of different ages may or may not be kept apart; boys may or may not be separated from girls. And according to the closeness of the supervision they organize gangs, carry out vendettas, place people in Coventry, gamble, bribe, blackmail, squabble, bully, and fight. The real nature of young boys has long been apparent to us, or so it has seemed. We have only to travel in a crowded school bus to be conscious of their belligerency, the extraordinary way they have of assailing each other, verbally and physically, each child feeling — perhaps with reason — that it is necessary to keep his end up against the rest. We know from accounts of previous generations with what good reason the great boarding schools, and other schools following, limited boys' free time, and made supervized games a compulsory part of the curriculum. As Sydney Smith wrote in 1810, it had become an 'immemorial custom' in the public schools that every boy should be alternately tyrant and slave. The tyranny of the monitors at Christ's Hospital, wrote Lamb, was 'heart-sickening to call to recollection'. Southey's friend who went to Charterhouse was nearly killed by the cruelty of the other boys who 'used to lay him before the fire till he was scorched, and shut him in a trunk with sawdust till he had nearly expired with suffocation'. Even at Marlborough, not founded until 1843, a new boy might be branded with an anchor by means of a red-hot poker. And at so tranquil-seeming an establishment as Harnish Rectory, run by the Rev Robert Kilvert, some of the boys were 'a set of little monsters' in their depravity. 'The first evening I was there,' recalled Augustus Hare, 'at nine years old, I was compelled to eat Eve's apple quite up — indeed, the Tree of Knowledge of Good and Evil was stripped absolutely bare: there was no fruit left to gather.'

Such accounts, which can usually be reinforced by personal experience of school life, have increasingly influenced educational practice over the past hundred years, leading us to believe that a *Lord of the Flies* mentality is inherent in the young. Yet there is no certainty that this judgment is well founded. In one respect we remain as perverse as we were in Spencer's day, devoting more time to observing the ways of animals than of our own young. Thus recent extensive studies of apes and monkeys have shown, perhaps not unexpectedly, that animal behaviour in captivity is not the same as in the wild. In the natural habitat the welfare of the troop as a whole is paramount, the authority of the experienced animal is accepted, the idiosyncrasies of members of the troop are respected. But when the same species is confined and overcrowded the toughest and least-sensitive animal comes to the top, a pecking order develops, bullying and debauchery become common, and each creature when abused takes his revenge on the creature next weakest to himself. In brief, it appears that when lower primates are in the wild, and fending for themselves, their behaviour is 'civilized', certainly in comparison with their behaviour when they are confined and cared for, which is when they most behave 'like animals'.

Our observations of children lead us to believe that much the same is true of our own species. We have noticed that when children are herded together in the playground, which is where the educationalists and the psychologists and the social scientists gather to observe them, their play is markedly more aggressive than when they are in the street or in the wild places. At school they play 'Ball He', 'Dodge

Ball', 'Chain Swing', and 'Bull in the Ring'. They indulge in duels such as 'Slappies', 'Knuckles', and 'Stinging', in which the pleasure, if not the purpose, of the game is to dominate another player and inflict pain. In a playground it is impracticable to play the free-ranging games like 'Hide and Seek' and 'Relievo' and 'Kick the Can', that are, as Stevenson said, the 'well-spring of romance', and are natural to children in the wastelands.

Often, when we have asked children what games they played in the playground we have been told 'We just go round aggravating people.' Nine-year-old boys make-believe they are Black Riders and in a mob charge on the girls. They play 'Coshes' with knotted handkerchiefs, they snatch the girls' ties or hair ribbons and call it 'Strip Tease', they join hands in a line and rush round the playground shouting 'Anyone who gets in our way will get knocked over', they play 'Tweaking', running behind a person and tweaking the lobe of his ear as they run off. One teacher, who asked her own 6-year-old what game he really enjoyed at school, was surprised to find it was 'getting gangs on to people'. He said, 'We get in a line and slap our sides as we run, and push down or bump a child.'

Such behaviour would not be tolerated amongst the players in the street or the wasteland; and for a long time we had difficulty reconciling these accounts with the thoughtfulness and respect for the juvenile code that we had noticed in the quiet places. Then we recollected how, in our own day, children who had seemed unpleasant at school (whose term-time behaviour at boarding school had indeed been barbarous), turned out to be surprisingly civilized when we met them in the holidays. We remembered hearing how certain inmates of institutions, and even people in concentration camps during the war, far from having a feeling of camaraderie, were liable to seek their pleasure in making life still more intolerable for those who were confined with them (see, for instance, Pierre d'Harcourt, *The Real Enemy*). It seems to us that something is lacking in our understanding of the child community, that we have forgotten Cowper's dictum that 'Great schools suit best the sturdy and the rough', and that in our continual search for efficient units of educational administration we have overlooked that the most precious gift we can give the young is social space: the necessary space — or privacy — in which to become human beings.

The wastelands

There is no doubt that the first world war and the coming of the
motor car killed, I suppose for ever, the playing of street games
in this country.

H. E. Bates

Children are all about us, living in our own homes, eating at our tables,
and it might be wondered how we ever supposed (along with H. E.
Bates, J. B. Priestley, Richard Church, Howard Spring, and other profes-
sional observers of the social scene) that they had stopped playing in the
way we ourselves used to play. Yet the belief that traditional games are
dying out is itself traditional; it was received opinion even when those
who now regret the passing of the games were themselves vigorously
playing them. We overlook the fact that as we have grown older our
interests have changed, we have given up haunting the places where children play, we no longer have eyes for the games, and not noticing them
suppose them to have vanished. We forget that children's amusements
are not always ones that attract attention. They are not prearranged ritu-
als for which the players wear distinctive uniforms, freshly laundered.
Unlike the obtrusive sports of grown men, for which ground has to be
permanently set aside and perpetually tended, children's games are ones
which the players adapt to their surroundings and the time available. In
fact most street games are as happily played in the dark as in the light. To
a child 'sport is sweetest when there be no spectators'. The places they
like best for play are the secret places 'where no one else goes'.

The literature of childhood abounds with evidence that the peaks of
a child's experience are not visits to a cinema, or even family outings to
the sea, but occasions when he escapes into places that are disused and
overgrown and silent. To a child there is more joy in a rubbish tip than
a flowering rockery, in a fallen tree than a piece of statuary, in a muddy
track than a gravel path. Like Stanley Spencer he may 'see more in a
dustbin in his village than in a cathedral abroad'. Yet the cult amongst
his elders is to trim, to pave, to smooth out, to clean-up, to prettify, to
convert to economic advantage — as if 'the maximum utilization of sur-
rounding amenities' had become a line of poetry.

Ironically the bombing of London was a blessing to the youthful
generations that followed. 'We live facing a bombsite where boys throw
stones, light fires, make camps and roast potatoes', writes an 11-year-
old. 'In my neighbourhood,' wrote a Peckham child in 1955, 'the sites

of Hitler's bombs are many, and the bigger sites with a certain amount of rubble provide very good grounds for Hide and Seek and Tin Can Tommy.' To a child the best parts of a park are the parts that are the least maintained. It is his nature to be attracted to the slopes, the bushes, the long grass, the waterside. 'Ours is a good park there are still places in it that are wild', observed a 10-year-old. But what do the authorities do? They exploit our wealth to make improvements for the worse. They invade the parks, erecting kiosks and tea gardens, and side-shows for those who require their entertainments ready-made. It is not only Battersea Park (the enchanted garden of our childhood) that has been turned into a honky-tonk. The trend is universal. In one small town we know there are some municipal gardens, the only place where children can play, and on the largest lawn they have laid-out and fenced off an immense bowling green for the summer pleasure of the middle-aged. The centre of our own home town possessed, miraculously, until two years ago, a small dark wood adjoining a car park. If an adult entered its shade he might imagine he was alone, unless he became aware that the trees above his head were a playground for Lilliputians. Now the trees have been cut down, the ground levelled, a stream canalized, and the area flooded with asphalt to make an extension to the car park. Should we be surprised if children play around the cars, if cars get damaged, if sometimes boys are tempted to more serious offences? Having cleared away the places that are naturally wild it is becoming the fashion to set aside other places, deposit junk in them, and create 'Adventure Playgrounds', so called, the equivalent of creating Whipsnades for wild life instead of erecting actual cages. The next need is to advertize in *The Times Educational Supplement* (for example 8 February 1963) for Play Leaders at 32*s.* for 2½ hours: apply Chief Officer (A/B/197/2) L.C.C. Parks Department, County Hall, S.E. 1. (WAT 5000 Ext. 7621) P.K. A2. Or, more recently (24 January 1969) for 'Senior Play Leader' at 40*s.* 6*d.* for 2½ hours: apply Parks Department, Cavell House, 2a Charing Cross Rd., W.C. 2, 836 5464, Ext. 144. The provision of playmates for the young has become an item of public expenditure.

In the past, traditional games were thought to be dying out, few people cared, and the games continued to flourish. In the present day we assume children to have lost the ability to entertain themselves, we become concerned, and are liable, by our concern, to make what is not true a reality. In the long run, nothing extinguishes self-organized play more effectively than does action to promote it. It is not only natural but beneficial that there should be a gulf between the generations in their choice of recreation. Those people are happiest who can most rely on their own resources; and it is to be wondered whether middle-class children in the United States will ever reach maturity 'whose playtime has become almost as completely organized and supervized as their study' (Carl Withers). If children's games are tamed and made part of school curricula, if wastelands are turned into playing-fields for the benefit of those who conform and ape their elders, if children are given the idea that they cannot enjoy themselves without being provided with the 'proper' equipment, we need blame only ourselves when we produce a generation who have lost their dignity, who are ever dissatisfied, and who descend for their sport to the easy excitement of rioting, or pilfering, or vandalism. But to say that children should be allowed this last freedom, to play their own games in their own way, is scarcely to say more than John Locke said almost three centuries ago:

> Children have as much a Mind to shew that they are free, that
> their own good Actions come from themselves, that they are abso-
> lute and independent, as any of the proudest of your grown Men.

And speaking of their recreation he observed how it was freedom 'they extreamly affect'; it was 'that Liberty alone which gives the true Relish and Delight to their ordinary Play Games'.

1. Starting a Game

'Zig zag zooligar
Zim zam bum.'

A Manchester 'dip'

Such is the capacity of the young for turning whatever they do into a sport, that collecting players for a game can be a game in itself. Two or three children, arms round each other's shoulders, reel across the playground chanting in the way they have heard other children chant before them: 'Who wants a game of *Sticky Toffee*? Who wants a game of *Sticky Toffee*?' Those who want to play attach themselves to the line, the line becomes unwieldy, the chant becomes a roar, there are more than enough players for the game, yet nobody now seems in the least inclined to break the line and begin playing. 'Sticky Toffee', or whatever the game proposed, has been forgotten in the very success of their summons to play it, a summons which varies according to local prescription, for instance: 'All join-ee join-ee up', or 'Arly-arly-in, who's a playing?', or 'All in, all in — hands in the dip'. In Pontypool:

All in, all in, a bottle of gin,
All out, all out, a bottle of stout.

In Brighouse:

All here who's laiking [playing],
Mary Ann's baking.

And in Whalsay, Shetland, when a game of 'Aggie Waggie' is proposed:

'Whā's cŏmĭn ĭ wīr fŭn āggĭe wāggĭe?'

('They seem able to fit any name into the rhythm', commented their teacher.)

Sometimes, however, playground recruitment is less voluntary. Two or three youngsters form a ring round a solitary child and threaten: 'Have a smack or join in the ring', or 'Pinch, punch, or join the bunch', or,

> Pinch, punch, join in the ring,
> Pinch, punch, no girls in.

('Please, miss,' said a little girl to the teacher on playground duty, 'that boy keeps hitting me and says it's a game.')

In some places the press-gang think they will be successful if they demand, 'Join the ring or tell us your sweetheart's name.' In Chingford:

> Pinch or punch or join in the ring,
> If you don't you'll have to sing
> Or tell us your true love's name.

And in East Dulwich:

> Pinch or punch or join in the ring,
> Or tell us the name of your sweetheart,
> Or do you believe in Santa Claus,
> Or have you a house of your own?

While in Hinckley, Leicestershire, they ask — with what counts in the playground as craft — 'Eggs or Bacon or join the ring?' If the child chooses either eggs or bacon he is told they are 'Not done yet', and he is, they feel, left with no option but to join the ring.

Avoidance of disliked role

On occasion a game starts in a flash, the players themselves hardly knowing how it began. More often children feel a game is not a proper one if such matters have not first been settled as who is to be allowed to play, what the boundaries are to be, and whether dropping-out is to be permitted. Yet the chief impediment to a swift start is the fact that in most games one player has to take a part that is different from the rest; and all children have, or affect to have, an insurmountable objection to being the first one to take this part. Tradition, if not inclination, demands that they do whatever they can to avoid being the chaser, or the seeker, or the one who, as they express it, is 'on', 'on it', 'he', or 'it'. Thus it is recognized throughout Britain (by everyone except the slowcoach) that the last person to exempt himself shall be the first to be 'on'; and this rule is so embedded in children's minds that their immediate response to the proposal of a game is to cry out 'Bags no on', 'I bags not on it', 'Me fains first', 'Foggy not on', or whatever is the locally accepted term of exemption. (In Banbury it is 'Baggy laggy', in Bishop Auckland 'Nanny on', in Forfar 'Chap no out', in Wigan 'Brit'.) On occasion, even the person suggesting the game may feel he must safeguard himself by saying in one gulp, 'Let's-play-Tig-fains-I-be-on-it'.

Yet, in some places, words are not enough to give exemption. In Norfolk the person who becomes the chaser is the one who last bobs down to the ground saying 'Vains'. In Putney it is he or she who last touches the ground, turns around, and says 'Bags I'm not on it'. In Swansea it is the child who last says and acts upon the words 'Not on this tippits', touching his shoe-cap; or 'Tippits, touch the ground, turn around, no back answers, one, two, three'. In Ruthin one child holds out his arms in a circle in front of him, shouting 'Hands in the bucket', and the last person to put his hands in the circle is 'out'. In many places one child will cry 'Last off ground is it' or 'Last on high is it'. Alternatively they have a race to a lamppost or to the end of the playground and the last to arrive is made the chaser; for it is apparently felt not unsatisfactory that the slowest runner should be the one who has to pursue them in the game. And sometimes, according to time-honoured precedent, the last person to arrive for the game finds himself welcomed with genuine warmth, for it is he who has to take the unwanted role.[3]

Such methods of settling who shall be 'on' appear eminently fair to the alert; and they will try any device to make someone other than themselves be he. They say, 'A, B, C, D, F, G, H. What have I missed out?' and when some half-awake replies 'E', he is told 'That's right, you are!' They say 'Whose shoes are the shiniest?' and when a player claims the distinction he is promptly given the important role. They shout 'Cannon' or 'Quick Fire', and the player who is dolt enough to inquire what this means will have talked himself into a job. In parts of Lincolnshire (e.g. Cleethorpes and Market Rasen) the children who are to play a game silently form a circle, giving each other instructions by signs, and even pushing each other into place without saying anything, for 'the first person to speak is *it*'. In some places, indeed, a player may require fortitude if he is to avoid the obnoxious role. In Sale, after the boys have formed a circle, one of them walks round pretending to kick each lad on the shins, and 'the one who flinches is on'. At Chapeltown, near Sheffield, the boys make a circle, putting one foot forward into the ring, and a player takes round a brick which he pretends to drop on their foot to make one of them move. And at Lydney, says a 13-year-old boy, there is no pretending about it:

> 'When you want to start a game you pick a stone and
> throw it at the people's feet. The first to jump back or say
> anything is on it.'

He-names

Children's dislike of being the player with a certain power in a game, of being the one, that is, from whom the others flee or hide, has led some folklorists to suppose that this player originally represented a being who was evil or supernatural. They observe that in France and Germany such a player is sometimes termed a wolf, that in Spain he is 'El Dimoni', and in Japan, likewise, 'Oni'. In some games in Britain, too, the chaser is 'Old Mr Wolf', 'Old Mother Witch', or 'the Devil'; yet in the majority of instances there seems little reason to think these roles have, or ever had, much significance. When awe of the Evil One is genuine, people fear even to pronounce his name. They refer to him obliquely as 'Old Harry', 'Old Nick', 'Old Splitfoot', 'Old Scratch', 'the old one', 'the gentleman downstairs', or use even more indirect terms. Parish, for instance, in his *Sussex Dialect*, 1875, noted that the devil was always spoken of as 'he', with a special emphasis. ('In the Downs there's a golden calf buried.' 'Then why döant they dig it up?' 'Oh, it is not allowed; *he* would not let them.')

It is, of course, true that in London and southern England the player is usually called 'he' (often spelt 'hee', although pronounced 'ee', and sometimes actually believed to be 'E'); and that in the south-west, the midlands, and north, the ordinary term is 'it'. (The player who is 'it' is then said to be either 'on' or 'on it'. Thus a child may say 'Who's going to be it?' Everyone cries 'No it!' and the last person to say 'no it' is 'on it'.) But although these expressions have a regional bias (see maps), it is difficult to learn much about their age. They have, it seems, always been exclusive to children, and consequently their appearances in literature are rare. The following are the terms that have been found in Britain for the player with the operative power in a game, or for the state of having this power.

Catcher. Surprisingly rare as the standard term, other than in Orkney, Shetland, Norwich, and Widecombe-in-the-Moor.

Daddy. In the district of the Lenches, near Evesham, the chaser was known as 'Daddy' in such games as 'Catch and Kill', 'Cabbage and Bacon', 'Jack Fox', and 'Daddy Daddy Touchwood' (*A Worcestershire Book*, 1932, pp. 45–50). It is not clear whether the term comes from the dialect *dad*, to hit or touch, as appears from such names as 'Off-Ground Daddy' and 'Cross Dadder'; or whether it is from *Daddy* meaning Father, see under 'Daddy Whacker'.

Done. Perth and district. 'We say a grace to see who is to be done' (Boy, 11). ' "You're done" is one of the many terms used at school. It simply means you are "het" ' (Girl, 11). 'This rhyme is said when you are picking one out to be done' (Girl, 11, Luncarty).

Has it on. Kirkwall, Orkney. 'One person has it on and must try to catch the rest' (Boy, 12). 'The catcher tries to touch someone and when she does the player who was touched then has it on' (Girl, 12).

He. The chaser seems to have been known as 'he' before the game was called 'He'. In *The Boy's Handy Book of Sports*, 1863, the chaser in a game of 'Touch' is specifically called *he* 'to use the approved schoolboy expression'. Earlier, in *Games and Sports for Young Boys*, 1859, the chaser is referred to as *touch* or *he*. In *Gammer Gurton's Garland*, 1810, a counting-out rhyme is given ending:

> Stick, stock, stone dead,
> Blind man can't see,
> Every knave will have a slave,
> You or I must be HE.

Het. Apparently produced by the Scots practice of broadening *i* into *e*, and prefixing an *h* to a word beginning with a vowel. 'The players race to a certain object and the last person there is "het" ' (Kinlochleven). 'The person that is heat has to run after it' (Edinburgh, also 'het', 'hit', and 'it'). 'If you are touched by the het-man you are then het' (Isle of Bute). 'The last person there has to go het' (Cumnock). Compare children in Holland, 'Ik ben het'.

Him. Whalsay, Shetland. 'I like when the person is him and when he chases me around. I don't like when I am him because I sometimes can't catch them' (Boy, *c.* 10).

Hit. Scotland, see *het.* But it is also to be heard in southern England in places such as Portsmouth.

In. Current around Axminster, Devon, in the 1920s. 'Two has to be in and run after the others.' Cf. *on.*

It. Apparently as widespread in the nineteenth century as it is today (see map). Robert Chambers, born in Peebles in 1802, says of a game such as 'Hid-ee': 'The *tig* usually catches and touches some one upon the crown, before all are in — otherwise he has to be *it* for another game' (*Popular Rhymes of Scotland*, 1842, p. 62). A Devonshire writer in 1864 reported that the player chosen for a game was said to be 'of it' (*Notes and Queries*, 3rd ser., vol. v, p. 395). Cf. the German child's 'Es', and the French child's 'Il l'est', a term of long standing (it appears in *Les Jeux des jeunes garçons*, *c.* 1810).

King. The accepted term in Orkney, the Isle of Lewis, and parts of Caithness, for as long as man can remember. Also common in Scotland for the chief player in a game such as 'You can't cross the Golden River', and formerly in the game 'England and Scotland' where, says Cromek, 'a king is chosen as leader of either party' (*Remains of Nithsdale and Galloway Song*, 1810, p. 251). In ancient Greece and Rome the leader of a game, or the player who did best, was called 'king', the duffer or player who did worst being the 'ass'. Thus in Plato's *Theaetetus*, § 10:

> He that mistakes, and as often as anyone mistakes, shall sit as an
> ass, as the boys say when they play at ball; but whoever shall get
> the better without making a mistake shall be our king, and shall
> order any question he pleases to be answered.

Man, mannie, old man. Scotland, north country, Liverpool, Lincolnshire, East Anglia. 'First we decide who is to be "mannie", which just means the person who is to be out or the person who is the catcher' (Girl, *c.* 11, Aberdeen). 'When you are caught three times you are old man then it is your turn to chase the others' (Boy, 13, Attleborough, Norfolk). Hence

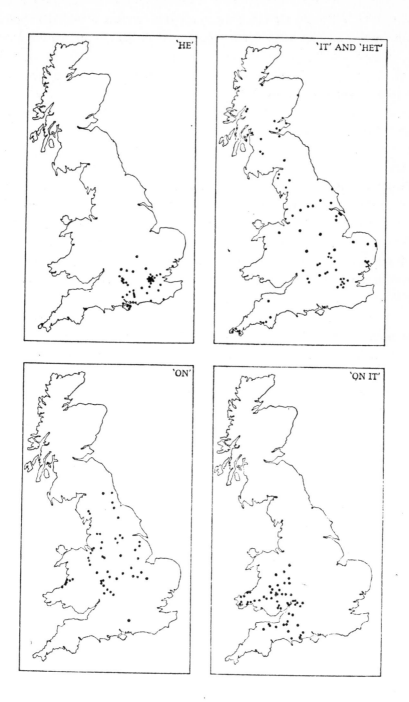

Places where the terms 'He', 'It' and 'Het', 'On', and 'On it' predominate

the trick boys have in Liverpool of asking players if they are man or woman: 'If they say man they are man and have to chase you'. Doubtless the term has long been in use, but it has not been found before 1894 when a South Shields correspondent to *Notes and Queries*, 8th ser., vol. vi, p. 155, wrote: 'In this neighbourhood there used to be, and I dare say still is, a game which we called "tiggy touch wood", where if the "man" succeeded in touching a boy before he could touch wood, he in turn became the "man".'

On or **on it.** To be 'on' or 'on it' is to be in the state of being the player who has special power within the game, other than leadership. 'We play Tag. It starts by somebody touching another and saying "Touch, you're on it" ' (Girl, 14, Newbridge, Monmouthshire). 'If there are a lot of people playing you will need two people on' (Girl, 9, Wolstanton). It will be seen from the maps on page 43 that 'on' predominates in the north and midlands, 'on it' in south Wales and Wessex. Cf. the German 'dran'.

Outer. London. The common name for the player who is separated from the rest in games such as 'Kerb or Wall' or 'Peep Behind the Curtain'.

Tag, Tagger, Ticker, Tig, Tigger, Tiggy. A chaser was formerly often known as 'tag', 'tig', or sometimes 'tiggy'. 'The moment this person is touched, he or she becomes *Tig*' (*Scottish Dictionary*, 1825). 'The boy he has touched is made tiggy until he can pay the compliment to some other boy' (*Youth's Own Book*, 1845, p. 217). Today, although not often, such a player is the tigger, tagger, or ticker. 'One person is the tagger and has to count to thirty' (Girl, *c.* 11, Plympton St Mary). 'The last one out is ticker' (Boy, 10, Oundle).

Ten. Flotta, Orkney. 'If he is caught he has to go ten with the one who was ten first' (Boy, 11). From *Ta'en*?

Touch. Formerly common, now rare. 'One volunteers to be the player who is called Touch; it is the object of the other players to run from and avoid him' (*Boy's Own Book*, 1829, p. 24). 'Last one across the road has got to be Touch' (Boy, 14, Ipswich).

Under. Liverpool and the Potteries. 'The one who was caught first is under in the next game' (Girl, 11, Stoke-on-Trent).

Up. Laverstock, Maidenhead, Portsmouth. 'We get a lot of boys and dip who's going to be up' (Boy, 9, Maidenhead).

Selection made by chance

When players exert themselves to avoid being 'on' the procedure is simple, the execution quick, but it is not always decisive, and not invariably the saving in time and temper that it ought to be. 'We all shout "no on", and we keep shouting "no on", and we go on and on until it is near the end of playtime and we don't start the game at all, like', confessed one lad. In consequence most children prefer the allotment of the disliked role to be a matter of chance. They feel that if the choice has been made by providence there is no possibility of argument, especially if the choice has fallen on someone other than themselves. Thus one boy will stand in the middle of a circle, shut his eyes, hold out his arm, and turn round and round until he has no idea which way he is facing. The player he is pointing at when he stops is 'on'. Likewise a player turns round and round with his eyes shut and throws a ball, and whoever he happens to hit is 'on'. Or a player bounces a ball in the middle of a circle, each player having his legs wide apart, and the one through whose legs the ball rolls is 'on' (see further under 'Kingy', p. 140f). Or a boy puts his hand behind his back, holds up a certain number of fingers, and the child who is unlucky enough to say the correct number is 'on'. Or one player goes out of hearing, the rest pick colours, including a colour for the person who is away, and when the person comes back and names a colour, the player who has chosen that colour is declared 'on'.

Such methods of determining who is to take the unpopular role are obvious enough, and might occur to anyone. Yet children also indulge in practices that are not likely to come to the minds of any but the initiated, and which, indeed, have something in common with old forms of divination now supposedly forgotten. Thus girls in South Elmsall, aged nine and ten, sometimes use mud to decide who is to be the chaser.

> 'We dip our fingers in the mud and the people playing choose
> a finger each first, and if the finger they have chosen come
> out with the most mud that person is "on".'

And again:

> 'A person wets all her fingers and wipes them on the
> ground. The one that is wettest, for example the fourth,
> well the fourth girl is "on".'[4]

Sometimes the procedures they adopt to ascertain the whim of fate on such a minor matter seem unnecessarily tortuous. One player will be appointed to make six piles of soil, or as many piles as there are players, each pile to look exactly alike, but one pile to conceal a stone. Each player then chooses a pile and picks it up, and 'the one who picks up the stone is "on" '. And again, one player makes a pool of spit on the back of his hand, smacks it with his index finger, and everyone notes in whose direction the spittle flies.[5] And, not uncommonly, they engage in the old and international practice of drawing lots or 'cuts'. They collect straws, or plantain stalks, or pieces of twig, or matchsticks, or ice-lolly sticks, and make one a different length from the rest. Then one person holds them in his fist so that only the ends show, and each player takes one. The player who draws the length that is different from the rest (which may be the shortest or the longest) finds himself with no option but to be the chaser.

§ In such a manner Chaucer's Canterbury pilgrims decided who should tell the first tale (*Prologue*, 835–6):

> Now draweth cut, er that we ferrer twynne;
> He which that hath the shorteste shal bigynne.

And in our own time, the girls in Mary McCarthy's *The Group*, 1963, ch. i, arranged by drawing straws who should take on the joyless duty of inviting Kay home for the holidays.

In Japan, too, boys habitually decide their disputes by drawing straws, which they call 'kuji'. In China (Canton) the practice of drawing straws is or was prevalent, and called 'Ts'ím ts'ò' (Stewart Culin, *Korean Games*, 1895, p. 52). In Macedonia Turkish children were found choosing sides with a long and a short straw in the 1920s (*Folk-Lore Society Jubilee Congress*, 1930, p. 156). In bar rooms in South Africa, we are informed, men may be seen drawing matchsticks to decide who shall stand the next round, just as drinkers in France did in the Middle Ages with straws. The game 'Erbelette', referred to by Froissart, may have been a sport of this kind, although the more usual names in medieval France seem to have been 'Courtes-pailles', 'Longs festuz', and 'Court festu'. In fact Jehan Palsgrave, *Lesclarcissement de la langue françoyse*, 1530, is explicit: 'I drawe lottes, or drawe cuttes, as folkes do for sporte, *je joue au court festu.'*

Odd man out

Another way a player can condemn himself to the unwanted role is by the process known as 'Chinging up' or 'Odd Man Out'. For this operation, much resorted to in Greater London, the players stand in a circle facing inwards, with their hands behind their backs, and chant in unison certain words, which vary from district to district, but are in Walworth, for example:

> 'Allee in the middle, and the odd man's out!'

On the word *out* they whip their hands from behind their backs, holding them in front for all to see, either with their fists clenched, or with their fingers stretched out palms downwards, or with their hands clenched but first two fingers spread out. They then look round to see if one player is 'odd', that is to say holding his hands in one of the three positions but different from everyone else, in which case that player becomes 'ee'. If no one is odd they try again; and sometimes increase the likelihood of one player being odd by introducing a fourth finger position, known as 'grab' or 'crane', in which the fingers point downwards.

Alternatively, the players pair off and play against each other, either bringing their hands out from behind their backs, or dabbing them in the air three times in front of them, and making the finger formation at the third dab, synchronizing their movements with three vocables such as 'Ick, ack, *ock*'. The finger formations they present now have significance: the clenched fist represents 'stone', the flat hand 'paper', and the two extended fingers 'scissors'. If both players chance to produce the same sign it is a 'wash out', and they try again. But if they produce different signs one of them inevitably wins since it is held that 'stone' blunts and thus beats 'scissors'; 'scissors' cut and thus conquer 'paper'; and 'paper' wraps round and thus triumphs over 'stone'. Each winner then plays another winner until there is only one boy left. This form of elimination often goes under the name of the sounds with which they synchronize their movements, thus 'Ching, Chang, Cholly' (South London), 'Chu Chin Chow' (Enfield), 'Dib, Dob, Dab' (Camberwell), 'Ding, Dang, Dong', 'Dish, Dash, Dosh', or 'Zig, Zag, Zog' (Southwark), 'E.I.O.', or 'Ick, Ack, Ock' (Croydon), 'Hick, Hack, Hock' (East Barnet), 'Eee, Pas, Vous' (Lambeth), and 'Stink, Stank, Stoller' (Brixton).

In Manchester, where the procedure is known as 'Flee, Fly, Flo, Bank', the players divide into groups of three, and act slightly differently. They swoop their fists from side to side while chanting 'Flee, fly, flo', and then on '*bank*' they flatten out their hands, either palms up or palms down. The odd man in each group then plays the odd men of two other groups; while if there are only two players left the decision is made with what they term 'Sizz, back, or brick', which in practice is 'scissors, paper, or stone', although the players themselves do not think of their words as having any representational significance, and we admit we did not understand them ourselves at first.

As is well known 'Paper, Scissors, Stone', or 'Rock, Paper, Scissors', can also be a diversion between friends to while away the time and see who wins most often; and it is also the basis of the rather less friendly contest known as 'Stinging', which is described in Volume 2 on p. 69 under Duels.

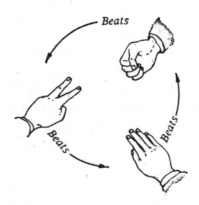

A diagram showing the well known 'Paper, Scissors, Stone'

§ Children in London have a fixed idea that 'chinging up' is oriental, and for once a folk-theory may be correct. In Japan it is a commonplace for children to determine priorities, or settle disputes, by waving a closed hand in the air three times, while chanting the meaningless words 'Jan Ken Pon', and then making exactly the same finger formations that British children do, and with the same signification, 'hasami' (scissors), 'kami' (paper), 'ishi' (stone), or in dialect, 'choki, pä, gu:'. Indeed 'Jan Ken Pon' is so ordinary in Japan that even professors resort to it to decide, for instance, which of them shall drink the next drink at a draught, or which of them wash up afterwards. Likewise in the great ports of China, if not elsewhere, children and grown-ups alike resort to 'Chai Ken' to decide anything trivial, the decision (in Shanghai) usually being the best of three. In Hong Kong, where men commonly play for drinks, the only observable difference in the finger signs is that for 'paper' the flat hand is held vertically, not horizontally as in England. Similarly in Indonesia, a traveller has told us of her astonishment at seeing children squatting in the shade playing the game she remembered from her childhood in a north London suburb (she knew it as 'Hic Haec Hoc'), although in Indonesia the game is 'earwig, man, and elephant', the earwig overcoming the elephant by crawling through his brain. In Abyssinia it appears they compete against each other with up to eight finger formations of different value; in Choa, for instance, they have needle, sword, scissors, hammer, the Emperor's razor, sea, altar, and sky (*Jeux abyssins*, M. Griaule, 1935, p. 189). In Egypt, too, children play a finger-sign game, placing their hands in a pile, palms downwards, and then on the command 'Eat okra', pulling their hands from the pile and holding them either with palms upwards or palms downwards, they then look around to see which player is different from the rest, precisely as young Mancunians do when playing 'Flee Fly Flo Bank'. Furthermore, judging by a scene in one of the tombs at Beni Hassan in Middle Egypt, it appears that finger-flashing games have been known in Egypt since about 2000 BC. According to Wilkinson's delineations in *Ancient Egyptians*, vol. i, 1878, p. 32, two players are shown flashing a certain number of fingers simultaneously, and it is probable that both guessed what their total would be, as in the game 'Micatia' or 'micare digitis', played in ancient Rome, and 'Morra' played in Italy today — as also 'Ch'ái múi' in China, and 'Tōjin Ken' in Japan. This well-known gambling game, although not in itself closely related to 'Odd Man Out', is yet part of the story, since in classical times it seems to have been the recognized method for deciding who should have — or avoid having — first turn in a game. Thus Calpurnius Siculus, about AD 60, describes two shepherds agreeing to play the best of three goes ('ter quisque manus jactate micantes'), to determine which of them should sing first in a contest (*Bucolica* ii. 26). And the poet Nonnus (fifth century AD) tells of Eros and Hymen deciding by the same process which should have first throw in the wine-throwing game 'Cottabe', explaining, even, that they did this with the varied movements of the fingers, holding out some, while keeping others pressed to the palm of the hand (*Dionysiaca* xxxiii. 77–80).

Dipping

Fanciful as it would seem to somebody who had never been a child, the normal way the young decide who is to have the unpopular part in a game is to form the players up in a line or circle, and count along the line the number of counts prescribed by the accented syllables of some little rhyme, such as the following which has fifteen counts:

> Err'ie, orr'ie, round' the ta'ble,
> Eat' as much' as you' are a'ble;
> If' you're a'ble eat' the ta'ble,
> Err'ie, orr'ie; *out!*

One child gabbles the words at speed, pointing briefly at each player in turn as he does so, and if there are less than fifteen players, he continues round the circle or along the line a second time, counting himself in first. The player the last count falls on is then either made the chaser, and the game begins; or, more often, he is counted 'out' and stands aside while the rhyme is repeated and a second player eliminated, and so on, until only one player remains — on whom the count has never fallen — and that player is the unlucky one. Virtually every child in England now calls this procedure 'dipping', a term that seems to have become general only in the early 1940s. It has not been known to our older correspondents; it does not appear in the accounts of games we possess written by children in the 1920s and 1930s; and it is not current in Scotland, Canada, or the USA. In the 1920s and 1930s, however, children used to touch the ground or point at the ground when they began counting, saying 'Dip' as they did so: 'Dip — Eeny, meeny, miney, mo', 'Dip — Each, peach, pear, plum'; and it is possible that this gave rise to the term, 'dipping' being easier to say than 'counting-out'.[6] Such a derivation would be in keeping with the origin of several other juvenile terms. For instance, games sometimes acquire their names from rhymes repeated when playing them (e.g. 'Blackthorn', 'Peter Pan', and 'North, South, East, West'); and there are earlier terms for counting-out whose origins appear to be analogous. In Kettering, about 1920, the process of counting-out was known as 'imbering', from the then popular rhyme 'Imber ormer dasma dormer'; in Workington, about the same time, children spoke of 'inking it out', presumably with reference to the old rhyme 'Ink, pink, pen and ink'; and in Aberdeen where the term dipping remains unknown, a 13-year-old girl told us she 'coonted a gipsy to see who was the mannie', meaning that to find who would be the chaser she used the rhyme:

> Gipsy, gipsy, lived in a tent,
> Couldn't afford to pay the rent,
> When the rent man came next day,
> Gipsy, gipsy, ran away.

Other names there are or have been for dipping include:

Chappin' out. Mentioned by Robert Chambers, *Popular Rhymes of Scotland*, 1842, p. 62: 'He is chosen by lot, or, as the boys express it, by chappin out.'

Counting a pie. The usual term in Aberdeen. 'French Tick and Tack is played by counting a pie and the odd man out is the mannie' (Girl, 13). In the nineteenth century counting-out was often conducted by each boy putting a finger in somebody's cap, where the fingers were then counted, and the counter was not readily able to identify whose finger he counted out. This was known as 'putting in the pie'.

Counting-out. The usual term in Scotland, some parts of the north country, and in the United States. Also general amongst those who write about children. 'The operation of counting-out is a very important mystery in many puerile games', observed J. O. Halliwell in 1849.

Deeming. Current about 1925 at Hurworth, County Durham.

Dishing up. In Walworth children speak of 'dipping out', 'dipping up', or 'dishing up'.

Picking. Current in the West Riding. Thus in Leeds when a player wishes to do the counting he cries 'Ferry for picking!' In Hull in the 1890s it was 'picking out' or 'knocking out'.

Telling out. The editor of *Gammer Gurton's Garland*, 1810, gives the heading 'Telling out' to the counting-out rhyme 'One-ery, two-ery, ziccary zan'. Mrs Baker, in her *Northamptonshire Glossary*, 1854, calls such rhymes *tells*. 'One of the number repeats a *tell*, touching each play-mate in succession with the forefinger as she repeats each word, spelling the last, and the one whom the last letter falls to is to commence the game, or to preside over it.'

Titting out. Boys in the south of Scotland and in the Lake District were said to be 'titted out' when eliminated with the rhyme:

> Tit, tat, toe, here I go,
> And if I miss I pitch on this.
> *Mill Hill Magazine, vol. v, 1877, p. 95*

Dips

> 'There are so many dips that I've lost count.'
> *Girl, 9, West Ham*

To the outsider it appears that any wretched doggerel will do for a dipping rhyme. A 'dip', it seems, can be of almost any length, cast in almost any mould, be either sense or nonsense (usually the latter), and need not even be a rhyme.[7] On occasion the dipper may merely count to twenty-one, and whoever the number twenty-one falls on becomes the catcher. He may recite the alphabet to the twenty-first letter, 'A, B, C, D, E, F, G, H, I, J, K, L, M, N, O, P, Q, R, S, T, *You*', or just repeat the vowels, 'A, E, I, O, *You*', or say 'One, two, sky blue, all out but you', or 'Red, white, and blue, all out but you', or occasionally 'A, B, C, D, E, F, G, H, I, J, K,

L, M, N, O, P, Q, R, S, T, U — are — He'; or in areas where the chaser is known as 'it' — A, B, C, D, E, F, G, H, I for It' (Pendeen), or 'I – T spells it, thou art it' (Blackburn), or 'Tom Tit you are it' (Cleethorpes).

More often, as we have already said, the process of dipping is more anxious and time-taking: the dip has to be repeated as many times, less one, as there are players, since the player the dip ends on is not selected but eliminated:

> Ip, dip, sky blue,
> Who's it? Not you.
> God's words are true,
> It must not be *you*.
> *East Dulwich*

The person pointed to stands aside, and the rest face the ordeal of being counted again. Thus certain phrases are thought appropriate simply because they end with the word *out*, as 'Pig's snout, walk out', and 'Boy Scout walk out' which sometimes gets extended to:

> Boy Scout walk out,
> Girl Guide step aside.
>   *Or;*
> Boy Scout walk out
> With your breeches inside out.

(In Glasgow, 'Oot Scoot you're oot'.) Likewise: 'Ice cream sold out', 'Wring the dirty dishcloth out', 'Egg shells inside out', 'Wee jelly biscuit is out', 'In pin, safety pin, in pin out', 'Little Minnie washed her pinnie in-side-out', 'I-N spells in, O-U-T spells out'. Sometimes they have nothing more original to offer than 'Horsie cartie rumble oot' (Aberdeen), 'Eggs and ham, out you scram' (Lydney), 'Elephant trunk, out you bunk' (Market Rasen), 'Smack, wallop, thump, you're knocked out' (Wilmslow), 'A car went up the hill and conked out' (Bristol), and 'Black shoe, brown shoe, black shoe, out' (Barrow-in-Furness). Yet, despite appearances, it is clearly not true that any phrase will do; for unless the children being counted are already familiar with the words the dipper is using, they cannot be sure that he is being fair. In consequence we find the same formulas used over and over again not only in one place by one group of children, but by many children over wide areas, and even around the English-speaking world. Further it appears that this has long been the case; and many of the dips familiar today have been doing playground duty for longer than the oldest teacher can remember. The words 'One, two, sky blue, all out but you', may be nonsensical, but their eight counts have been found to rule playgrounds alike in Manchester and Maryland, and appear to have ordained which child should be chaser at least since Victorian days (see Bolton, 1888, p. 92, and Gregor, 1891, p. 30). Likewise 'Red, white, and blue, all out but you', is known to have been recited in America as well as Britain for eighty years or more, and it was not necessarily new when Bolton came across it in Pennsylvania in 1888. The ubiquitous 'Pig's snout, walk out', has been recollected by correspondents who were at school in 1910; and the equally improbable 'Egg shells inside out' was already on the lips of Lancastrian children in the 1920s. The Scottish 'Wee jelly biscuit is out', collected today in Luncarty, Helensburgh, and Bute, has been current at least since 1911 (*Rymour Club Miscellanea*, vol. ii, p. 70). And children in Alton were still commemorating in the 1960s the long defunct Board of Education:

London County Council, L.C.C.,
Board of Education, you are he.

The durable nature of these dips becomes still more evident when versions of a single rhyme, or rhyme-form, are set side by side. For instance, children have delighted in the following spell-like jingle for the past eighty years; and the recordings show both how the number of counts in a dip can remain constant, despite differences in wording and even meaning; and how variations can in themselves be traditional and, as it were, 'correct' for particular areas.

Iggy oggy,
Black froggy,
Iggy oggy out.
Girl, 13, Dulwich

Iddy oddy,
Dog's body,
Iddy oddy out.
Girl, 13, Ruthin

Iddy oddy,
Dog's body,
Inside out.

Lancashire, 1920s

Iddy oddy,
Cock's body,
Inside out.

Northumberland, c. 1890

Iddle oddle,
Black poddle,
Iddle oddle out.

Somerset, 1922

Ibble obble,
Black bobble,
Ibble obble out.

*Gloucester, Forest of Dean, Lydney, Newport, South
Molton, Welshpool, and Croydon*

Ibble ubble,
Black bubble,
Ibble ubble out.

Children, Hampstead

Eettle ottle,
Black bottle,
Eettle ottle out.

*Girl, 12, Aberdeen; also from Helensburgh and Orkney,
1961, Berwick, c. 1935, Forfar, c. 1910, Stromness, 1909*

Eettle ottle,
Black bottle,
You are out.

Girl, 12, Edinburgh; and Gregor, 1891, Edinburgh

Eettle ottle,

Black bottle,
My dog's deid.
Forfar, c. 1910; and Gregor, 1891, Fraserburgh

Ickle ockle,
Black bottle,
Ickle ockle out.
Girls, Swansea

Ickle ockle,
Ink bottle,
Out goes she.
New York, Lincolnshire, c. 1930

Ickle ockle,
Chockle bockle,
Ickle ockle out.
9-year-olds, Titchmarsh, Northamptonshire

Ickle ockle,
Chockle chockle,
Ickle ockle out.
Witherslack, Westmorland, 1937

Ickle ockle,
Chocolate bottle,
Ickle ockle out.
Manchester and Radcliffe; also Oldham, c. 1933

Iggle oggle,
Blue bottle,
Iggle oggle out.
Girl, 14, Ruthin

Iggle oggle,
Black bottle,
Iggle oggle out.
Girl, Truro
Eetter otter,

Potter bottle,
Out jumps the cork.

Boy, 10, Dublin

Eetie ottie,
Horses are naughty,
Eetie ottie out.

Girl, 14, Aberdeen

Ingle angle,
Silver bangle,
Ingle angle out.

*Children, c. 10, Newcastle upon Tyne, North Shields,
Birmingham, Welshpool*

Ingle angle,
Golden bangle,
Ingle angle out.

Boy, 12, Golspie

From these examples it will be seen that the 'Eettle ottle' versions belong
to Scotland, that the ones beginning 'Iddy oddy' are traditional in the
north-west, and that 'Ibble obble' appears to centre on the Severn. In addition, extended forms of these jingles have long coexisted, for example:

Eettle, ottle, black bottle,
Eettle ottle out;
If you want a piece and jam,
Please step out.

*Aberdeen, Ballingry, Edinburgh, Flotta, Forfar, Golspie,
Kirkcaldy, Luncarty, and Stromness*

Eettle ottle, black bottle,
Fishes in the sea,
If you want a pretty one,
Just catch — me!

Young children, Ballingry

Ickle, ockle, black bockle,
Fishes in the sea,
If you want a pretty maid,
Please choose me.

> *James Kirkup, 'The Only Child', p. 147, referring to South Shields, c. 1926*

Ingle angle, silver bangle,
Ingle angle out,
Turn the dirty dish cloth
In - side - out.

> *Forest of Dean*

Hibble hobble, black bobble,
Hibble hobble out,
Turn the dirty dish cloth
In - side - out.

> *Forest of Dean*

Eettle ottle, black bottle,
Eettle ottle out.
If you had been where I had been,
You would not have been out.

> *Kirkcaldy; also Glasgow, c. 1925*

Eettle ottle, black bottle,
Eettle ottle out,
Tea and sugar is my delight,
And o-u-t spells out.

> *Edinburgh; also Midlothian, c. 1905*

Ickle ockle, blue bottle,
Fishes in the sea,
If you want a pretty maid,
Please choose me.

> *Girl, 13, Spennymoor*

Ickle ockle, black bottle,
Ickle ockle out,
If you want a lump of jelly,
Please walk out.

Knighton, and similar Ruthin

Ickle ockle, blue bottle,
Ickle ockle out,
If you see a policeman,
Punch him on the snout.

Girl, c. 9, Ipswich

Ingle angle, silver bangle,
Ingle angle out,
If you want another bangle,
Please walk out.

Girls, c. 11, Swansea

Eatle autle, blue bottle,
Eatle autle out,
Tea and sugar's my delight,
Tea and sugar's out.

Children, Kirkcudbright, 1904

Eettle ottle, black bottle,
Eettle ottle out,
Shines on the mantelpiece,
Just like a threepenny piece,
O-U-T spells out.

Girl, c. 11, Aberdeen

Eetle ottle, black bottle,
Eetle ottle out,
Standing on the mantelpiece,
Like a shining threepenny piece,
Eetle ottle, black bottle,
Eetle ottle out.

Edinburgh, c. 1900, and Caithness, c. 1915[8]

Needless to say these rhymes with additional lines are ill received if the players do not expect them. They know the count will now fall on a different person, and feel certain they are being imposed upon if the person the count falls upon is themselves. In many places a special ending is customary, and there can be no cause for complaint. The dipper regularly ends a rhyme with the words 'o'-u'-t' spells' out', and' out' you' must' go", or 'o'-u'-t' spells' out', please' walk' out", or 'One', two', three', out' goes' she". In parts of Aberdeen the counterman may add:

> Out goes a bonny lass, out goes she,
> Out goes a bonny lass, one, two, three.

In Harrogate:

> Raggle taggle dish cloth torn in two,
> Out goes you.

In Gloucester:

> o-u-t spells out, so out you must go,
> With a dirty dish cloth on your head
>   because I said so.

And in Market Rasen:

> o-u-t spells out, so out you must go,
> With a dirty wet dish cloth wrapped
>   round your big toe.[9]

In Liverpool the authority of the dip is felt to be enhanced when the dipper adds:

> o-u-t spells out, and out you must go,
> Because the king and queen says so.

In Birmingham the dipper may add:

> And out you go with a jolly good clout
> Upon your ear-hole spout;

and he tries to put his words into practice; as he also does in Blackburn, when he says:

> If you do not want to play

> Go away with a jolly good slap across
> your face like that.

And in Manchester, as in many other places, the dipper ends:

> And if you do not want to play
> Just take your hoop and run away.[10]

But should a girl from Portsmouth be on holiday, and extend a rhyme with lines her country cousins have not heard before, they are not likely to be impressed with their fairness, even if the words she says are:

> As fair as fair as it can be,
> The king of Egypt said to me,
> The one that comes to number three
> Must be he. One - two - three.

The most-used dips

In general the best-known dips today were also the favourites fifty and sixty years ago; and the following verses though not the most beautiful compositions in the English language, must be some of the most useful.

> Eeny, meeny, miney, mo,
> Catch a — by the toe,
> If he squeals let him go,
> Eeny, meeny, miney, mo.
>> *Current for at least eighty years. See 'Oxford Dictionary of Nursery Rhymes', pp. 156–7*

> Eeny, meeny, miney, mo,
> Sit the baby on the po,
> When he's done
> Wipe his bum,
> Tell his mummy what he's done.
>> *Current since the nineteenth century*

Each, peach, pear, plum,
Out goes Tom Thumb;
Tom Thumb won't do,
Out goes Betty Blue;
Betty Blue won't go,
So out goes you.

The first couplet, at least, has been current since c. 1915

Inky, pinky, ponky,
My daddy bought a donkey,
The donkey died,
Daddy cried,
Inky, pinky, ponky.

Current since c. 1900

If you had been where I'd been
You'd have seen the fairy queen;
If you'd been where I've been
You'd have been out.

Possibly a descendant of the Jacobite song 'Killiecrankie':
(An' ye had been where I ha'e been
Ye wadna been sae cantie, O;
An' ye had seen what I ha'e seen,
I' the braes o' Killiecrankie, O.)

Oh deary me,
Mother caught a flea,
Put it in the kettle
To make a cup of tea.
The flea jumped out,
And bit mother's snout,
In come daddy
With his shirt hanging out.

As well known in late nineteenth century as today. See
also 'Lore and Language of Schoolchildren', p. 19

Paddy on the railway
Picking up stones;
Along came an engine
And broke Paddy's bones.

Oh, said Paddy,
That's not fair.
Pooh, said the engine-driver,
I don't care.
>   *Current since the beginning of the century*[11]

Old Father Christmas,
What do you think he did?
He upset the cradle,
And out fell the kid.
The kid began to bubble,
He hit it with a shovel,
o-u-t spells out.
>   *All recordings from north of the Wash, other than one*
>   *from Cape Town. Known in Halifax, c. 1900*

Two, four, six, eight,
Mary's at the cottage gate,
Eating cherries off a plate,
Two, four, six, eight.
>   *Cf. 'Oxford Dictionary of Nursery Rhymes', p. 334, where*
>   *the rhyme is traced back to Regency days*

Oranges, Oranges, four a penny,
All went down the donkey's belly;
The donkey's belly was full of jelly,
Out goes you.
>   *The first line introduced several other puerile rhymes in*
>   *the nineteenth century*

Ink, pink, pen and ink,
Who made that dirty stink?
My mother said it was you.
>   *Current for at least fifty years*[12]

Dipping rhymes are not often rude, although small facetiae such as 'Ip, dip, bull's shit, you are not it', and 'Blib, blob, hoss tod, blib, blob, out', are repeated with open humour.

A pennorth of chips
To grease your lips.
Out goes one,
Out goes two,
Out goes the little boy
Dressed in blue.

   Current since the 1920s

Dip, dip, dip,
My blue ship,
Sailing on the water
Like a cup and saucer
Dip, dip, dip,
You are not it.

   Current for fifty years, and possibly the most popular dip
   today amongst small girls. (Alternatively: Dash, dash,
   dash, My blue sash, etc)

Red, white, and blue,
The cat's got the flu,
The baby has the whooping cough
And out goes you.

   Cf. 'Lore and Language of Schoolchildren', p. 106

Round and round the butter dish
One, two, three,
If you like a nice girl,
Please pick me.

   A version, 'Round about the punch bowl', appears in
   'Traditional Games', vol. ii, 1898, p. 84

I know a washerwoman,
She knows me.
She invited me to tea.
Have a cup of tea, ma'm?
No, ma'm.
Why, ma'm?

Because I have a cold, ma'm.
Out goes she.

> *Current since before the First World War. Part quoted in*
> *'London Street Games', 1916, p. 60*

Have a cigarette, sir?
No, sir.
Why, sir?
Because I've got a cold, sir.
Let me hear you cough, sir.
Very bad indeed, sir.
You ought to be in bed, sir.
o-u-t spells out.

> *Robert Graves printed a version, 'I have a little cough, sir',*
> *in his 'Less Familiar Nursery Rhymes', 1926*

One, two, three, four, five, six, seven,
All good children go to heaven.
Penny on the water,
Tuppence on the sea,
Threepence on the railway,
Out goes she.

> *Current since the 1880s*

Hickety pickety i sillickety
Pompalorum jig,
Every man who has no hair
Generally wears a wig.
One, two, three,
Out goes he.

> *General since nineteenth century*[13]

Three white horses
In a stable,
Pick one out
And call it Mabel.

> *Best known in the north country*

The following are favourites in Scotland:

> Skinty, tinty, my black hen,
> Lays an egg for gentlemen,
> Sometimes nine, and sometimes ten,
> Skinty, tinty, my black hen.
>
> > *Already current in 1853. See 'Oxford Dictionary of Nursery Rhymes', pp. 201–2*

> Engine, engine, number nine,
> Runs along the bogey line,
> Pea scoot, you're oot,
> Engine, engine, number nine.
>
> > *This version has been repeated since the 1920s. Others date back to nineteenth century[14]*

> Three wee tatties in a pot,
> Tak ain oot and see if it's hot,
> If it's hot cut its throat,
> Three wee tatties in a pot.
>
> > *The first couplet was known in Philadelphia by 1888. Bolton no. 716*

> Eachie, peachie, pearie, plum,
> Throw the tatties up the lum.
> Santa Claus got one on the bum,
> Eachie, peachie, pearie, plum.
>
> > *Ayr, Cumnock, Flotta, Forfar, and Golspie*

> Eenty, teenty, orry, ram, tam, toosh,
> Ging in alow the bed, an catch a wee fat moose.
> Cut it up in slices, and fry it in a pan,
> Mind and keep the gravy for the wee fat man.
>
> > *Aberdeen and Edinburgh*

> Oh dear me,
> Ma grannie catcht a flea,

> She roastit it an toastit it,
> An' took it till her tea.
>
> *Popular throughout this century, and recited by J. J. Bell's*
> *'Wee Macgreegor', 1902. 'Sich vulgarity!' exclaimed Aunt*
> *Purdie*

§ Presumably there was once a time when children were so eager to begin their games that they could do so without the benefit of rhyme, but it is difficult now to imagine. There were, or so it seems, special formulas for counting-out in the seventeenth century, anyway in France. Cotgrave in 1611 described the game 'Defendo' as:

> A play with bits of bread (ranked one by another) which
> the player counts with certaine words, and the last his
> words end on, he takes, whither it be little or great.

Some rhymes which are known to be old, such as 'Who comes here? A Grenadier' (part-quoted 1725), and 'Hickory, Dickory, Dock' (recorded 1744), are or have been at one time used for dipping. But no English counting-out rhyme, as such, is known to us earlier than the one the antiquary Francis Douce collected from his 'pretty little Sister Emily Corry' in 1795 (Bodley, Douce Adds. R 227):

> Doctor Foster was a good man,
> He whipped his scholars now and then,
> And when he had done he took a dance
> Out of England into France;
> He had a brave beaver with a fine snout,
> Stand you there out.

It is possible, however, that the 'certaine words' which Cotgrave knew were not words merely discounting sense, such as we have recorded so far, but were an example of the outright gibberish that some children still favour for counting-out.

Chinese counting

'This is one you won't know,' said a 10-year-old, 'because it has only just been made up:

> Addi, addi, chickari, chickari,
> Oonie, poonie, om pom alarie,
> Ala wala whiskey,
> Chinese chunk.'

It was not for us to tell her that children knew it in other parts of the country, and said it was 'Chinese counting'; that children knew this or similar nonsense in the United States, and thought it was 'Indian counting'; that its progenitor had been known in Britain and America when her great-grandmother was a child;[15] and that people had often wondered about such gibberish and were not certain where it came from, but tended to honour it with an ancestry more remarkable than the imaginings of any child.

Possessing now, as we do, above a thousand recordings of gibberish counting-out rhymes, the possibility is alluring that something will be discovered if the rhymes are ordered geographically, or chronologically, or like-with-like, or indeed all these ways at once. It has been found, for instance, that there is one piece of gibberish that reigns supreme in British playgrounds, and that it is everywhere recited with extraordinarily little variation. Thus in Scotland:

> Eeny, meeny, macca, racca,
> Rae, rye, doma, anca,
> Chicca, racca,
> Old Tom Thumb.
> > *Girl, c. 11, Aberdeen*

> Eeny, meeny, macker, acker,
> Ere, o, dominacker,
> Ala packa, pucker acker,
> Um, pum, push.
> > *Girl, c. 12, Kirkcaldy*

Eeny, meeny, maca, racar,
Er, I, domeraca,
Ali baba, sugaraca,
Om, tom, toosh.

Girl, c. 11, Helensburgh

Eany, meany, maca, raca,
Red rose, doma naca,
Ali Baba, suva naca,
Rum, tum, toosh.

Boy, 12, Langholm

In England, proceeding southwards:

Eeny, meeny, mack-a, rack-a,
Rare, o, domino,
Ala-balla, jooba-lalla,
Hom, pom, flesh.

Boy, 13, Bishop Auckland

Eeny, meeny, mackeracka,
Rari, jackeracka,
Rari, sackeracka,
Pon, pom, puss.

Girl, 11, South Elmsall

Eeni, meeni, macaraca,
Rare, ri, domeraca,
Chiceraca,
Rom, pom, push.

Girl, 9, Ipswich

Iney, meney, macker, acker,
Air, I, donnal macker,
Chica chica, wolla wolla,
Om, pom, push.

Boy, 11, Oxford

Ena, mena, macka, racka,
Rai, ri, domi nacka,
Chika lolla, lolla poppa,
Wiz, bang, push.
Girl, 13, Cleethorpes

Eenie, meenie, macca, racca,
Ie, rie, dumma racca,
Ticka racca, lollipop,
Rum, pum, push.
Children, c. 10, Birmingham

Eenimeenimackeracka,
Airidominacka,
Chickawallalollipopa,
Ompompush.
Boy, 12, Croydon

Eani, meani, macker, racker,
I, o, domin acker,
Chicka pocka, lolipoppa,
Om, pom, push.
Boy, c. 12, Portsmouth

In Wales:

Ina, mina, maca, raca,
Re a, rom, domi naca,
Chica pica, lollie popa,
Om, pom, push.
Children, Amlwch, Anglesey

Ina, mina, macaraca,
Ri a rie, a dominacer,
Chica boccer, lollipoper,
Rum, tum, tush.
Girl, 13, Ruthin

In Australia:

Eena, meena, micka, macka,
Eyre, eye, domma nacka,

> Icky chicky,
> Om, pom, puss.
> *Children, Melbourne, 1922*

> Eny, meeny, maca, racka,
> Rare ri, dom er racka,
> Chic a packa, lollipap,
> You are out.
> *Girl, c. 12, Welshpool*

> Eeny, meeny, macca, racca,
> Ere, ree, dominacca,
> Icaracca, omaracca,
> Om, pom, push.
> *Girls, c. 12, Swansea*

In New Zealand:

> Eeny, meeny, macka, racka,
> Rare, rye, domma nacka,
> Chicka pocka, ellie focka,
> Om, pom, puss.
> *Girl, 11, Wellington*

Each day of the year hundreds of children must initiate their chosen game with a recital of this count, sometimes leading into the gibberish with the words:

> I went to a Chinese laundry
> To buy a loaf of bread;
> They wrapped it up in a tablecloth
> And this is what they said:
> Eenie, meenie, macca, racca, etc.

There are many children who know no other gibberish rhyme like 'Eenie, meenie, macca, racca'. They are amused by it, intrigued by it, and treasure it as an old and special possession. Indeed the meaningless words would appear to have been carefully passed down to them by previous generations as a talisman from the long ago, when it might be presumed to have been understood, and to have had wonderful significance, were it not that its recorded history goes back no further than our own day.

'Eenie, meenie, macca, racca' was not known to Bolton in 1888, nor to Gregor in 1891, nor to the alert members of the Rymour Club collecting before the First World War. We have no records of it ourselves before the 1920s. Earlier than this it is found only in embryo:

> Eener, deener, abber, dasher,
> Ooner, eye-sher,
> Om, pom, tosh:
> Iggery-eye, iggery-eye,
> Pop the vinegar in the pie,
> Harum scarum, pop canarum,
> Skin it.
> > *London, c. 1910 (two recordings)*

> Haberdasher, isher asher,
> Om, pom, tosh.
> > *London Street Games, 1916, p. 95*

> Ena, dena, dasha, doma,
> Hong, pong, toss.
> > *Stromness, 1909. 'Notes and Queries', 10th ser., vol. xi, p. 446.*

Further, 'Eenie, meenie, macca, racca' seems to be unknown, or little known, in the United States, where the nearest equivalents popular today have some soda added:

> Icka backa, icka backa,
> Icka backa boo;
> Icka backa, soda cracka,
> Out goes you.

> Acker backer, soda cracker,
> Acker backer boo;
> If your father chews tobacco
> He's a dirty Jew.

The seeds of 'Eenie, meenie, macca, racca' are nowhere to be discovered, unless they are present in a rhyme which now has only local currency:

Inty, minty, tipedy, fig,
Delia, doilia, all munig,
Eicha, peicha, dol muneicha,
Om, pom, tush.
Girl, 11, Ruthin

Inty, minty, tipsy, tee,
I-la, dila, dominee,
Occapusha, dominusha,
Hi, tom, tush.
Yorkshire, 3 recordings

Yet 'Inty minty' is a count that has always had a more lively existence in America than in Britain. Not only did Bolton collect thirty versions in the United States in 1888, but the rhyme appears to have been as well known there in the mid nineteenth century as in the mid twentieth century:

Eeny, meeny, tipty, te,
Teena, dinah, domine,
Hocca, proach, domma, noach,
Hi, pon, tus.
Philadelphia, 'Notes and Queries', 1st ser., vol. xi, 1855, p. 113

Inty, minty, tippety, fig,
Delia, dilia, dominig;
Otcha, potcha, dominotcha,
Hi, pon, tusk.
Huldy, guldy, boo,
Out goes you.
Hartford, Connecticut. Bolton, 1888, no. 624

Inty, minty, tibbity, fee,
Delia, doma, domini;
Eenchi, peenchi, domineechi,
Alm, palm, pus,
Alicka, balicka, boo,
Out goes Y-O-U.
New York City, 1938. Dorothy Howard MSS.

Aila, maila, tip-tee tee,
Dila, dila, dominee,
Oka, poka, dominoka,
High prong tusk …

> *The American Boy's Book, 1864, p. 32*

Eenie, meenie, tipsy, toe,
Olla, bolla, domino;
Okka, pocha, dominocha,
Hy, pon, tush.
o-u-t spells out goes he,
Right in the middle of the dark blue sea.

> *Washington, D.C. Bolton, 1888, no. 621*

Imwty, dimpty, tibbity fig,
Delia, dauma, nauma, nig,
Heitcha, peitcha, dauma neitcha,
Ein, pine, pug,
Ullaga, bullaga, boo,
Out goes YOU.

> *San Francisco. Patricia Evans, 'Who's It?' 1956, p. 17*

Where then did such a formula come from? If every known version was fed into a computer would its original home be found on the continent of Europe? Compare:

Eenie, meenie, tipsey, tee,
Alabama, dominee,
Hocus, pocus, deminocus,
I pon tust.

> *Pasadena, California, 1938. Dorothy Howard MSS.*

Engete pengete zukate me
Abri fabri domine
Enx penx
Du bist drauss.

> *Hungary. 'Zeitschrift für deutsche Mythologie', vol. ii, 1855, p. 218*

Anemane, mikkelemee,
Hobbel, den dobbel, den dominee,
Flik, flak, floot, eik en lood,
Jij bent dood.

> *'Nederlandsche Baker en Kinderrijmen', 1874, cited by Bolton*

Eckati peckati zuckati me,
Awi schwavi domine,
Quitum quitum habine
Nuss puff kern
Du bist drauss.

> *Austro-Czechoslovakian border. 'Ztschr. d. Myth', ii, p. 218*

However, the opening phrases that have been predominant — 'Inty minty' and 'Eenie meenie' — recall other rhymes of English-speaking children that seem to have been well known to earlier generations: the Scots 'Inty tinty tethery methery' and 'Eenty teenty figerty feg'; the American charm that was Eugene Field's song of a far-off year:

Intry-mintry, cutrey-corn,
Apple-seed and apple-thorn ...

and 'Eenie, Meenee, Mainee, and Mo', that Kipling declared were the First Big Four of the Long Ago.

Kipling was well aware, nevertheless, that 'the terrible rune', whose edict no boy or girl dare disobey, was not the verse of comparatively modern evolution concerning a hapless African but its forerunner of mysterious meaning, or no meaning, that was documented before his day:

Any, many, mony, my,
Barcelony, stony, sty,
Harum, scarum, frownum ack,
Harricum, barricum, wee, wi, wo, wack.

> *'Northamptonshire Glossary', vol. ii, 1854, p. 333*

Hana, mana, mona, mike,
Barcelona, bona, strike,

Hare, ware, frown, venac,
Harrico, warrico, we, wo, wac.

New York, 1815. 'Notes and Queries', 1st ser., vol. xi, p. 352

Eeny, meeny, moany, mite,
Butter, lather, boney, strike,
Hair, bit, frost, neck,
Harrico, barrico, we, wo, wack.

Philadelphia. 'Notes and Queries', 1st ser., vol. xi, 1855, p. 113

Eena, meena, mona, my,
Pasca, lara, bona, by,
Elke, belke, boh,
Eggs, butter, cheese, bread,
Stick, stock, stone dead.

F.W.P. Jago, 'Dialect of Cornwall', 1882

Elimination rhymes which are sound-related, to say the least, are found in France, Germany, Austria, Romania, Holland, and Poland, for example:

Une, mine, mane, mo,
Une, fine, fane, fo,
Maticaire et matico,
Mets la main derrière ton dos.

Dauphind, Savoie. 'Les Comptines', 1961, p. 126

Ene, tene, mone, mei,
Paster, lone, bone, strei,
Ene, fune, herke, berke,
Wer? Wie? Wo? Was?

E. Fiedler, 'Volksreime in Anhalt-Dessau', 1847, p. 53

Additional interest attaches to the following rhyme current in Norway in which the second line starts 'Katta', in the way it starts 'Cat a' or 'Cat'll-a' in some English versions, the presumed starting-point of 'Catch a' when the lines were anglicized. Compare:

Ina mina maina mau
Katta lita bobbi sau

Di va nokså gau.
Ina mina maina mau.

Bergen, Norway. Helge Bfrseth, 'Min mann Mass', 1959, p. 12

Ena deena dinah doe,
*Cat a*weazel awhile awoe
Spit, spot, must be done,
Twiddlum, twaddlum, twenty-one.

Children in Somerset, 1922. Macmillan MSS.

Zaina, daina, dina, disk,
Kittla, faila, fila, fisk,
Each, peach, must be done,
Tweedlum, twadlum, twenty-one.

North-east Scotland. Gregor, 1891, p. 31

Eena, meena, mina, mona,
Jack the jeena, jina, jona,
Ah me, count 'em along.
You shall be the soldier's man
To ride the horse, to beat the drum,
To tell the soldiers when to come,
One, two, three,
Out goes thee.

S. O. Addy, 'Household Tales', 1895, p. 148

Een-a, deen-a, dine-a, dust,
Cat'll-a, ween-a, wine-a, wust,
Spin, spon, must be done,
Twiddlum, twaddlum, twenty-one.
o-u-t, spells out,
A nasty dirty dish-clout;
Out boys out!

'Games and Sports for Young Boys', 1859, p. 68

It appears that the theory that these rhymes are centuries old is not to be lightly dismissed. It will ever be a wonder that children who cannot remember their eight-times table for half-an-hour, can nevertheless carry in their heads assemblages of rhythmical sounds, and do so with such constancy that gibberish remains recognizable although repeated in different centuries, in different countries, and by children speaking different languages.

> Eeny, meeny, mink, monk,
> Chink, chonk, charla,
> Isa visa varla,
> Vick.
> > *Girl, 11, Lydney*

> Eeny, meeny, mink, monk,
> Chink, chonk, chow,
> Oozy boozy, vacadooza
> Vay, vie, vo, — vanish
> > *Children, Canberra, Australia*

> Ene, mene, mink, mank,
> Klink, Klank,
> Ose, Pose, Packedich,
> Eia, weia, weh.
> > *Karl Simrock, 'Das deutsche Kinderbuch', 1857; also two similar versions from Berlin correspondents*

> Ene, mene, ming, mang,
> Kling klang,
> Osse bosse bakke disse,
> Eje, veje, vaek.
> > *Glostrup, Denmark. E. K. Nielsen, 'Det lille Folk', 1965, p. 96. Also Swedish version, p. 118*

> Eena, meena, ming, mong,
> Ting, tay, tong,
> Ooza, vooza, voka, tooza,
> Vis, vos, vay.
> > *White children, Rhodesia*

Ala mala ming mong,
Ming mong mosey,
Oosey, oosey, ackedy,
I, vi, vack.
Boys, Enfield

Yet, as we have seen, there is no certainty that a formula that is known in one country, or even in several, will be repeated in a neighbouring country. The following which is current in Germany and Denmark, which is part of the American child's repertory and has been so since Bolton's day (1888), and which has been familiar in north-east Scotland for the past fifty or sixty years, has for some reason never permeated England:

Ipetty, sipetty, ippetty sap,
Ipetty, sipetty, kinella kinack,
Kinella up, kinella down,
Kinella round the monkey o' town.
Girls, Aberdeen. Well known north-east Scotland

Ellerli, Sellerli, Sigerli, Sa,
Ribedi, Rabedi, Knoll.
Maria Kühn, 'Alte deutsche Kinderlieder', 1950, p. 170

Ibbity, bibbity, sibbity, sa,
Ibbity, bibbity, vanilla.
Dictionary, down the ferry.
Fun, fun, American gum
Eighteen hundred ninety-one.
Chicago. Margaret Taylor, 'Did You Feed My Cow?', 1956, p. 78

Iberdi, biberdi, ziberdi, zab,
Iberdi, biberdi, kanalie.
Denmark. E. K. Nielsen, 'Det lille Folk', 1965, p. 97

This count is recognizable both by its rhythm and by the ending of the second line where Danish children say *kanalie*, German *knoll* (pronounced *kenoll*), Scots *kinella*, and American, consulting their pleasure, say *vanilla*. The only rhyme having any resemblance in England is one that is also known in Scotland independently of 'Ippetty, sippetty', and thus is probably of separate origin:

> Ibsy, bibsy, ibsy, I,
> Ibsy, bibsy, sago.
> > *Girl, 12, Ford, Shropshire*

> Ibse, ibse, ibse, ah,
> Ibse, ibse, zebo.
> > *Boy, 15, Forfar*

Mishearings may, for instance, easily have made this concoction from the words Mrs Baker knew in 1854 as 'a Tell, to decide who is to commence a game':

> Izzard, izzard, izzard, I,
> Izzard, izzard, izzard, I.
> > *'Northamptonshire Glossary', vol. i, p. 352*

The rhyme 'Inty tinty tethery methery', also known as 'Eenty teenty ithery bithery' and 'Zeenty teenty tether a mether', etc., and first recorded in 1820, was remarkably popular in Scotland in the nineteenth century (it has not been found outside Scotland except amongst emigrants), and remains moderately well known, the following two specimens being separated by at least one and a half centuries:

> Zinti, tinti,
> Tethera, methera,
> Bumfa, litera,
> Hover, dover,
> Dicket, dicket,
> As I sat on my sooty kin
> I saw the king of Irel pirel
> Playing upon Jerusalem pipes.
> > *Charles Taylor, 'The Chatterings of the Pica', 1820, p. 31,*
> > *where described as being old*

Zeenty teenty
Heathery bethery
Bumful oorie
Over Dover
Saw the King of easel diesel
Jumping over Jerusalem wall.
Black fish, white trout,
Eerie, oarie, you are out.

Girl, c. 13, Cumnock

This basic rhyme has a companion that is remarkable as much for its survival amongst children in Glasgow for a hundred years without wear and tear, as for the traces it retains of its ancestry:

Eenty teenty haligalum,
The cat went out to get some fun,
It got some fun on Toddys grond,
Eenty teenty haligalum.

Girl, c. 9, Glasgow

Eenty-peenty, halligo lum,
The cat gaed oot to get some fun;
It got some fun on Toddy's grun —
Eenty-peenty, halligo lum.

Calder Ironworks, nr. Glasgow, c. 1855. 'Rymour Club', vol. i, 1906, p. 5

Eenty teenty tuppenny bun.
The cat went oot to hae a fun.
Hae a fun, play the drum,
Eenty teenty tuppenny bun.

Girl, 12, Aberdeen

Cf. Indi tindi alego Mary,
Ax toe, alligo slum.
Orgy porgy, peel-a-gum;
Itty gritty, francis itty,
Ordellum joodlum pipes.

Victoria, Australia, c. 1895[16]

The starting-point, or inspiration, or source of occasional words in 'Eenty teenty' and its associates, would appear to be versions of the 'shepherd's score', so called, the numerals reputedly employed in past times by shepherds counting their sheep, by fishermen assessing their catch, and by old knitting women minding their stitches. These scores have been found principally, but not exclusively, in Yorkshire, Lancashire, Westmorland, and Cumberland. In the neighbourhood of Keswick they remain so familiar they are known not only to the old folk but to children, both boys and girls, who acknowledge 'When we are at school we count in Cumbrian when we are dippin'.' According to a 12-year-old girl in Borrowdale, tape-recorded for us by Father Damian Webb, their count proceeds in fives:

1	yan	11	yan-dick
2	tan	12	tan-dick
3	tethera	13	tether-dick
4	methera	14	mether-dick
5	pimp	15	bunfit (or bumfit)
6	sethera	16	yaner-bunfit
7	lethera	17	taner-bunfit
8	hothera	18	tethera-bunfit
9	dothera	19	methera-bunfit
10	dick	20	gigert

A boy, who did not state where he came from, gave the numerals slightly differently: 'Yan, tan, tethera, methera, pimp, othera, sothera, hin, twin, dick.' A girl from Braithwaite, however, confirmed the first girl's version, other than 'overa' for 'hothera', and this version is, in fact, virtually the same as the Borrowdale version collected in 1877, which was said to have been obtained from shepherds in the vale sixty years previously, in 1818 (*Transactions of the Philological Society*, 1878, p. 354).

Since these scores have an unfamiliar sound, appear to be old, and are still something of a philological mystery, theories about them abound. It has been suggested they were brought from Wales by drovers in late medieval times; that they are a relic of the language spoken by the ancient rulers of Strathclyde, or more particularly of Cumbria; that they

Welsh numerals	Score from Borrowdale	Score from Bishopdale	Score from Litchfield, Connecticut	Score from Wales	Rox'shire count
1 Un	Yan	Een	Rene	Ainy	Zeendi
2 Dau	Tan	Teen	Tene	Bainy	Teendi
3 Tri	Tethera	Peever	Tother	Banny	Taedheri
4 Pedwar	Methera	Pepperer	Feather	Batry	Muudheri
5 Pump	Pimp	Pence	Fib	Bin	Baombe
6 Chwech	Sethera	Sather	Solter	Aithy	Heeturi
7 Saith	Lethera	Lather	Lolter	Karthy	Zeeturi
8 Wyth	Hothera	Luther	Poler	Kary	Aover
9 Naw	Dothera	Nogger-go-lence	Deborah	Katry	Daover
10 Deg	Dick	Hine-er-giggle	Dit	Kin	Dek
11 Un-ar-ddeg	Yan-dick	Tine-er-giggle	Rene-dit	Ainy kin	Mu
12 Deuddeg	Tan-dick	Pear-er-giggle	Tene-dit	Bainy kin	Daonul
13 Tri-ar-ddeg	Tether-dick	Pepper-er-giggle	Tother-dit	Banny kin	Rahn
14 Pedwar-ar-ddeg	Mether-dick	Pomfit	Feather-dit	Batry kin	Tahn
15 Pymtheg	Bunfit (or Bumfit)	Heen-er-bun	Bumpum	Bwmfa	Toosh
16 Un-ar-bymtheg	Yaner-bunfit	Teen-er-bun	Rene-bumpum	Ainy bwmfa	
17 Dau-ar-bymtheg	Taner-bunfit	Pear-er-bun	Tene-bumpum	Bainy bwmfa	
18 Deunaw	Tethera-bunfit	Mepper-er-bun	Tother-bumpum	Banny bwmfa	
19 Pedwar-ar-bymtheg	Methera-bunfit	Pepper-er-bun	Feather-bumpum	Batry bwmfa	
20 Ugain	Gigert	Figgit	Giggit	Icka	

are a survival of the language preserved by the Celts when they retreated into the hills from the Anglo-Saxon invaders; and, more popularly, that they were the charms of white witches or the incantations of the ancient Druids. Certainly the scores bear relationship to the Welsh numerals: the words for 4, 5, 10, and 15, in particular, have resemblance; the counting proceeds 1+10, 2+10, 3+10, 4+10, 15, 1+15, 2+15, 3+15, 4+15, while in other languages, even in other Celtic languages, the count from 15 is 6+10, 7+10, 8+10, 9+10. On the other hand, no records of the score have been found in Wales other than the one here printed for the first time, and this is reputedly an importation. It has always been in the northwest and in Yorkshire that the tradition of old men counting with curious numerals has been strongest.[17] And the word for twenty suggests the Gaelic *fichead*, the equivalent of the Latin *viginti*. Remembering that Froissart in his journey south from Scotland, about 1364, noted that the common people in Westmorland still spoke the ancient British tongue, there may be weight in Henry Bradley's assertion that the numerals 'are entitled to be regarded as a genuine remnant of the British dialect of the north-west of England, and as proving that the dialect was nearly identical with the oldest known Welsh' (*The Academy*, vol. xv, 1879, p. 438). Comparison can best be made if the modern Welsh numerals are set in column beside some of the scores.

Very many recordings of sheep-scoring numerals have been made over the past hundred years. The above examples, other than the Borrowdale score still known today, have been selected not for their conformity but their variety.[18]

The relation hip between the children's rhymes and the shepherds' scores is not close. Yet it may be felt that the opening of the rhyme 'Zinti, tinti, tethera, methera' is closer to the Roxburghshire count 'Zeendi, teendi, taedheri, muudheri', and indeed to the Cumberland score 'Yan, tan, tethera, methera', than are any of the scores to the Welsh numerals. The similarity of the fifth and sixth counts 'bumfa, litera' and 'baombe heeturi' is not remarkable in itself, but becomes increasingly apparent the greater are the number of children's rhymes collected, as 'bamfy, leetery', 'bamfaleerie', 'bamber oozer', 'bumpanary', and 'bump and airy'. Further 'bumfa, litera' and 'bamfy, leetery, heetery' (Bolton, no. 873), bear comparison with 'mimph, hithher, lithher', which are five, six, and seven in a Wensleydale knitter's score (*Notes and Queries*, 3rd ser., vol. iv, 1863, p. 205); while 'hover, dover, dicket' of the rhyme would seem to be related to 'hothera, dothera, dick', eight, nine, and ten, of the Cumberland score, as also, perhaps, to the nursery rhyme 'Hickory, dickory, dock'.

In the companion counting-out rhyme, the first line 'Eenty, teenty, tuppenny bun' may be no more than a 'sound' coincidence with 'Een, teen … teen-er-bun' of the Bishopdale score. Likewise only an unpoetic ear, perhaps, will hear an echo of the Welsh numerals 'Un, dau, tri, ped-war, pump' (pronounced *een, daay, tree, pai'dwaar, pimp*) in the Scots rhyme 'Eetum, peetum, penny pump'; but it is a rhyme which takes a diversity of forms:

> Eetum, peetum, penny pump,
> A' the laadies in a lump,
> Sax or saiven in a clew,
> A' made wi' candy glue.
>
> *W. Gregor, 'Folk-Lore in North-east Scotland', 1881, p. 169*

> Eatum, peatum, penny, pie,
> Pop a lorum, jettum I,
> Ease, oze, ease ink,
> Pease porridge, man's drink.
>
> *Argyllshire. 'Folk-Lore', vol. xvi, 1905, p. 450*

Heetum peetum penny pie,
Populorum gingum gie,
East, West, North, South,
Kirby, Kendal, Cock him out.

> *J. O. Halliwell, 'Nursery Rhymes', 1853, p. 188*

Zeetum, peetum, penny, pie,
Poppy-lorry, jinkum, jie,
Fish guts, caller troot,
Gibbie, gabbie, ye're oot.

> *Edinburgh. 'Rymour Club', vol. i, 1911, p. 90*

Eetum, peetum, penny pie
Popaloorum chicken chie,
Black pudding, white troot,
I choose the first one oot.

> *Boy, 10, Stromness, 1961*

Eatum, peetem, penny pie,
Pop-a-lorie jinkie jye,
Stan' ee oot bye
For a bonny aipple pie,
Black fish, fite troot,
Eery airy ee're oot.

> *Huntly district, Aberdeenshire, c. 1920*

Ikey pikey penny pie,
Popalorum jiggum jye,
Stand thee oot lug.

> *W. Dickinson, 'Cumberland Glossary', 1881*

Eetem, peetem, penny pie,
Cock a lorie, jenky jye,
Ah, day, doot,
Staan ye there oot bye.

> *New Deer. Gregor, 1891, p. 15*

The objection that the shepherds' numerals, like the Welsh numerals, are based on the digital system, reckoning in groups of five, while the count-ing-out rhymes are in verse form, usually with four beats to the line, and that this precludes kinship, does not seem to us insurmountable. When children count out before a game they do not count on their fingers, as they do in school, for no sums are involved. They are not trying to seek a total as men ordinarily do when they are counting sheep, or otherwise wrestling with numerals. Children are merely marking-off; their requirement is rhyme and regular rhythm to help the memory, and four beats seem to come more naturally than five (compare 'Tinker, tailor, soldier, sailor' and 'Silk, satin, cotton, rags'); their pleasure is in assonance, and reduplication ('eenie meenie', 'zinty tinty', 'heetum peetum', 'om pom'). These factors can easily affect the measure. There is, in addition, as in all forms of oral transmission, a tendency to rationalize, to substitute known words for unknown. Thus a score learnt by a lady in Bransdale, near Scarborough, went:

> Yan, teean, tethera, methera, pip,
> Seeaza, leeaza, catra, coan, dick.

But the words a shepherd in Weardale is said to have used were:

> Yen, tane, tether me, leather me, dick,
> Caesar, lazy cat, or a horn, or a tick.

What is noticeable is that the counting-out rhymes that are native to Scotland are the ones which bear most resemblance to the scores. The following rhyme was common enough in the late nineteenth century, and remains so today:

> Zeenty, teenty, figery, fell,
> Ell, dell, dominel,
> Urky, purky, taury rope,
> An, tan, tousy, joke,
> You are oot.
>> *Boy, 12, Helensburgh*

> Inty, tinty, figgery, fell,
> Ell, dell, rumble dell,
> Ucky, pucky, toosie row,
> An, tan, toosie row.
>> *Girl, 14, Flotta, Orkney*

> Eenty, teeny, figury, fell,
> Ell, dell, dominell,
> Irky, pirky, tarry rope,
> An, tan, tousy, Jock.
> > *Girl, 14, Kirkcaldy*

> Zeeny, meeny, feeny, fig,
> El del dominy ig,
> Zanty panty hithery mithery,
> Bafaleery over dover
> Nicky divy den.
> > *Girl, 15, Musselburgh*

No record of it has been found before 1880, so it may derive from another rhyme, rather than from a score. But the thirteenth, fourteenth, and fifteenth counts, 'an, tan, toosie', are reminiscent of the thirteenth, fourteenth, and fifteenth counts of the Roxburghshire numerals 'rahn, tahn, toosh', which were communicated to A. J. Ellis by the editor of *The Oxford English Dictionary*, J. A. H. Murray, born at Hawick in 1837, and may be presumed to be a childhood memory. And if the third count is dropped from the first five of a score known near Penrith, about 1840, 'Iny, tiny … fethery, phips' (Ellis, F. 1), or from a Rhode Island 'Indian' count of about the same date 'Ene, tene … fether, pip' (Ellis, F. 5), we are not much removed from 'Inty, tinty, figgery, fell' and 'Zeeny, meeny, feeny, fig'. No relationship is apparent, however, between the scores and the gibberish rhymes which circulate in southern Britain. The following, for instance, of which two strains are discernible (the 'X, Q' strain and the 'Dutch cheese' strain), is particularly popular around London, and has not been found north of Manchester.

> Inkey pinkey ellakamar,
> X, Q, santa mar,
> Santa mar, ellacafa,
> Sham.
> > *Student, Luton*

> Inky pinky ellakama,
> X, Q, santa fa,

Santa fa, ellakama,
Trot, trot, trot.
  Student, Plymouth

Inka vinka vinegar,
X ma, polinimar,
Polinimar, franc, franc.
  Girl, c. 11, Lydney

Inka ponka pinka pa,
Tish U, allah-ma-gah,
Inka ponka pinka pa.
  *10-year-olds, Headington, who believed the rhyme was
  exclusive to themselves*

Ip, dip, dalabadi,
Dutch cheese, santami,
Santa mi, dalabadi,
Sham.
  Children, Enfield

Ip, dip, alaba da,
Dutch cheese, chentie ma,
Chentie ma, alaba da,
Dutch cheese, Scram.
  Girls, c. 12, Wembley

Dip, dip, alla ber da,
Dutch cheese, sentima,
Sentima, alla ber da,
Dutch cheese, scram.
  Girl, 11, Aberystwyth

Dip, dip, allabedar,
Duck shee, shantamar,
Shantamar, allebedar,
Duck shee, shantamar.
  Boys, c. 12, Sale

These rhymes have been conveyed moderately carefully by oral tradition from late Victorian times, when they seem to have been particularly well known in the Portsmouth area.

> Ickledee, pickledee, elleka-mah,
> Dex Q elleka-fah,
> Awnty Sawnty, elleka-see,
> Trance.
> *Portsmouth, 1895–1900; Gosport, c. 1900*

> Ecklie, picklie, eleka fa,
> Fix, Q, salty fa,
> Sonti fonti, eleka fee,
> Trons.
> *Portsmouth, c. 1915*

But their pedigree can be traced back no further, unless the family came from America where counts such as the following seem to have flourished:

> Ickama, dickama, aliga, mo,
> Dixue, aliga, sum,
> Hulka, pulka, Peter's gun,
> Francis.
> *San Francisco. Bolton, 1888, no. 675*

> Ikkamy, dukkamy, alligar mole,
> Dick slew alligar slum,
> Hukka, pukka, Peter's gum,
> Francis.
> *Massachusetts and Baltimore, 1848–58. Bolton, no. 674[19]*

Very different, however, is the recorded life-span, now over, of rhymes beginning 'Onery, twoery' or 'Anery, twaery'. Early in the nineteenth century when antiquarians first became interested in children's gibberish rhymes, nearly every example they collected or recollected began 'Onery, twoery'.

One-ery, two-ery, ziccary, zan;
Hollow bone, crackabone ninery ten:
Spittery spot, it must be done;
Twiddleum twaddleum Twenty one.
Hink spink, the puddings stink,
The fat begins to fry,
Nobody's at home, but jumping Joan,
Father, mother and I.
Stick, stock, stone dead,
Blind men can't see,
Every knave will have a slave,
You or I must be HE.

    'Gammer Gurton's Garland', 1810, p. 31

One-ery, oo-ry, ick-ry, an,
Bipsy, bopsy, little Sir Jan,
Queery, quaury,
Virgin Mary,
Nick, tick, toloman tick,
o-u-t, out,
Rotten, totten, dish-clout,
Out jumps — He.

    Philip Gosse, Dorsetshire schooldays, c. 1820, 'Longman's Magazine', 1889

Anery, twaery, tickery, seven,
Aliby, crackiby, ten or eleven;
Pin-pan, muskidan,
Tweedlum, twodlum, twenty-one.

    Current in Edinburgh, 1821, and also a generation earlier. 'Blackwood's Magazine', August (Part II), 1821, p. 36

One-erie, two-erie, tickerie, seven,
Allabone, crackabone, ten or eleven;
Pot, pan, must be done;
Tweedle-come, tweedle-come, twenty-one.

    Surrey, England. Jamieson's 'Scottish Dictionary, Supplement', vol. ii, 1825, p. 169

> Onery, uery, ickory, Ann,
> Filisy, folasy, Nicholas John,
> Queevy, quavy, Irish Mary,
> Stingalum, stangalum, buck.
>
> *New England, c. 1820. Newell, 'Games of American
> Children', 1883, p. 197*

No explanation is readily forthcoming why the most popular gibberish rhyme of the nineteenth century (Bolton gives eighty versions) should be unknown to children today; while the gibberish that is now most common, 'Eenie, meenie, macca, racca', was unknown in the nineteenth century. Children certainly enjoy 'Chinese' counting as much today as they ever did; and they retain the ability, as we have seen from 'Eenie, meenie, macca, racca', to transmit gibberish with little variation. Further, they are not keen on novelty for the sake of novelty since, as far as the children are aware — and as far as anyone else was aware — 'Eenie, meenie, macca, racca' is ancient. We know only that dips, even magical-sounding dips in which not a word is understandable, are not necessarily old, and need not originally have been for elimination. The well-known nonsense refrain of the song 'The Frog and the Mouse' has been pressed into service for counting-out; specimens of secret language, 'Ifficky Ikey hadikey mikey gunnicky', have been used for counting-out; so have scraps of mock Latin, 'Orcum, porcum, unicorcum, herricum, merricum, buzz'. The dipping rhyme 'Addi, addi, chickari, chickari' probably started life as the chorus of a music-hall song. And in recent times children have adopted the flight of nonsense 'Teenie, weenie, yellow polka-dot bikini'.

Rhymes, sayings, and beliefs do not have to be old to become traditional, nor do they have to have had any special significance. We have shown elsewhere how an item can become traditional merely because it fits the requirements of a particular channel of communication. Children obviously have a disposition for the authority that attaches to a rhyme which seems to be in a foreign tongue. As Southey remarked, if such rhymes are 'not in a known tongue, they may by possibility be in an unknown one'. Children saying 'Eenie, meenie, macca, racca' or 'Icketty, picketty, eye selicketty umpelaira jig' can have the pleasurable feeling that although the words sound like nonsense, if a Chinaman chanced along *he* would understand what they were saying. We suggest that the counts beginning 'Onery, twoery' lost their attraction simply because they were too ordinary; the words 'Onery, twoery, ickery, Ann' were coming to sound too much like straightforward English.

Counting fists or feet

Not infrequently children feel that the process of dipping is fairer — which means less likely to go against them — if each player counts as two, and his hands are counted rather than his person. The dipper (or 'spudder') cries 'Spuds up'. The players hold out their clenched fists, thumbs uppermost, and the dipper taps each fist in turn, counting as he does so,

> One' potato (pronounced *bertater*), two'
> potato,
> Three' potato, four',
> Five' potato, six' potato,
> Seven' potato, more'.

He includes himself by banging his right fist on his left, and his left fist on his right, and the eighth fist he comes to, with the word 'more', he bangs harder than the rest, and the player puts the fist behind his back. The dipper goes on counting round eliminating further fists (in some places his words are 'One spud, two spud, three spud, four ...' and in the north '... five potato, six potato, seven potato, *raw*'), and when both of a player's fists have been knocked down that player is out, and the count continues among the rest until only one player is left holding up a spud.

This system increases the suspense, makes more of a game of finding who is to be on, leaves less time for the playing of the chosen game, and — such love has the younger part of mankind for complicating a ritual — is resorted to almost more often than ordinary dipping. 'One potato, two potato' has been in constant use throughout the twentieth century; it is much employed in America; and counting fists is also standard practice in many European countries, where, as in Britain, the operation is generally associated with a particular rhyme.

In France:

> Sancta fémina goda,
> Caracas et Quito,
> Villes principales Cayenne

Et Paramaribo.
Cache ton poing derrière ton dos.

'Les Comptines', 1961, p. 102; also oral collection, Vichy, 1965

In Holland:

Olleke, bolleke,
Rubisolleke,
Olleke, bolleke,
Knol.

Current since nineteenth century

And since for the past fifty years children in Britain have had a second rhyme which they regularly associate with counting fists, a gibberish count (recordings from places as far apart as Aberdeen, Amlwch, and East Barnet), which goes —

Olicka bolicka,
Susan solicka,
Olicka bolicka,
Nob

— it appears that the young in Britain and Holland have been associating the same actions with the same meaningless words for the past two or three generations, and thus unwittingly giving further evidence of the internationality of the juvenile community.

When fists are counted the number of participants in the dip, as we have seen, is effectively doubled; when feet are counted the process is slightly less time-consuming, since each player in the circle puts forward only one foot at a time. Each player puts out his right foot, and the dipper crouches on the ground and touches each toe-cap in turn, saying:

'Your' shoes' are' dirty', please' change'
them'.'

The player whose shoe is touched at 'them' changes his feet, putting forward his left foot. The dipper continues round with 'Your shoes are dirty, please change them', and when his words end on someone's left foot that person is out. Counting feet is now as popular, or more so, than counting fists (children may feel that the dipper, doing his work at speed amongst their shoes, does not always know whose feet he is counting out); and slight variations to the formula are current, as 'My mother says your shoes are dirty, please change your feet', and 'Your shoes need cleaning with Cherry Blossom Black Boot Polish', and at Accrington:

> Your shoes are dirty, your shoes are clean,
> Your shoes are not fit to be seen by the
> 　　Queen,
> Please change them.

§ Elimination by counting-out players' feet has not been long recorded in England, but it is well known elsewhere. At Vichy in France the formula is compounded of nonsense syllables:

> Di pi tic,
> Di pi toc,
> Carabou azinel,
> Vire, vire, forekel.

In Italy a nonsense rhyme is used beginning 'Pe u, pe do, pe tre', and the counting-out becomes a game in itself (*Conte, cantilene e filastrocche*, 1965, p. 24). In Abyssinia the players pray to be first to withdraw their feet, 'I pray, Mother Marie, that mine shall be first', for such a player is acclaimed master or 'fortunate one'; while the child whose foot remains out longest is punished, his only choice being whether he will be punished 'in the sky or on the earth'. If he replies 'in the sky' his foot is held high, but is allowed to hit the ground lightly; if he says 'earth', his foot is lifted less high but brought down with force (Marcel Cohen, *Jeux abyssins*, 1912, pp. 13–17). Games have also been played on this principle in Scotland. In the Highlands one of the company counted out the players' feet using a Gaelic gibberish rhyme, beginning:

> Ladhar-pocan,
> Ladhar-pocan,
> Pocan seipinn
> Seipinn Seonaid
> Da mheur mheadhon.

When only one player remained his foot was placed in the hook used for hanging the cooking-pot over the fire. A further rhyme was recited to determine whether he should be punished, and if the player was again unlucky he was blindfolded and made to kneel down. The leader would then hold something over his head asking 'Ciod e so os-cionn am bodach?' If the player who was blindfolded guessed correctly what was being held over his head he was freed; but if his guess was incorrect, the article (perhaps a peat) was laid on his back, and he had to attempt to guess some other object (Maclagan, *Games of Argyleshire*, 1901, pp. 92–3). In Ireland, too, where the sport was known as 'Trom, trom, cad tá os do chionn?' ('Heavy, heavy, what is on your back?'), the men at a wake would sit on their haunches and extend one leg; and one of the company would count out their feet with a doggerel, either in English or Irish, and he whose foot was not counted out had to bend down and be loaded with objects until he guessed one of them (Sean O Súilleabháin, *Irish Wake Amusements*, 1967, p. 120). It is remarkable that this amusement is almost exactly duplicated at the furthermost point of Europe, in Armenia. In 1888, or thereabouts, one of Bolton's correspondents stationed at Harput reported that the local children sat in a circle putting their feet forward, and one of the party repeated a jingle, touching a foot at each word. The jingle ended,

> Alághěná,
> Chalághěná,
> Akh dedí,
> Chekh dedí,

and the foot upon which the last word was pronounced was withdrawn. The player who was left at the end with a foot not counted out was compelled to stoop over, while the rest of the players stacked their hands on his back. Then, as in Scotland and Ireland, the player was given a chance to escape punishment. He was asked whose hand was topmost. If his guess was correct he was freed, and there was a new counting-out of the feet. But if he guessed incorrectly the hands were lifted in a body and brought down with a thump upon his back.

Participation dips

Part of the schoolchild's genius (as also of others whose minds have not grown with their bodies) is to be perpetually troubled by possibilities of unfairness, and ever to be contriving methods to overcome them. The player who frequently takes the part of dipper is soon suspected of knowing how the dip will work out, and a safeguard is felt to be necessary. The dip takes the form of a question:

> My mother made a nice seedy cake:
> Guess how many seeds were in the *cake*?

The player reached with the word *cake* gives any number he likes, and the dipper has then to continue dipping for that number of counts. Participation dips are thought rather jolly, which in fact they are:

> Old Mother Ink
> Fell down the sink,
> How many miles
> Did she fall?
> — *Three.*
> One, two, *three.*

> Dic - dic - tation,
> Cor - por - ation,
> How many buses
> Are in the station?
> — *Five.*
> One, two, three, four, *five.*

> Charlie Chaplin
> Sat on a pin,
> How many inches
> Did it go in?
> — *Four.*
> One, two, three, *four.*

> Dic-a dic-a dation,
> My operation,
> How many stitches
> Did I have?
> — *Six.*
> One, two, three, four, five, *six.*

However, the suspicious-minded become aware that a new danger has replaced the old one. The child who gives the number can, with a little preparatory mathematics, make the dip fall on whomever he wishes, even himself. It is therefore felt more satisfactory if the player's answer is spelt round.

> Engine, engine, on the line,
> Wasting petrol all the time.
> How many gallons does it take,
> Five, six, seven, or eight?
> — *Eight.*
> E-I-G-H-T spells *eight.*

Even this is not manipulation-proof, and it is noticeable that in most of the older dips the spelling of the number or of a colour does not immediately conclude the dip.

> As I went down the Icky Picky lane
> I met some Icky Picky people,
> What colour were they dressed in —
> Red, white, or blue?
> — *Red.*
> R-E-D spells red.
> And that's as fair as fair can be
> That you are not to be *it.*
>
> > *Manchester, Welshpool, Trowbridge, Enfield, Shrewsbury, Ruthin. Known in Gloucestershire in 1898*

> My mother bought me a nice new dress.
> What colour do you guess?
> — *Green.*
> G-R-E-E-N was the colour of the *dress.*
>
> > *Manchester. Current since Edwardian days. 'Rymour Club', vol. i, 1906–11, p. 105*

I know a doctor,
He knows me.
He invited me to tea.
Have a cigarette, sir?
No, sir.
Why, sir?
Because I've got a cold, sir.
How many blankets do you need?
— *Three.*
One, two, three, and out you must *go.*

> Well known in the Home Counties. Alternatively 'How
> many tablets do you need?' and 'How many weeks did
> you stay in bed?' Part quoted 'London Street Games',
> 1916, p. 91

As I went up the Piccadilly hill
I met some Piccadilly children,
They asked me this, they asked me that,
They asked me the colour of my best hat.
— *Green.*
G-R-E-E-N spells green, and O-U-T spells *out.*

> Swansea, Golspie, St Peter Port. Known in Somerset, 1922

Father Christmas
Grew some whiskers,
How many inches long?
— Four.
One, two, three, four.
And if you do not want to play
Just take your joy and run away
With a jolly good smack across your face
Just like *this.*

> St Peter Port and Wakefield

Engine, engine, number nine,
Running on Chicago line.
If the train should jump the track
Do you want your money back?
— *Yes.*

Y-E-S spells Yes,
So if you do not want to play
Please take your hoop and run *away*.

> *Wilmslow. Also Harrogate and Dublin; Melbourne and*
> *Philadelphia. First couplet goes back to 1890 in the*
> *United States*

Fear of fraud may be further allayed if the respondent is made to shut his eyes.

Up the ladder, down the ladder,
See the monkeys chew tobacco,
How many ounces did they chew?
Shut your eyes and think.
— *Six.*
One, two, three, four, five, six,
And out you must go for saying so.

> *Ubiquitous since 1920s*

Mickey Mouse bought a house,
What colour did he paint it?
Shut your eyes and think.
— *Red.*
R-E-D spells red,
And out you must go for saying so
With a clip across your ear-hole.

> *Berry Hill version. Widely known. Earliest recording 1936*

My mother and your mother
Were hanging out the clothes,
My mother gave your mother
A punch on the nose.
What colour was the blood?
Shut your eyes and think.
— *Blue.*
B-L-U-E spells blue, and out you go
With a jolly good clout upon your big nose.

> *Birmingham version. Apparently known everywhere,*
> *but a particular favourite in Scotland. An Edinburgh*
> *version appears in 'Rymour Club Miscellanea', vol. i,*
> *1906–11, p. 107*

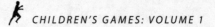

Sometimes the condition is made that the player on whom the count ends must be wearing the colour named, otherwise he — or more likely she, for this is a feminine diversion — is not allowed to be out.

> My mother and your mother
> Were chopping up sticks.
> My mother cut her finger tips.
> What colour was the blood?
> — *Pink.*
> P-I-N-K spells pink,
> So pink you must have on.
> > *Swansea*

> My wee Jeanie
> Had a nice clean peenie,
> And guess what colour it was.
> — *Blue.*
> B-L-U-E spells blue,
> That bonny bonny colour of blue,
> And if you have it on you are out.
> > *Edinburgh. Versions throughout Scotland*[20]

Any deceit that may still be supposed possible, is finally frustrated if the question asked in the dipping rhyme is one to which a player can give only one answer, and which yet varies with the player asked, for instance his birth date.

> Eachie, peachie, pear, plum
> When does your birthday come?
> — *Fourteenth of December.*
> 1, 2, 3, 4, 5, 6, 7, 8, 9, 10, 11, 12, 13, 14,
> D-E-C-E-M-B-E-R. You are out.

The most ardent disciplinarian should be satisfied with a dip such as this, even if he finds after carrying it out that no time remains for playing the game to which it was intended to be a preliminary. But this, he will find, troubles only the serious-minded. It is evident that even participation dips are repeated as much for fun as for fairness. The two participation dips that follow are almost the most popular of all, yet the responses they elicit have no effect on the count whatever.

There's a party on the hill, will you come?
Bring your own cup and saucer and a bun.
Dipper aside: What's your sweetheart's
   name?
Player: Mary.
Mary will be there with a ribbon in her hair,
Will you come to the party will you come?

> *Versions current throughout Britain. Based on a nineteenth-century song 'Will you come to my wedding, will you come?'*

As I climbed up the apple tree
All the apples fell on me.
Bake an apple, bake a pie,
Have you ever told a lie?
— No.
Yes you did, you know you did,
You broke your mother's teapot-lid.
What colour was it?
— Blue.
No it wasn't, it was gold,
That's another lie you've told.

> *Well known in England, Scotland, Wales, and the United States, since nineteenth century*

To the majority of young players dipping is not so much a means of getting a game started as part of the game itself. When children describe a game they may spend as much time giving details of how they decide who is to be on as they do in describing the game; and these details they will very properly repeat with renewed earnestness when they describe further games. Preliminaries such as we have given here precede most games in which one player has a part different from the rest. It will however be appreciated that in the descriptions of games that follow we have — with the impatience of juvenile affairs which is a well-known adult characteristic — not felt it necessary to recount these preliminaries each time.

2. Chasing Games

'The rules are very simple, if you are ticked on any part of the
body, you are man. But that's when the trouble starts. Some
players deny that they were took, and a fight starts.'

Boy, 13, Liverpool

In chasing games a touch with the tip of the finger is enough to trans-
form a player's part in the game. It is as if the chaser was evil, or magic,
or diseased, and his touch was contagious. His touch can immobilize
a player, or make him clutch his body as if hurt, or put him out of the
game. Simultaneously it can free the chaser of his task, and enable
him to be an ordinary player again. It is not even necessary that the
touch be given fairly for it to be effective ('Sometimes when I can't
catch anyone I pretend to be giving up in a huff,' said an 8-year-old,
'then I turn round quickly'). Nor is it necessary that a player be aware
who is the chaser (in one game, 'Tig No Tell', this is deliberately kept
obscure). Rather the touch seems to have power in itself; and chasing
games could well be termed 'contaminating games' were it not that the
children themselves do not, on the whole, think of the chaser's touch as
being strange or contagious. Their pleasure in chasing games seems to
lie simply in the exercise and excitement of chasing and being chased;
and the contagious element, which possibly had significance in the past,
is today uppermost in their minds only in some unpleasant aberrations,
which are here relegated to a subsection.

Touch

The basic game, in which one person chases the rest, can start almost
spontaneously, be played virtually anywhere, and once started, is self-
perpetuating. 'It is an endless game', as one child observed. No sooner
has the chaser succeeded in touching someone (and perhaps said 'it' or
'tick' to emphasize the touch) than that person becomes the new chaser.
Sometimes the unceasingness of the game is stressed by a name such
as 'No Barlies Tick' (Welshpool), making it clear that players are not
permitted to drop out or claim respite, even after using the truce word
'Barley'. Indeed girls sometimes complain that the game goes on until

they are puffed out: 'The only thing you can do if you want to stop is run into the toilets.' The game is usually played within a defined area. The only other restrictions are that the chaser must not keep after the same person all the time; and that when a person is touched or 'tigged' he cannot 'tig back', or, as they express it in many places 'You can't tig your butcher', or, at Hemsworth, 'No sharps'. The player must first chase someone else.[21]

If, however, the chaser is slow, or seems uncertain whom to follow, the game is liable to be enlivened by some confident fellow flaunting himself in front of the chaser, or by the introduction of vocal stimuli. The chaser is goaded with little rhymes that are no less traditional for being witless, the usual couplet (recited in places as far apart as Swansea and Golspie) being:

> Ha, ha, ha, hee, hee, hee,
> Can't catch me for a bumble bee.

Or, with little difference, in Helensburgh and Forfar:

> Ha, ha, ha, hee, hee, hee,
> You canna catch me for a wee bawbee.

Or, in Birmingham, 'You can't catch me for a penny cup of tea'; or in Leamington Spa, Banbury, Oxford, and Alton, even more senselessly, 'You can't catch me for a toffee flea'. In Nottingham they upbraid the half-hearted player with the Midlands term 'mardy':

> Mardy, mardy mustard,
> You can't eat custard;
> Hee, hee, hee,
> You can't catch me.

In Harrogate they chant:

> Look at 'im, look at 'im,
> Chuck a bit of muck at 'im.

And in Bristol, according to a 10-year-old:

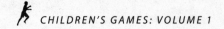

> Hurry up, hurry up, step on the pace,
> You silly old, silly old squashed tomato
> face.

But if, states our informant, the chaser succeeds in touching his tormentor he exclaims, 'You're the squashed tomato now. If ever there was a nit it was you.'

The language of the chase

In juvenile speech the word for the significant touch that affects another player is not synonymous with either of the standard English words *touch* or *catch*. Children in the north country, for instance, 'tig' each other, but they do not say they 'tig' wood, even when they touch it significantly for protection in 'Tiggy Tiggy Touchwood'. Again, 'tig' cannot be equated to *catch* when, in a game such as 'Tig and Relevo', a person has to be 'tigged' to be released. The word 'tig', which is now used only by the young, subsists throughout the greater part of northern Britain, the past tense very often being 'tug' or 'tugged' or even, in New Cumnock, 'tuggen'. However, in the far north of Scotland (Golspie, Inverness, Stornoway), and in parts of Wales (e.g. Fishguard and Ruthin), they 'tip' a person. In the west midlands they 'tick' him, and he is then said to have been 'took', 'tuck', or sometimes 'tucked'.[22] In Monmouthshire, Gloucestershire, and Oxfordshire, they speak of 'tagging' each other, and the person who 'tags' may be called 'tag' or 'the tagger', as he also is in the United States, not only in chasing games but in baseball when a runner is put out by being 'tagged' with the ball.[23] In Nottingham children 'dob' each other, in Romsey they 'dab', in the Forest of Dean they 'dap', at Hereford and Crickhowell they always 'tap', and in Jersey they 'take' ('First of all you dip to find out who takes'). In London, and fairly generally in the south-eastern counties, the 'He' or 'Ee' who chases strives to 'have' someone, a term which gives rise to such verbal infelicities as:

> 'He has to "have" another boy, if he "has" one the boy he
> "has" has to hold the place where he was "had".'
>
> *Boy, 13, Croydon, describing 'French He'*

And:

> 'We played He and I was had, so I had to be he.'
> *Girl, 8, Dulwich, describing 'He'*

Occasionally the past tense 'had' itself becomes the verb and the English language is placed under considerable strain:

> 'If she hads a person when she is he the person she hads becomes he.'
> *Girl, 11, West Ham, on 'Ball He'*

Further confusion may arise, at least in the adult mind, in Devon, Lincolnshire, and parts of Scotland where, no matter how lightly a person is touched, he is said to be 'hit'. When you get 'it on the shoulder you hold the place where you got 'it' (Girl, 9, Plympton St Mary, describing 'Fleabite Its'). 'If the man does hit him he must stand with his legs parted' (Girl, 13, Whalsay, where the chaser — whether boy or girl — is always 'man'). And confusion may turn to alarm in Orkney, where the word for tigging is 'stoning', if a child is overheard saying, 'When somebody stones you, you have got to go and stone somebody else.'

The following are the names for the ordinary game of Touch:

Catch, Catching, Catchings, Catchy. Probably of no dialect significance but all our recordings are from Norfolk, e.g. 'We dip to find the catcher in catchings' (Norwich). In the 1930s a common name for the game in Norwich was 'Adjins' (Had-yous).

Catchers. Widecombe-in-the-Moor, Devon.

Chase, Chasers, Chasey, Chasing, Chasings. Current here and there throughout Britain, for instance, the above names were found respectively in Cleethorpes, Lossiemouth, Alton, Runcorn, and Plympton St Mary. Sometimes they are alternative names, or present only in compounds, such as 'One-Chase-All' (Dulwich) and 'Chase me Charlie' (a name for 'Touch' in Ipswich, when played in the water).

Dets or *Detter.* Recently current in West Sussex and the Avon Valley. *EDD* gives 'Ditter' in Wiltshire and Dorset. William Barnes, the Dorset poet, knew it as 'Datter'.

Dipanonit. Contraction of 'Dip-and-on-it'. The only name known to boys at Henstridge, in south-east Somerset.

Dobby. From *dob*, to touch or tig, Nottingham. Hence such games as 'Dobby Off-Ground'. (In the southernmost parts of Yorkshire the *dobby* is the den or home.)

He. The predominant name in London and the Home Counties. Norman Douglas found his urchins knew only the names 'Touch' and 'He' — 'Called Ee: all touch-games are "he" games, and this is the grandfather of the whole family'. Understandably a writer in *The Yorkshire Post*, 18 April 1961, who had always thought of the game as being *Tig*, found the name incomprehensible when he came to teach at a south London school. But it is, or appears to be, a relatively modern name (late nineteenth century?), the chaser being known as 'he' long before the game was so called.

It. Common in the west country, and relatively uncommon elsewhere, except in Cambridgeshire and Huntingdonshire.

Kip. The local name in Cardigan and nearby Blaenanerch. Cf. *Tip*.

Nag. Given by one juvenile informant as a name in Birmingham.

Picka. Stromness, Orkney. Hence 'High Picka', 'Funny Picka' (French He), and such-like names. 'Picka' was listed amongst games played at Stromness in 1909 (*Notes and Queries*, 10th ser., vol. xi, p. 445). Cf. *Stony Picko*.

Picky. Scalloway, Shetland. To *pick* is to strike or touch.

Runabout-Tig. Name to distinguish ordinary *Tig* from the types with 'dens'. Isle of Bute.

Skibbie. Caithness, nineteenth century (*EDD*). A correspondent says 'Skibbie Lickie'. In Golspie it was 'Skeby'. Thus a 13-year-old girl: 'The girl who is skeby ... tries to give them skeby. If she gives them skeby then they are skeby' (*Golspie*, E. W. B. Nicholson, 1897, p. 120). *Stony Picko*. The usual name at Kirkwall, Orkney. The term for touching is 'stoning', so 'Stony Picko' is equivalent to saying 'Touch Touch'. ***Tackie.*** 'A game in which one is appointed to pursue and catch the others.

Often played in the stack-yard, and it is then commonly called "tackie amo' the rucks" ' (Gregor, *Dialect of Banffshire*, 1866). In Aberdeen, today, it is generally 'Tick an' Tack'.

Tag. Predominant name in Monmouthshire, south Herefordshire, south Worcestershire, Gloucestershire, and north Wiltshire. Hungerford seems to be on the border between Tag and He. It was formerly much more widespread, even a generation ago; and at one time may have been the usual name in southern England, as it is today in Canada and the United States. However it has not been found earlier than in *The Craftsman*, 4 February 1738; and in Henry Brooke's *The Fool of Quality*, vol. i, 1766, p. 177, where 'they all played Tagg till they were well warmed'. (Brooke was brought up in Ireland.)

Takesit. St Helier, Jersey, where to *take* is to chase and touch, and the one who does this is the *taker*.

Tapped You Last. Talgarth, Breconshire.

Tick. The usual name in Northamptonshire, Warwickshire, north Worcestershire (in Kidderminster it is 'Tick-on-tag'), Shropshire, Staffordshire, Cheshire, and south Lancashire. In some places, as Wigan and Manchester, it is often or usually 'Ticky'. In 1905 *EDD* gave *Tick* much the same area. Michael Drayton, born 1563 at Hartshill, near Atherstone in north Warwickshire, seems to have known the game as 'Tick':

> The Mountaine Nymphs ... doe giue each other chase,
> At Hoode-winke, Barley-breake, at Tick, or Prison-base ('*Poly-Olbion*', *1622, xxx, p. 144*)

'Tick' is also general in north Wales (alternative 'Tip') including Anglesey, and as far south as Radnorshire.

Tig. Prevailing name from the Wash to the Hebrides; also in Birmingham, around Aberystwyth, in Cornwall, and in Guernsey.[24] The recordings in *EDD* indicate that *Tig* was similarly the standard name in north Britain and in Cornwall in the nineteenth century. Compounds such as 'High Tig', 'Chainy Tig', 'Tig on Lines', are common. A writer in *Blackwoods*, no. liv, 1821, p. 38, mentioned 'Tig me if you can' played in Edinburgh. Jamieson (1825) said that in Fife when one child touched another he said 'Ye bear my tig'.

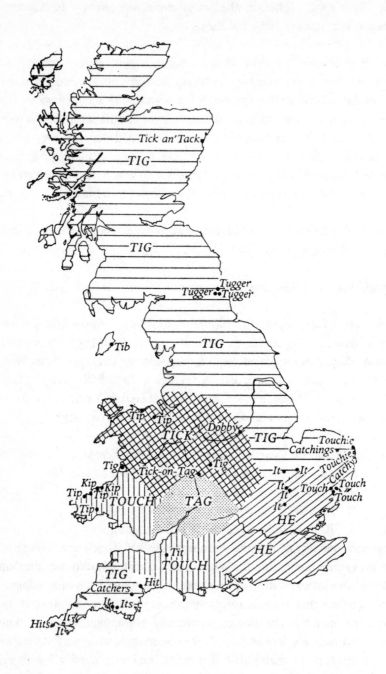

Predominant names for touch-chasing in Great Britain

Tiggy. The usual name in York, and an occasional alternative to 'Tig' elsewhere, especially in the north country. In Manchester it is sometimes 'Stiggy'; in Hexham, Northumberland, it becomes 'Tuggy' (the *u* as in *soot*). Common in Australia.

Tip. Alternative name in parts of Wales, hence 'French Tip', 'Ball Tip', etc. In Lewis, Orkney, and the north of Scotland (e.g. Golspie), where the children 'tip' each other, the game is sometimes called 'Tippy' or 'Tippies' instead of 'Chasers' or 'Tig'.

Tit. The name for ordinary chasing at Bridgwater, Somerset, where they also play 'Off Ground Tit', 'Tree Tit', 'Cabbage Tit' and so on.

Touch. This was the standard name in juvenile books of games in the nineteenth century, e.g. *The Boy's Own Book*, 4th ed., 1829, p. 24. Sometimes the name was extended to 'Touch and Run' (Lady Granville, *Letters*, vol. i, 1894, p. 80, referring to 1815), 'Touchlast' (given by Jamieson in 1825 as the English equivalent to the Scottish 'Tig'), and 'Touch and Catch' (Morris's *Glossary of Furness*, 1869). In Brighton today the game is sometimes 'Touch Chasing'. The chief areas for 'Touch' in the present day are south Wales, Bristol, Somerset, Dorset, the New Forest, and parts of East Anglia, hence 'Release Touch' (Ipswich), 'Sticky Touch' (Rushmere), 'Off Ground Touchie' (Yarmouth).

Tugger. Prevailing name in Gateshead and Newcastle upon Tyne (the chaser being said to be 'on'); sometimes it is 'Tigger'.

Players restricted to particular way of moving

In some chasing games the ordinary rules of Touch are maintained, but all players, including the chaser, are restricted in the way they may move. They play 'Walking He' in which no player may run, 'Hopping He' in which no player may put both feet on the ground at once, and 'Bob He' in which the players squat, and progress is made by bunny jumps ('it is quite a hot game'). At Timberscombe in Somerset the game of the moment when we paid a visit in 1964 was 'Spider Touch', the players progressing on all fours, but with their fronts facing the sky. In Lincolnshire, where a popular game is 'Crab Tiggy', the players attain

the 'crab' position by doing a handstand and dropping backwards on to
their feet, so that their bodies are *arched* inside out. (A headmaster commented: 'If we tried to *make* them do this, parents would write to their
M.P.s'.) In Camberwell, where one of the games is 'Butterfly He', they run
in pairs holding hands, but with one player back to front. And another form
of Touch in which the players move in pairs is 'Piggyback He' (otherwise
known as 'Donkey Touch' or 'Horsie Tig'), in which the important rule
is that the chaser must be properly mounted, or his touch does not count.
The same rule applies in 'Bike He' (in Wigan known as 'Ticky on Bikes'),
but in this game the chaser's art is to steer his bike across the front of the
person he is chasing, thus forcing the rider to put a foot on the ground,
which makes him the chaser as effectively as if he had been touched. Each
of these games is best played in a small area (even 'Bike He'), and with
plenty of players, although there must not be too many players in 'Bike
He', or the result is hair-raising, or, more precisely, knee-grazing.

Chases in a difficult environment

In some chasing games the players are free to move as they will, but running is difficult or impossible because of the environment in which they
are played. In 'Tree He', for instance, otherwise known as 'Tree Touch',
or 'Tree Tiggy':

> 'All the people but the person who is on climbs up a tree,
> and the person who is on gives them a minute and then
> climbs up after them. If he touches someone that person is
> on, but they cross over to some more trees while he is up
> the first tree.'
>
> *Boy, 12, Market Rasen*

Likewise in 'Monkey Tig', played in Orkney 'in a place where there
are plenty of walls', the children clamber from one elevation to another
and 'if the catcher catches one of the "offers" (those who have gone
off) that person is "king" '. But as in every game of chase played above
ground level, 'if an offer goes off the wall, he or she is king' (Girl,
10, Stromness), that is to say, if a player puts a foot on the ground he
becomes the chaser just as if he had been touched. The domestic form
of 'Tree Touch' or 'Monkey Tig' is generally known as 'Pirates' or

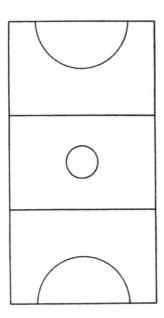
'Shipwrecks', and is sometimes played in gymnasiums and sometimes, but not always happily, attempted at home. Every chair, table, cupboard, and stool that can be found is spread about the room, so that the pirate who chases, and the rest of the players who attempt to scramble from him, can clamber from one object to the next without putting a foot on the ground, for the floor is the sea, and anyone who steps in the sea has to become the pirate.

In the playground the younger children commonly play 'Line Touch' on the painted lines of the netball courts. All players have to stay on the lines and keep moving forward. 'You mayn't turn back even if the boy is coming towards you.' Those being chased may only change direction when they come to the end of a transverse line, while the semicircle in front of each goal is generally taken to be a place of safety. (Other names: 'Ticky Line', 'Tiggy on Lines', 'White Line Touch'.) Likewise in the street they play 'Policeman, Policeman, on the Bridge' (Birmingham), drawing chalk lines on the road, one line leading to another, and saying there is water between the lines, and anyone who steps on the road will get wet.

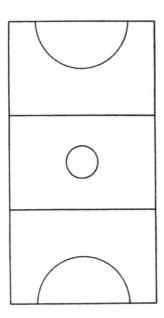

Netball court. These lines are often used for games other then netball.

In the park they play 'Swing Tig' (called 'Yo-ho' in Glasgow), in which they have one more player than they have swings, and this player is chaser:

> 'The person "out" runs round about the swings and tries to tig any of the people who are either swinging or have their feet on the concrete slabs. When the runner approaches the person on the swing she swings to the slab at the other side. If a person is tigged or puts her feet down in the middle the runner shouts 'Yo-ho' and takes her place in the swing.'
>
> *Girl, 13, Glasgow*

And they play 'Roundabout Tiggy' on the little roundabouts in the park playgrounds. The chaser stands on the ground inside the roundabout with his eyes shut, and tries to touch someone as the ring of the roundabout goes round. Anybody who is touched, or who falls off the roundabout while avoiding being touched, takes the chaser's place in the middle.

Touch conveyed by substitute for hand

In some chasing games the touch is made not with the hand but with an object carried in the hand, or with the hands carried in such a way that they represent something else.

Bull

In West Ham young children play a game in which the chaser, known as 'the bull', has to keep his hands clasped together in front of him, with two fingers pointing forwards for horns. Although he runs after the others and tries to touch one of them with his hand, as in ordinary chase, his touch is ineffective if his hands are not held properly, and if the touch is not made with one of the two outstretched fingers. 'The bull has to touch you with his horn, and if he touches you, you are the bull, and then you have to catch us', explained an 8-year-old boy. And the new chaser, too, must hold a proper pair of horns in front of him the whole time he chases, or his touch will not count.

This game has not been reported from elsewhere in England, but it is played in Kirkcaldy, in exactly the same way, although there known as 'Hornie'.

§ The requirement that the chaser keeps his hands clasped in front of him as he chases is clearly not a rule that has been made up by the players. It not only occurs in several other games (see under 'Widdy' and 'Bully Horn') but appears to be the game described in 1813 in *A Nosegay, for the Trouble of Culling*, under the name 'Staggy Warner':

> 'The boy chosen for the stag, clasps his hands together, and
> holding them out threatens his companions as though pursuing
> them with horns ... he who is struck by the stag's horns (or more
> properly speaking *hands*) becomes stag in his turn.'

Horned animals, other than bulls, are more often chased than avoided; but horned creatures of little earthly form, horned men, or horned gods, seem to be as old as the caveman's drawing at Ariège; and like 'Auld Hornie' himself have constantly brought consternation to men's gatherings. It may be pertinent that in *Notes and Queries*, 11th ser., vol. viii, 1913, p. 34, a Lincolnshire game is described in which the pursuer strikes his captive on the back, calling 'Horney, Horney, Horney'; and that a further writer (vol. viii, p. 115), recalled that when he was a lad a game was in vogue called 'Hunt the Devil to Highgate' in which 'He', as he ran, was flicked with the ends of moistened pocket handkerchiefs. At Painswick in Gloucestershire children used formerly to rush down the street crying 'Highgates', after taking part in the ancient ceremony of 'Clipping the Church', conceivably a survival of the Roman festival of *Lupercalia*, when youths struck every woman they met with thongs made of goat skin. It is probably no more than a coincidence that in the earliest description of Touch known to us, in Ammann's *26 nichtigen Kinderspiele*, 1657, the children are chased by one of their number, who tries to slap a player with his hand and then run away; and the name of the game was 'Zicken', the chaser being said to be a goat.

Whacko

In Hanley, and other districts in the Potteries, children play the game 'Whacko', in which the power of touch rests in a scarf. Two boys twist the scarf as tight as they can, and then bring the ends together so that it 'twists itself', and makes a serviceable weapon that can be held in one hand. The boy who is 'on' carries the scarf and has to chase and hit someone with it, who then takes the scarf and chases someone else.

In Senghenydd, Glamorganshire, the game is known as 'Slopper'.

§ To twist a piece of material so that it can be used for hitting someone seems to be traditional also in France. In the game 'Mère Garuche', a form of 'Warney', each player arms himself with a handkerchief 'en garuche, en le pliant et le tressant en anguille' (*200 Jeux d'enfants, c.* 1892, p. 132).

Daddy whacker

In some chasing games in which a stick or whip is used to make the effective touch, there remains an atmosphere of the days when working men and apprentices took part in these sports, and rough play was tolerated. In Wigan, where children play a game called 'Stick', the pursuer has the right to chastise whom he touches. 'The person who is "it",' says a 10-year-old, 'finds a small stick about the size of a clothes peg and a long one about the size of a poker.' He 'tries to hit one of the others with the small stick or by throwing or by any other way. When the chaser has succeeded in hitting somebody with the small stick, he whacks them with the long one.' The player has to stand submissively to receive this punishment, after which the chaser 'hands the long stick to the person he has just hit and throws the short one away. The boy he has just caught is then "It" and has to find the small stick before he can begin chasing'.

In Annesley, on the edge of Sherwood Forest, where the children speak of 'running' somebody, rather than of chasing them ('The girls run us, then the boys run the girls'), the game is called 'Running' and the chastisement is known as giving a person 'his dubbins'. Here, however, the chaser does not forfeit his wand of office: 'When he catches you he hits you with the stick and when he has finished hitting the person he lets them go and he counts ten and starts running you again.'

In Monmouthshire where the game is known as 'Daddy' or 'Daddy Whacker', the play is further ritualized: 'When they are caught once the boy who is chasing them gives them three whackings, then lets them go, but when they are caught the third time they have to take the place of the one who is "on it" ' (Caerleon).

Other names: 'Stick Tig' (Kinlochleven), 'Stick Touch' (Newbridge, Monmouthshire), and 'Whips' (Golspie).

§ This game appears to be depicted in a rhyming-alphabet chapbook *The First Step to Learning*, printed by J. Catnach about 1820. The woodcut illustration to the letter 'O' shows a boy running with a stick in his hand, and two other children who are perhaps trying to avoid him. The inscription reads 'O was Old Daddy, who shall he be?' It thus appears that 'Daddy' is a traditional name for the chaser, and this seems to be confirmed by a version of 'Ticky, Ticky Touchwood' reported in *Notes and Queries*, 11th ser., vol. viii, 1913, p. 34, in which the children taunted their pursuer 'Daddy! Daddy! I don't touch wood'. Whether or not coincidental, this challenge used also to be made in Silesia and Switzerland, where in a game of touch-iron the cry was 'Father, I have no iron, hit me' (H. Handelmann, *Volks-und Kinder-Spiele aus Schleswig-Holstein*, 1874, p. 66, quoted by Newell); and the saying in France that a player who has just been touched 'ne peut reprendre son père' will already have been noted. D. Parry-Jones, *Welsh Children's Games*, 1964, pp. 110–11, says that in Pembrokeshire the game was known as 'Data Meddw' (Drunken Daddy), and in Glamorgan it was 'Daddy Gransher' and 'Padi-racsyn' (Paddy the ragged). See also under *Daddy*, p. 41, and 'Daddy Grandshire', p. 227.

Ball he

In 'Ball He' the ball becomes an extension of the chaser; he may run with it, throw it when he likes at whom he likes (or dislikes), and if he hits someone that person becomes the chaser; but if he misses he has the wearisome task of fetching the ball himself while the others run off to the other end of the playground. It is a game that is liable to exhaust both body and temper. It seems to be played only when boys are cooped up together with nothing better to do; and it is a game which an unusual number of children speak of as being rough and breeding disputes. 'Sometimes someone throws the ball too hard and a fight starts or the person gets mad and goes after the person to get his own back' (Boy, 13, Liverpool). 'Usually there are some black eyes or bleeding noses.

Also, if the ball just scrapes you or somebody and "they" say it did and you say it didn't, there is a "free for all" fight, fighting "all in" ' (Boy, 15, Guernsey). Sometimes it is the rule that players must be hit below the knee for it to count; and generally anyone who touches the ball, even accidentally, automatically becomes the chaser, although in some places players are allowed to fist the ball away as in 'Kingy' (q.v.), and in Bristol they have a version called 'Scoop' in which the ball may be scooped up and thrown away with the cupped hands.

Names for the game are mostly as would be expected: 'Ball Tag', 'Ball Tig', 'Ball Touch', 'Ball Chase', 'Tiggy Ball', and 'He with the Ball'. In Welshpool the game is known as 'Poison Ball'; in Selborne it is 'Stingy'; and in some places it is 'Dodge Ball', although 'Dodge Ball' is usually the game in which one boy is in the middle of a circle of players, trying to dodge the ball.

It is not necessary, of course, that the object thrown be a ball. 'The most exciting game of tig that there is, is "Slipper Tig",' says a Lincolnshire lad, 'where one boy gets a slipper and chases the others and tries to hit them by throwing the slipper at them.' And at one school in Greater London 'Coke He' is the popular game, partly, it seems, because of the availability of large supplies of boiler fuel, and partly because 'it is against the rule of the school to throw coke about in the playground'.

Three lives

In 'Three Lives', which is a more civilized game than 'Ball He' and played principally in Scotland, no player is appointed chaser, and it is as if the ball itself was 'het'. Whoever is nearest the ball throws it at some-one else, and whoever is hit by the ball below the thigh loses a 'life'. The game usually begins with the players standing in a small circle with their feet apart touching the feet of their neighbours on either side. One player bounces the ball in the middle of the circle, and as soon as the ball rolls under somebody's legs, that player picks it up while the rest run. Staying where he is he throws the ball at someone, trying to hit him. Thereafter anyone near the ball can pick it up and fling it at any other player, but a person must not move with the ball in his hand. The other players can run where they like within bounds. Each person has three lives, and may continue in the game until he has been hit a third time, when he usually has to stand aside until only one player is left, who starts the next game.

But at Stornoway in Lewis a player who loses three lives becomes the centre of attention. 'When the ball has hit you three times below the knee you go through the mill. Everyone puts one hand against a wall and the person runs through and everyone gives him a smack on the back.'

Names: In Aberdeen, where the game is tremendously popular, it is called 'Sappy Soldiers'; in Perth it is 'Wounded, Dying, Dead' (the first time a person is hit he is wounded, the second time dying, and the third time he is dead and out of the game); in Langholm it is called 'Deadies'; in New Cumnock it is 'Chipped, Cracked, and Broken' ('When you are broken you have a last throw and if you hit anyone you have to be broken again, but if you miss you are out of the game'); and in Glastonbury it is 'Multiplication Touch' ('If you are touched once you are "double one", if you are touched twice you are "treble two", if touched three times you are "treble three", but if you are touched four times you are out').

The touch having noxious effect

French touch

The fancy that a chaser's touch is contagious or even wounding is here given logical expression. The game starts as ordinary 'Touch', but when the chaser succeeds in touching someone, the new chaser has to keep one hand covering the spot where he was touched until he, in his turn, manages to touch someone else. The sport, therefore, is for the chaser not merely to touch another player, but to touch him on a part of his anatomy that will be an embarrassment to him to keep a hand on while he is chasing, for instance, the top of his head, his nose, backside, a shoulder-blade, elbow, knee, or foot. 'It looks so funny when someone is tuck on the foot and one sees him hopping about', remarks a 12-year-old. In fact one of the joys of the game seems to be envisaging the awkward places where a person might be touched. 'He might be tug on the eyes then he won't be able to see. Then he can't tig us at all', suggested a Birmingham 8-year-old. It is, of course, a strict rule of the game that the chaser has no power of touch unless one of his hands is covering the affected spot.

Names: The majority are evocative of the game, for instance: 'Hospital Touch', 'Poison Touch', 'Poisonous Tiggy', 'Body Tick', 'Flea-Bite Its', 'Ticky Wounded', 'Wounded Tiggy', 'Doctor Touch', 'Lame Tig', 'Ticky Lame Horse', 'Sticky Touch', 'Sticky Glue Touch', and, in Kirkwall,

'Funny Picko'. The name 'French Touch' probably reflects the feeling that a touch which is so pernicious must be an importation. This is also implicit in the names 'London Touch' (in Bristol) and 'Chinese Touch' (in London). And it is consistent that children in Berlin think of it as foreign too. They call it 'Englisch Zeck' or 'Englisch Einkriege' (Reinhard Peesch, *Das Berliner Kinderspiel der Gegenwart*, 1957, p. 34).

The dreaded Lurgi

There has long been and still remains a sinister side to the game of Touch. Generation after generation of children have, at certain times, felt that something evil or sickening was transmitted by the chaser when he made his touch, and this especially when he touched a person on the skin. The headmistress of a village school in Wiltshire writes: 'For several years we have occasionally seen "P.A.L." written in ink on arms and legs. Our children are usually embroidered with something or other, and "Wash it off" was the nearest we had to conversation on the subject. If we had thought about it we should have assumed it was merely a gang sign or a hero's initials. In any event it was so small and blurred that we did not always recognize it as being "P.A.L.". Recently, however, a small girl was crying because everybody said she had "it". I could not find out what "it" was, and was really exasperated before a boy volunteered that "it" was "Lurgy", and, thereafter, that "Lurgy" was "it". This was deadlock, until, rolling up the leg of his shorts, the boy said, "She should have had this — P.A.L. — Protection Against Lurgy".'

Following on this report, inquiries have shown that a number of schools, large and small, have been troubled with the complaint. 'The dreaded Lurgi' is passed on by touching a person's skin, or, sometimes, by throwing a small contaminated parcel at him (as in 'Ball Tig'). Clearly the immediate source of infection has been 'The Goon Show'. On 9 November 1954 an edition of 'The Goon Show' (a BBC sound programme featuring Peter Sellers, Harry Secombe, and Spike Milligan) was entitled 'The Lurgi strikes Britain', and 'the dreaded Lurgi' became a by-word in subsequent programmes.[25] It seems, however, that diseases, even imaginary ones, do not occur spontaneously. In Norwich we found the word 'lurgy' in everyday use amongst children — 'You're lurgy' — but with the restricted inference that the person was 'stupid, goofy, looney, nuts, a nit' ('nit' was a favourite word in the early sixties). Boys in Norwich also said to each other, 'You've got the touch', 'the flea touch', 'the silly touch', or 'the lurgy touch', and this touch was one that could be passed on. Almost certainly they were not referring to the 'dreaded lurgi', but sustaining the dialect *lurgy* and *lurgy fever*, which have long been in use in East Anglia to distinguish the idle, and the ailment from which they suffer.

In Hampshire we found children who had the feeling that a person's characteristics could be transmitted by touch. Thus in one school, there was a girl whom we shall call Jill Benney, with the reputation of a cry-baby, it was felt any child could be contaminated who was given the 'Benney touch'. In Liss children transmit something, which only they can understand, when they make the 'aggie touch'; and the touch may even be passed on by the deceit of shaking hands. In Wolstanton children play a game called 'Germ':

> 'Germ is a kind of tick you dip and the person that is out
> has the germ but if he ticks somebody that person is on
> and it goes on like that.'
>
> *Boy, 9*

In Glastonbury they play 'Minge', a game in which players can obtain no protection from the touch, as they ordinarily can, by saying their truce-term 'fens':

> 'In the game Minge someone is on-it, and the person that
> is on-it has a disease. But if the person who's on-it touches
> somebody else they've got the disease and they chase.
> There is no fens in the game.'
>
> *Boy, 11*

In Swansea girls obtain a morbid thrill playing 'The Plague'; in Cranford, Middlesex, the game is called 'Fever'; in Sale, Manchester, it is 'The Poo' ('the one that has it at the end of the day smells'); at Castel in Guernsey it is 'Poisonous Fungi'; and at St Peter Port it is 'Lodgers':

> 'A bundle of paper is wrapped up tightly in a ball and one
> person is on. He throws the ball of paper at somebody
> while the others shout out "How much do they pay a
> week?" or "How many have you got?" The person who is on
> is supposed to have fleas.'
>
> *Boy, 11*

And while these games are being played, and even afterwards, the suspension of disbelief in the game's pretence can be absolute: the feeling is unfeigned that the chaser's touch is unhealthy.

§ Such games seem to be played around the world. In Auckland, New Zealand, when a boy is tagged by a girl, the others deride him shouting 'You've got girl fleas'. In Valencia the ordinary game of chase is 'Tu portes la pusa' (You carry the flea). At Massa in the Bay of Naples, the game is 'Peste'. And in Madagascar, according to *The Folk-Lore Journal*, vol. i, 1883, p. 102, the child who did the chasing was *bôka*, a leper, and when he touched someone his leprosy was conveyed to the one he touched, who in turn tried to rid himself of the disease on someone else. At the end of the game all the children spat, saying '*Poà*, for it is not I who am a leper'.

Indeed the importance to a child of not being the one who receives the 'last touch' has frequently been noticed, particularly in the nineteenth century. (See, for example, 'Last Bat' in Brockett's *North Country Words*, 1825, and 'Tig' in Patterson's *Antrim Glossary*, 1880.) It has been observed that a child who received the 'last touch' on the way home from school, when he has no way of passing it on, was liable to feel genuinely ill at ease. But as Blakeborough pointed out in his *Wit of the North Riding*, 1898, 'this last tig had to be given on the skin, not on the jacket, or the boy would call out, "I wasn't born with my clothes on" '.

Immunity from the touch

In the following games those being chased can make themselves immune to the 'Touch' merely by themselves touching a particular substance, or by staying in a specific place, or by adopting a certain posture. It is, however, generally expected of a player that he will relinquish his security when the chaser has moved away; and in some games he has no option, as when a second fugitive arrives at his sanctuary and his departure is obligatory.

Touchwood

In 'Touchwood' security from the chaser is obtained by touching any object which can be termed 'wood', as a door, window-sill, fence, or trunk of a tree. Players run at will from one piece of wood to another, and even back to the piece of wood they have just left. The attraction of the game, as in all games of this type, is the chance it gives the less-good runner to feign boldness. He can taunt the chaser with the words 'Tiggy tiggy touchwood, I don't touch wood', and the moment the chaser turns on him scurry to a nearby sanctum which his pursuer has not observed. However, as an 11-year-old remarks, 'It is not fair if you carry wood about with you when you are playing this game. And it is not fair to climb up trees.'

Names: 'Touchwood' (general), 'Ticky Touchwood' (Ipswich), 'Tig-on-Wood' (Rossendale), 'Tiggy Tiggy Touchwood' (Thirsk), 'Tuggy Tuggy Touchwood' (Etton), 'Wood Tick' (Knighton), 'Wood Touch' (Timberscombe).

§ 'Touchwood' is less a favourite with children today than with antiquarian impresarios who wish to exhibit the game as evidence that wood anciently possessed religious or magical properties. Not that there is any evidence that the game is old. The earliest known reference to it is in Robert Anderson's *Ballads in the Cumberland Dialect*, 1805, p. 35, 'Tig-touch-wood' (*EDD*). Thereafter mention of it is made in *Blackwood's Magazine*, August 1821, p. 33, 'tig touch timmer'; *The Boy's Own Book*, 4th ed., 1829, p. 24; *Exercises for the Senses*, 1835, p. 123; and *The Book of Games, c.* 1837, p. 119. A joke about a boy carrying a pencil with him, which he produces from his pocket when touched, occurs in *The Youth's Own Book of Healthful Amusements*, 1845, pp. 217–18. All indications are that 'Touch Iron' is the older form of the game.

Touch iron

This is the same game as 'Touchwood' except that, as a Knottingley boy says, 'it is played in a good spot which has gratings, fences with nails, or any other iron objects', and 'the players are chased about until they see a metal object and grasp it'. However, in Knottingley, according to one informant, the game tends to become more virile than elsewhere, for 'it is up to the players to knock each other off the piece of iron to try to make them be on' (cf. 'Budge He' below). 'Touch Iron' is not as popular as it used to be. It seems to have fallen out of favour in the latter part of the nineteenth century, possibly because by then every boy had begun to carry iron with him in the nails of his boots, and recourse to iron had become too easy.

Other names: 'Iron Tig' (Blackburn), 'Metal Touch' (Bristol), 'Tig on Metal' (Bacup), 'Tiggy on Iron' (South Elmsall).

§ References to 'Touch Iron' considerably antedate 'Touchwood'. A humorous writer in *The Craftsman*, 4 February 1738, claiming access to an old manuscript, asserted 'In Queen Mary's Reign, Tag was all the Play; where the Lad saves himself by touching of cold iron.' The engraver of *Les Trente-six figures contenant tous les jeux*, 1587, shows boys saving themselves by holding on to the iron bars of windows while a chaser waits for them to let go; and the caption states it to be common for boys to play 'qui retiendra fer'. Florio gives 'Ferri' as 'a kind of play so called' in his Italian-English *Dictionarie*, 1611; and in Italy today, where iron is touched to give protection from the plague in the game 'Peste' (already noted), and where the touching of iron is common to counteract ill luck, the game is 'Tocca ferro'. In Britain it is of course notorious, as Robert Kirk wrote in 1691, that 'all uncouth, unknown wights are terrified by nothing earthly so much as cold iron'; and an amount of superstitious practice has developed in the light of this knowledge, specifically in the hanging of horseshoes over doorways. Peesch, in *Das Berliner Kinderspiel der Gegenwart*, 1957, p. 34, says that in the elementary form of 'Einkriege' players are safe who hold on to either wood or iron.

Touch colour

If 'Touch Iron' was the game of the eighteenth century, and 'Touchwood' of the nineteenth, 'Touch Colour' is the game that prevails today. Possibly because the architecture of contemporary school-playgrounds efficiently eliminates trees and other signs of nature, the children are forced to play 'Touch Colour', or, depressingly often, 'Green Touch' — the green being not grass but paint.

> 'At our school we have lots of green doors and posts and spots of green paint, so we run backwards and forwards to different spots of green.' *Boy, 10*

At other schools, according to the surroundings, they play 'Green Drainpipe Touch', 'Touch Stone Wall', and 'Door-knobby Tig', and such-like perversions of the traditional amusement, for although children will remain faithful to a traditional game for as long as they can, they are not slow to adapt if the environment makes an old game impracticable.

Other names: 'Tiggy Touch Colour' (Birmingham), 'Dobby Colours' (Nottingham), 'Ticky Off-Green' (Wilmslow), and, less common than 'Green Touch' — 'Black Touch', 'Brown Touch', 'Red Touch', etc.

§ A writer in *The Boy's Own Paper*, 5 November 1887, p. 88, describing his schooldays in the middle of the nineteenth century, recalled playing 'Touch-wood', 'Touch-iron', and 'many absurd Touches' including 'Touch-paint'. An 8-year-old Italian girl told us that she and her friends decide before beginning to play whether they will touch wood, touch iron, or touch a colour. 'Touch Colour' is also much played in Sweden; and, as in Britain, it is now played more often than either 'Touchwood' or 'Touch Iron'.

Colours

This is a variation of 'Touch Colour' in which the monotony of green is dispelled. Whoever is appointed chaser names the colour that will give immunity while he is chasing; and those players who are not wearing the colour, and cannot see any of it, have no alternative but to keep running (cf. 'Farmer, Farmer, May We Cross Your Golden River?'). When someone is caught and becomes the new chaser he chooses a new colour; and at Arncliffe in the West Riding the naming of the colour becomes a small ceremony. The children form a circle round the person who is 'on' and sing:

> Charlie over the water,
> Charlie over the sea,
> Charlie caught a blackbird, and can't
>   catch me.

The person in the middle calls out the colour (or it may be a type of object), and the players have to find it without being caught.

Names: 'Colours' (Bristol), 'Colour Tag' (Cwmbran), 'Colour Touch' (Swansea), and 'Charlie over the Water' (Arncliffe).

Off-ground he

'Off-Ground He' is such a favourite that in some places children give the impression it is the only chasing game they know. The motif is simple: a player cannot be caught if he is above the ordinary level of the ground. He is safe as long as he can balance on a brick, hang from the branch of a tree, straddle a fence, or climb on to a dustbin. Of course, should a player be half-falling from his perch the chaser will 'guard' him closely, and touch him the moment he falls; but, as several children remark, 'You must not pull someone off of the object they are on, and then touch them, that is cheating.'

Names: 'Dobby Off-Ground' (Nottingham), 'Feet Off Ground' (London and environs), 'High Picka' (Orkney), 'High Tig' (general in Scotland), 'Last Off Ground' (Aberystwyth), 'Jack Above' (Barrow-in-Furness, Barlby and Market Rasen), 'London Town' and 'No Feet' (alternative names in Norwich), 'Off-Ground Catch' (Gorleston), 'Off-Ground Daddy' (Poole), 'Off-Ground He' (general north and west Home Counties), 'Off-Ground Its' (Lizard), 'Off-Ground Tag' (Pontypool and Forest of Dean), 'Off-Ground Tick' (Frodsham, Wolstanton, Welshpool, Knighton), 'Off-Ground Tig' (Accrington and Halifax), 'Off-Ground Touch' (west country and East Anglia), 'Tick Off-Ground' (Upton Magna), 'Tig Off-Ground' (Bishop Auckland and St Peter Port), 'Tig on High' (Bacup), 'Tiggy Off-Ground' (Lincolnshire), 'Tiggy on High' (Cumberland and Durham), 'Tuggy, Tuggy, Off-Ground' (Etton).[26]

Occasionally the nature of the 'off-ground' sanctuary is specified, as at South Elmsall where they play 'Stone Tiggy' and, says a 10-year-old, 'they cannot tig us if we are on stone and we shout "Lick-Lock I'm in my den" '.

§ 'Feet Off-Ground' was one of the games listed in *Notes and Queries*, 11th ser., vol. i, p. 483, as being played by children in London elementary schools in 1910. It is also given in *200 Jeux d'enfants, c.* 1892, pp. 100–1, under the name 'Le Chat Perché'. It is known to be popular today in Sweden, Italy, and Spain, and is probably played throughout Europe; but it does not seem to have been common in the United States up to the early 1950s. Brewster mentions only 'Hang Tag', in which players obtain immunity by hanging from the branch of a tree.

Budge he

This is an elaboration of 'Off-Ground He', and — for the energetic — a more satisfactory game. Only one player may take refuge on any one elevation. If a second player comes to the safety-place, the first player is obliged to leave. Hence the game is played with a certain assertiveness:

> 'A person decides he wants to move, so he runs over to
> another person who is off-ground and says "Bunk you
> skunk". The other person has to move and the person who
> is on has to try and tig him.'   *Boy, 13, Market Rasen*

It is while the expelled player is considering whom, in his turn, he shall discompose with a visit, that the chaser commonly makes his touch.

The game can also be played with posts for sanctuaries (e.g. netball posts), or with the players standing on places which are distinguishable, although not elevated, such as the covers of drains and water hydrants. 'There can only be one person on a drain', explains a Fulham girl, 'but say a girl wanted to change drains she would run on to the next one and say "Buzz" and the person who was on that drain would have to get off, and most probably would be had.' 'I don't like playing "Buzzing Bee",' commented an 11-year-old Walworth girl, 'because in the summer the drains smell terribly.' In Kirkwall, Orkney, the game is known as 'Syre Buzz', a syre being a drain.

Other names, some of them aptly imperious, include: 'Scoot' (Widecombe-in-the-Moor), 'Scram' (Timberscombe), 'Shift' (Ipswich), 'Shoo' (St Martins), 'Buzz' (Bristol and parts of London), 'Bunk Tiggy' (Market Rasen), 'Tiggy Budge' (York), 'Off-Ground Budge' (Croydon), 'Hoppit' and 'Hook' (Norwich), 'Clear-Off He' (Yarmouth), 'No Two Birds in One Nest' (Shoreham-by-Sea), and 'Feet-Off-Ground-He-Scram' (Broadbridge Heath).

Twos and threes

'Twos and Threes' is the orderly adult-approved form of 'Budge He'. Children stand in pairs, one child behind the other, in a circle with all the players facing the centre, and an equal distance between each pair. One pair are appointed chaser and fugitive. The player being chased runs where he likes outside the circle or across the circle or dodging around the pairs, and he obtains safety by placing himself in front of any one of the pairs, whereon the person at the back of that pair becomes the new person to be chased. There are thus never more than two people running at once, but the game is non-stop, for should a player be caught he becomes the chaser and turns round and chases the one who caught him.

'Twos and Threes' is not a game children readily play on their own. Unlike 'Budge He' there must be not less than six players, their number must be even, the formation of the game does not occur spontaneously, and there is none of the subsidiary sport of moving at will from safety to evict somebody else. Indeed, when the game is played in the street, as in Putney, they do not bother about the circle, they simply 'cling together in pairs' and shout 'Help', and the game is called 'Help'.[27]

§ The name 'Twos and Threes' has predominated only in the twentieth century; earlier it was 'Round Tag' or, when the players stood in a line rather than a circle, 'Long Tag' (*Cassell's Sports and Pastimes*, 1888, p. 272). In polite society it was 'Fox and Goose', 'Faggots', 'Tertia', or 'Touch-Third' (Henry Dalton, *Drawing-Room Plays*, 1861, p. 329). Francis Kilvert seems to have known it as 'Thirds' (*Diary*, 31 August 1871). *The Cumberland Glossary*, 1881, has 'Hinmost o' Three', probably the same game, 'played on village greens'; *The Modern Playmate, c.* 1870, has 'Tierce'; and the usual name in the north country was apparently 'Tersy' or 'Tarsy' (*EDD*). This suggests that the game came from France where *le Tierce* or *le Tiers* has long been popular. The young Gargantua played 'au tiers' (1534); and, even earlier, the Ménagier de Paris, *c.* 1393, described young wives 'en la rue avecques leurs voisines jouans au *tiers*' (vol. i, 1847, p. 72). Moreover *le tiers* seems to have been a popular sport in medieval France, for Martial D'Auvergne makes it the occasion of some horseplay between young men and maids in *Les Arrêts d'Amour*, written about 1460–5, where a gallant complains of a girl shoving a handful of grass down the back of his neck; and the girl replies that she did so merely in the spirit of the game:

> 'Jouant au tiers en ung beau grant preau vert, et par
> joyeusete en courant par derriere elle mist audict gallant
> ung tantinet d'herbe entre la chemise et le dos, ce gallant
> se despita si terriblement que il lui vint incontinent bailler
> deux grans soufletz.'
>
> Edition c. 1520, 51st judgment, ll. 19–26

Descriptions of the game in the seventeenth and eighteenth centuries show it to have been played in much the same way as today, but with the pursued player keeping outside the circle until he moved in front of a pair, a rule still observed in some places (e.g. at Ardingly College), and particularly in the United States. In Germany the game was 'Das Drittenabschlagen' (J. C. F. Gutsmuths, *Spiele für die Jugend*, 1796, p. 276), and the chaser usually carried a *Plumpsack* or knotted handkerchief with which to hit the runner. Kampmüller says that in Austria the game has been superseded by a version 'Der dritte schlägt', in which the third in the row, instead of running away, chases the one who had been chasing (*Oberösterreichische Kinderspiele*, 1965, pp. 142–4).

In the United States the game is generally known as 'Three Deep', sometimes 'Third Man'. Mrs Child in *The Girl's Own Book*, Boston, 1832, called it 'Tiercé, or Touch the Third'.

Tom Tiddler's ground

'Tom Tiddler's ground' varies from other sanctuary-site games less in form than in emphasis, which is on the peril of entering the chaser's territory, rather than the security of being off it. The game has in fact an element of make-believe or exaggeration, and is mostly played by younger children. A straight line or a large circle is drawn on the ground, and beyond the line or within the circle is 'Tom Tiddler's ground'. The children gather along the edge of the forbidden territory, daring each other to dash in for a few moments when they think it safe, and calling attention to themselves when they do so, the traditional words being:

> I'm on Tom Tiddler's ground,
> Picking up gold and silver.

Tom has to stay within his ground, and touch someone who is upon it. This player then takes his place, or, very occasionally, is made prisoner and has to be rescued.

The name 'Tom Tiddler' is, however, sometimes forgotten. The game becomes more dramatic, and the ground more dangerous to step on, when the landowner is a vampire, a dragon, a ghost, or other bogie. In a Hampshire village young girls were seen playing 'Gorillas' beside the school toilets. There was a division in the wall between the boys' toilets and the girls', and when a player went beyond this mark she was on the gorilla's ground, and the gorilla tried to 'have' her. They put a foot into the gorilla's territory and withdrew it sharply when the gorilla lunged at them. One girl ran a semicircle through the gorilla's territory. Another invaded it by climbing along a ledge of the toilets. Several ran round the back of the little building and came out the other side. All the while they jeered, 'Silly old gorilla', 'Stupid old gorilla'. Almost the greatest part of the fun seemed to be thinking of rude things to say to the gorilla.

§ In a recollection of the game, played about 1803, one boy was 'Tom Tidler', and his ground was marked off with a boundary line:

> 'He had heaps of sticks, stones, &c., supposed to be his treasures. The game consisted of a lot of boys invading his ground, and attempting to carry off his treasures, each calling out, "Here I'm on Tom Tidler's ground, picking up gold and silver". Meanwhile Tom was by no means a sluggard, but briskly defended his property, and drove off the thieves with a whip or switch.' (*'Notes and Queries', 3rd ser., vol. iv, pp. 480–1)*

Yet the name of the groundlord was not always Tom Tiddler in the past, any more than it is today. In *The Craftsman*, 4 February 1738, and in Henry Carey's *Namby Pamby*, 1725, he was a friar:

> Now my Namby Pamby's found
> Sitting on the Friar's Ground,
> Picking Silver, picking Gold,
> Namby Pamby's never Old.

In Edward Moor's recollection of about 1780 he was 'Tom Tickler' (*Suffolk Words*, 1823); in Charlotte M. Yonge's *The Stokesley Secret*, 1861, ch. 2, he was 'Tommy Tittler'; in Mrs Child's *Girl's Own Book*, 1832, p. 44, he was 'Old Man in his Castle'; in the *Alphabet of Sports*, 1866, an 'Old Man in Orchard'.

Jamieson in his *Scottish Dictionary, Supplement*, 1825, describes the game under the names 'Canlie' ('a very common game in Aberdeenshire') and 'Willie Wastell'. Newell, *Games of American Children*, 1883, gives the alternative names 'Dixie's Land' (New York), 'Golden Pavement' (Philadelphia), 'Van Diemen's Land' (Connecticut), and 'Judge Jeffrey's

Land' (Devonshire, England). Gomme, *Traditional Games*, vol. ii, 1898, adds 'Old Daddy Bunchey' (Liverpool), and 'Pussy's Ground' (Norfolk). At Chirbury the game was called 'Boney' (i.e. Bonaparte), 'I am on Boney's ground' (*Shropshire Folk-Lore*, 1883, pp. 523–4). In Cornwall it was 'Mollish's Land' (*Folk-Lore Journal*, vol. v, 1887, p. 57). Correspondents have supplied the names 'I set my foot on Airlie's Green' (Strathmore, *c.* 1920), and 'Willy, Willy Wausey, I'm on your causey' (Carlton, *c.* 1898, Nottingham, *c.* 1925).[28] Perhaps it was Dickens who popularized the name 'Tom Tiddler'. The game seems to have been a favourite with him. In addition to the Christmas story 'Tom Tiddler's Ground', he refers to it in *Dombey and Son* and in *David Copperfield*.

On the Continent versions of the game seem to have a long history. It is apparently depicted in *Les Trente-six figures*, 1587, plate ix, under the name 'Je suis sur ta terre vilain'. It seems to be the game 'Man, man, ik ben op je blokhuys' listed in a Dutch translation of Rabelais, 1682. And in Swabia, where the protected territory was a 'kingdom', the invaders' cry was remarkably similar to the English:

> König, ich bin in deinem Land,
> Ich stehl dir Gold und Silbersand.
> E. Meier, 'Deutsche Kinder-Reime', 1851, p. 121

The variety of European parallels extant is well shown by Roger Pinon in *Arts et Traditions Populaires* (Strasburg), vol. ix, 1961, no. 1, pp. 16–23.

Shadow touch

Of all the methods of obtaining safety in a game, that in 'Shadow Touch' is the strangest, for it is a player's shadow that has to be touched, not his body; and to make himself safe a player has to make his shadow disappear. 'This is a tig for sunny days only, where a person tigs another person's shadow with his foot.' So it is that children are to be seen flattening themselves against the sides of houses, crouching beside cars, and crawling into bushes, for 'when a boy is in a shadowy spot the chaser cannot chase him no longer'. It is therefore not surprising, as one informant confided, that 'the person who is it may be it for a very long time'.

Despite the game's obvious defects (a shadow does not feel when it is trodden upon, nor remain under the chaser's foot for identification), 'Shadow Touch' is undoubtedly popular. Country children may complain that 'it is rather inconvenient because it can only be played when the sun is out'; but no such disadvantage mars the pleasure of the city child. 'When it is dark and the street lamps come on it is then we try to catch each others shadders', explained a 12-year-old.

Other names: 'Shadows' and 'Tig on Shadow'.

§ The game is also played in Canada and the United States ('Shadow Tag'), Australia ('Shadows'), and New Zealand ('Shadow Tick').
Norman Douglas noted it in *London Street Games*, 1916, p. 139.

Three stoops and run for ever

Security in this game is attained by posture. It starts as ordinary 'Touch' with one person chasing the rest, but any runner can make himself safe when he thinks he is about to be touched simply by crouching on the ground, and (usually) uttering some special word. This way of obtaining immunity is so easy, and so amusing to put into practice, that the attraction the game has for children is readily understandable. But it is, of course, too easy a way of becoming safe to make a good game. The amusement is infinitely frustrating for the chaser; and the number of times each person may stoop has to be strictly limited. A player who stoops more than the permitted number of times (usually three) is immediately penalized. He is made what he most dreads being — the new chaser; and he knows that he is likely to be the chaser for a long time, for once there is a new chaser the rest of the players are all allowed the pleasure of having three more stoops.

The great popularity of this game is reflected in the variety of names and local rules it possesses. The comments of the players on the spot, given in the following list, show, however, that the variations in the way the game is played are in manner rather than matter.

Bob Down Bunny. West Ham (a P.T. name). 'If you are had before you bob down you are still hee even if you haven't had one bob' (Girl, 11).

Bob Down Tick. Frodsham, Cheshire.
Bob Tig. Scarborough.

Bobbin. Berry Hill, Forest of Dean.

Bobs and Excuses. West Ham and Golders Green. 'When the person comes very close, and the person running away is out of breath he is allowed to bob down or make an excuse something like "Ah, my knee hurts" or "Oh, my side hurts". You are allowed to bob down three times and make three excuses. If you are had before you have said an excuse or made a bob you must be he' (Girl, 11).

Bops. Attleborough, Norfolk. 'Once you have bopped six times you are the old man' (Boy, 13). Cf. *Bop*, to dip, or duck suddenly, in Forby's *Vocabulary of East Anglia*, 1830.

Cabbage. Griffithstown, Monmouthshire. 'You get down on the floor and say "Cabbage" ' (Girl, 12).

Dippsy. Middleton Cheney.

Excuse me Touch. Ponders End, Enfield. 'Players say "Excuse me" when they duck.'

Fish and Chips. Swansea.

Ground Tiggy. South Elmsall. 'You bend and touch the ground with your hands' (Girl, 10).

Low Picko. Kirkwall, Orkney.

Low Tig. The usual name in Scotland. 'One sits on the ground if one does not want to be tug' (Girl, 14, Forfar). Cf. 'High Tig' p. 81.

Mercy Touch. Bristol, Truro, and Helston. 'You kneel on the ground and say "Mercy" ' (Girl, 10).

Pounds, Shillings, and Pence. Ramsey, Huntingdonshire. 'If you want a rest you shout out "Pounds" and sit on the ground. The second time … "Shillings". The third time you say "Pence". Then you must run because you can't have any more rests' (Girl, 12).

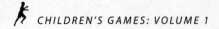

Six Stoops and Run for Ever. Broadbridge Heath.

Squashed Tomatoes. Euston. 'Bend down and say "Squashed Tomatoes" ' (Girl, 11).

Squat. Hounslow.

Stoop Tick or **Stoops.** Banbury.

Stooping Tick. Wolstanton, Staffordshire.

Teddybear's Touch. Glastonbury. 'You say "Teddybear" and sit down' (Boy, 10).

Ten Stoops and Run for Your Life. Alton. 'In some games there are no squibs [truce term] or homes, but if you stoop you're safe' (Boy, 9).

Three Bobs and Run for Your Life. Blackburn.

Three Bobs and Three Excuses. York.

Three Bobs and Two Pokers. Yarmouth. 'Stand stiffly at attention for pokers' (Girl, 12).

Three Bops and Run for Your Life. Ipswich. *See* 'Bops' above.

Three Squads and Three Excuses. Camberwell, Dulwich, and Peckham. 'When a new person is hee you start again with your squads and excuses' (Girl, 10).

Three Squats and Run for Your Life. Peckham Rye and Walworth.

Three Stoops and Run for Ever. Welwyn. 'We shout "Stoop" when we get into crouch position' (Boy, 11).

Three Stoops, Three Pokers, and Run for Your Life. Petersfield.

Three Stoops, Three Statues, and Run for Your Life. Banbury. 'You either stoop or stand like a statue or the person chasing you can have you' (Girl, 11).

Tick Cuckoo. Welshpool. 'The one that's on it comes after you and you duck down and call Cuckoo' (Girl, 12).

Ticky Bob-Down. Wilmslow.

Ticky Little Man, Ticky Stoop Down, Ticky Toadstool. Alternative names at Sale, Manchester.

Tiggy Bob-Down. South Elmsall. 'If you crouch down and shout "Cabbage", "Carrots", or "Turnip", you can't be tug' (Girl, 10).
Tomato. Vale, Guernsey. 'When you have bob down three times you must run for your life' (Girl, 10).

Touch Ground It. Helston.

Tuggy Little Man. Hexham, Northumberland.

§ Newell noted 'Squat Tag' being played in the United States in the nineteenth century (*Games of American Children*, 1883, p. 159), and 'Squat Tag' or 'Stoop Tag' seem to be the usual names there today. In Edmonton, Alberta, it is called 'Animal Squat Tag'. It seems that squatting gives protection in one chasing game or another in many parts of the world. Newell says that it does in Spain, and cites Maspons y Labrós, *Jochs de la Infancia*, 1874, p. 81. Lumbroso says it does in Lombardy in the game 'Cuciù' (*Giochi*, 1967, p. 306). Kampmüller says it does in Austria in the game 'Hockerlbot' (*Oberösterreichische Kinderspiele*, 1965, p. 136). Brewster says it does in India in the game 'Uthali' (1953, p. 64). Culin says it does in Korea in the game 'Syoun-ra' (*Korean Games*, 1895, p. 51).

Northall, in *A Warwickshire Word-Book*, 1896, gives the name 'Tick-and-tumbledown'.

Proliferation of chasers

In the following games the chaser is not relieved of his task when he touches someone. He continues chasing throughout the game, and those he touches become chasers with him. Thus at the climax of the game all the players are chasers except one.

Help chase

'Help Chase' is the straightforward game in this category: those who are touched by the chaser help him to chase the rest, or, as the children put it: 'If the man who is hee has another man, he is hee with him and so on.' 'Eventually all are had and the time comes to start again. The first one had in the last game is hee in the next.'

Names and variations: 'All Man He' (West Ham), 'Help Chase' (St Leonards-on-Sea and elsewhere), 'Tig and Help Chase' (Oxford), 'American Tig' (New Cumnock), 'Gorilla' (Fulham, 'Immediately one is court he becomes a goriller with the original one'), and 'Devil's Den' (Swansea, 'Whoever is caught becomes another devil').

In Stoke-on-Trent, where the game is called 'Scatter', a fair start is ensured by having the players stand round 'the one that is under' (i.e. the chaser) and each take hold of a piece of his clothing. They may not begin running until the one who is under says 'Scatter, scatter, scatter, one, two, three'. In Bishop Auckland the game often starts with two chasers, and is known as 'Two On' or 'Skip Jack'. To ensure that everybody starts at once the chasers cross their arms in front of them, and each player takes hold of a finger. To start the game the chaser then says 'Nash',[29] or 'Skip Jack, run and never come back'. When a person is caught the catcher says 'Skip Jack, help to catch, by one, two, three'.

Chain he

'Chain He' is a game which once, perhaps, possessed a sinister or otherworldly significance. When the chaser manages to touch somebody that person has to join hands with him, and from then onwards they run together. Each person touched joins the chasers, taking the hand of the person who touched him, so that there is an ever-lengthening 'chain' of chasers; although in one form of the game, now popular, when there are four chasers they split into pairs, and when these pairs catch two more players they split into further pairs. Both forms of the game have been described as 'the game of the moment', and both have the same rules: that a player can be 'tigged' or 'caught' only by a chaser's disengaged hand (i.e. the outside hand of a player at one or the other end of the chain); that a player cannot be caught if the chain is broken (the chasers must first join up again); and that the first person caught becomes the chaser in the next game.[30]

Of the two forms, the game in which the chasers split into pairs is the fastest; but the game with the long chain is the one that is memorable. When twelve or more players are linked together they make a formidable-looking chaser, and it is fortunate for those who are still free that the longer the chain grows the more awkward are its movements, and the more likely it is to break when the two ends strive to touch different players. Some children describe the wonder of playing the game at night under the street lamps, when a chain of children spreads out across the road and moves forward in the half-light to hem in those who are still free. The free players charge the chain, aiming at the weakest link, and time after time manage to break through before the ends can curl round to touch them. Other children tell how experienced players learn to close their ranks so that a charge from even the largest boy can be contained, and his chance of escape becomes slight. 'I do not like this game', complained a 10-year-old (probably a weak link in the chain), 'because when you keep 'old of 'ands the person who is on keeps dragging you and you easily get tired of it and if you leave loose of 'ands and tig somebody the person you tig is not caught.' But a 13-year-old Liverpool lad affirmed: 'It is an exciting game, and the last person to be caught is quite pleased with himself for being the last one.'

Names: The commonest names are descriptive, 'Chains', 'Chainy', 'Chain He', 'Chain Had', 'Chain Tig', 'Chain Touch', 'Ticky Chain', 'Ticky Join Up', 'Linky', 'Strings', 'String Tiggy', 'String Touch', 'Stringing Up' (Helston), and 'Altogether Tiggy' (Northampton). In some places more than one name is current, for instance, in Liverpool, 'Chain Tick', 'Stag-Eye', and 'Pea-Wak-Fly'. Around London the smart name is 'Sticky Toffee'.[31] At Chudleigh, Welshpool, Thirsk, and Stenness in Orkney, the game is 'Fishes in the Net', and when there are three or four people in the chain they must completely encircle a person to catch him. In Stromness it is 'Fisherman's Net' (cf. the French 'L'épervier' in which the first two chasers are termed 'les pêcheurs'). Most names are for either form of the game; but 'Couple Tag' (St Ives, Cornwall), and 'Pairs' (Scalloway, Shetland), can only refer to one form, while 'Long Ticker' (Spaldwick), 'Long Chain Tag' (Sleaford), and 'Dragon's Tail' (east Montgomeryshire), distinguish the other. At Annesley the game is called 'Fly' from the chaser's command to the players to start running (cf. 'Scatter'). And in Dulwich, where the game is called 'Sheep Dog', at Blaenavon, where it is 'Shepherds', and in Scarborough, where it is

'Shepherd's Crook', they chase only in pairs, and each captive is taken back to base to make an additional pair.

Other names current include: 'Aller Beyroot' (Neath), 'Buckle' (East Meon), 'Bully' (Caister-on-Sea), 'Clawer' (Tewkesbury), 'Corner to Corner' (Snelland), 'Cree' (Knighton), 'Cree-cree' (Llanfair Waterdine), 'Crackum' (Stamford, Lincolnshire), 'Doctor' (Cwmbran), 'Join up Bucket' (St Ives), 'Knocky-knole' (Llangunllo, Radnorshire), 'Stag' or 'Stags' (fairly common), and 'Tommy Early' (Presteigne). Also 'Hawks and Doves' and 'Fox and Rabbits', but pretty-pretty names usually come from teachers' manuals.

§ In the United States 'Chain Tag' or 'Link Tag'. In Austria 'Ketten-fan-gen' (Kampmüller, 1965, p. 151). Further names and antecedents appear in the next section.

Vestigial features in 'chain he' variants

In widely separated areas of Britain hand-linking touch continues to be played under strange names and fanciful-seeming rules that are possibly the consequence of custom and pastime in former days.

Chain a Wedding. In the neighbourhood of Pontypool the game of 'Chain a Wedding' begins with two children holding hands and running after the rest. They make a chain until all have been caught except one, whereupon they break up to catch the last player. First and last caught then become the chasing pair for the next game. It seems probable that the name 'Chain a Wedding' is an echo of the old practice, prevalent particularly in south Wales, of obstructing the wedding procession by a rope tied across the road, so that a toll could be exacted for allowing the otherwise happy pair to continue on their way (see Kilvert's *Diary*, 15 May 1875, and *The Lore and Language of Schoolchildren*, 1959, p. 304).

Warning. The special emphasis on the player who remains uncaught also occurs in Swansea, where the game is called 'Cock Warren' and the last child is similarly chased by all the others running freely. 'Cock Warren' appears to be a corruption of 'Cock Warning', a name for 'Chain He' in the Rhondda Valley; and the name of a 'favourite game' (undescribed) played at Sedgley Park School, Staffordshire, about 1805.[32] The game of 'Warning', otherwise known as 'Widdy', was popular throughout the nineteenth century. In *The Boy's Own Book*, 4th ed., 1829, pp. 23–4, it is described as a game in which one player, standing behind a line, delivers the following challenge or caution:

> Warning once, warning twice, warning
>   three times over;
> A bushel of wheat, a bushel of rye,
> When the cock crows, out jump I!
> Cock-a-doodle-doo! — Warning!

'He then runs out, and touches the first he can overtake, who must return to bounds with him. These two then (first crying "Warning" only) join hands, and each of them endeavours to touch another; he also returns to bounds, and at the next sally joins hands with the other two. Every player who is afterward touched by either of the outside ones, does the like, until the whole be thus touched and taken. It is not lawful to touch an out-player after the line is broken, either accidentally, or by the out-players attacking it, which they are permitted to do. Immediately a player is touched, the line separates, and the out-players endeavour to catch those belonging to it, who are compelled to carry those who capture them, on their backs, to bounds.'

Basically this is 'Chain He', but clearly a slower game since the chasers return to base each time they have touched someone (as in 'Shepherd's Crook' played today in Scarborough); and the quaint practice of those who have been chased retaliating by chasing their chasers in the hope of riding to the boundary on their backs, seems to have been vestigial even in George IV's time. When boys in ancient Greece played the game 'Ostrakinda' any fugitive they caught was called the '*ass*', this signifying that he had to carry them home (Pollux, ix. 111; and see further under 'Crust and Crumbs'). Indeed, a vestige of this practice survives to the present day in Grimsby, where the last one to be caught when playing 'Chains' is given an enforced ride on the shoulders of his companions. Further, at the Lizard, in the heel of Cornwall, an 11-year-old boy (seemingly posted there for visiting folklorists) made our journey worth while with the information that 'the game where you all join up in one long string, we call "Warney". The last person who's caught, he's Warney. He says, "Warney one, warney two, warney three", like that, up to ten, then he starts chasing'.

Staggy. In the Manchester borough of Sale a version of the game is known as 'Staggy in the Button Hole', and contains the singular feature that 'the one who was tuck first and is on next gets beaten on the back while the others chant:

> Staggy in the button hole, one, two, three,
> Staggy in the button hole, one, two, three,
> Staggy in the button hole, one, two, three,
> Staggy in the button hole, can't catch me.

Then the game starts again' (Boy, 12). This is almost identical to the treatment that awaits the newly appointed chaser at Accrington, who has first to allow himself to be hit ('but not very hard') ten times on the head before he begins chasing. And at Rossendale, also in east Lancashire, where the game is known as 'Stagger-Ragger-Roaney', the boy has to suffer being 'shaken up and down' while the rest of the players chant:

> Stagger-Ragger-Roaney, my fat pony,
> One, two, three, four, five, six, seven.

'They then let him go and run away, and when he has recovered he chases them.'[33] The names 'Stag', 'Staggy', 'Ticky-Stag' (and at Knighton 'Stagalonia') are not uncommon denominations for 'Chain He', although more often they refer to the catching game in which players run back and forth across some open space (pp. 128–30). It is curious that in the games 'Staggy in the Button Hole' and 'Stagger-Ragger-Roaney' there should be ceremonial discomfiture for the player who acquits himself poorly, when it is recollected that in the west country deceiving husbands or scolding wives used to be made the subject of a rough ceremony termed a 'Stag Hunt'.[34]

Widdy. At Rushmere St Andrew, near Ipswich, one of the places where the game is called 'Stag', the person who has been appointed 'it' clasps his hands together in front of him, counts slowly up to ten, and then announces his animation with the shout 'Squirrel'. Similarly, 600 miles away in Whalsay, one of the Shetland Islands, when the children play 'Humpty Dumpty' — said to be a corruption of 'Hunty Bunty' — the first chaser clasps his hands together in front of him and issues the innocuous-seeming warning or invitation 'Who's coming in my fun Humpty Dumpty?' and keeps his hands clasped, as he runs, until he tigs somebody, and joins up with him. In Peckham Rye the game is known as 'Chain Widdy', in Thirsk it is occasionally 'Whitee', in Helston it is 'Willie Willie Way'. The game 'Widdy', as set out in *Games and Sports for Young Boys*, 1859, pp. 1–2, is identical in all respects to 'Warning' except that the chaser is described as first clasping his hands together, calling out 'Widdy, widdy, way — cock warning!' and striving 'to overtake and touch one of the others without dividing his hands'.[35] It seems possible, as has been suggested under 'Bull', that this pursuit and 'touching' with clasped hands formerly had a greater significance than the mere hampering of the chaser. Jamieson gives the earliest account we have of touch-linking in the *Supplement* to his *Scottish Dictionary*, 1825, when he defines the Lothian game of 'Hornie' as:

'A game among children, in which one of the company runs after the rest, having his hands clasped, and his thumbs pushed out before him in resemblance of horns. The first person whom he touches with his thumbs, becomes his property, joins hands with him, and aids in attempting to catch the rest; and so on till they are all made captives. Those who are at liberty, still cry out, Hornie, Hornie!'

Jamieson wondered 'whether this play be a vestige of the very ancient custom of assuming the appearance and skins of brute animals, especially in the sports of Yule' (as described by Strutt), or whether it might 'symbolize the exertions made by the devil, often called *Hornie*, in making sinful man his prey, and employing fellow-men as his coadjutors in this work'. Whatever its antecedents may be, a children's game called 'Hornes Hornes' was listed by Randle Holme in 1688, and the name 'Hornie' for a linking game subsists to this day in Kirkcaldy; while in Stromness, where in 1909 'Long Horny' and 'Short Horny' were played, the name for 'Chain He' continues to be 'Horny'.

Bully Horn. In *The Book of Sports*, *c*. 1837, the editor, William Martin, who was born in 1801 at Woodbridge in Suffolk, recalls the game 'Stag

Out'.[36] The chaser is again likened to a stag. He 'clasps his hands before him and rushes at the other boys'; and the additional point is made that the other boys seem to 'taunt and bay him', yet, if the stag succeeds in touching one of the 'bayers', he can make him submit to the ordeal of bearing him (the stag) back to bounds, before the two of them rush out together with linked hands to touch another if they can. The game of 'Bully Horn', played to this day in Ballingry, Forfar, and Golspie, is remarkable in that it embodies not only the return to bounds with each new person 'tigged', but the tormenting of those caught, and the systematic goading of him — or it may be her — who chases. The players are thus preserving — unconsciously, but in no irresolute manner — all the rudimentary features of play in former times. The following is a description of 'Bully Horn' by a 12-year-old Forfar schoolgirl:

> 'In the winter about eight o'clock a gang of us get together
> the likes of Isabella, Sandra, Margaret, Mary, another
> Margaret, David, Gus or Angus, Harold, and Duncan. We
> all stand on the pavement and run to a lamp-post, the last
> one is out. The one that is out stands on the pavement
> and we shout names to her to annoy her, then she comes
> and chases us. When she gets someone they have to run
> to the pavement and we run after them and thump them,
> pull their hair, before they reach the pavement. We run
> up to the pavement and catch the one that is tigged. We
> twist her fingers and do everything we like till she says
> "Bully Horn". Then they join hands and try to get someone
> else out. If they let go hands we shout out aloud "Chainy
> Broken — Get them". We run and hit them again before
> they reach the pavement. This goes on till everybody is
> out. The one that was last out is first out next time.'

Kingy

This fast-moving game has all the qualifications for being considered the national game of British schoolboys: it is indigenous, it is sporting, it has fully evolved rules, it is immensely popular (almost every boy in England, Scotland, and Wales plays it), and no native of Britain appears to have troubled to record it.[37]

'Kingy' is a ball game in which those who are not He have the ball hurled at them, without means of retaliation, and against ever-increasing odds, an element that obviously appeals to the national character. Anyone who is hit by the ball straightway joins the He in trying to hit the rest of the players. Those who are throwing may not run with the ball in their hands, but pursue their quarry by passing the ball to each other. Those being thrown at may run and dodge as they like, and may also punch the ball away from them with their fists. For this purpose players sometimes wrap a handkerchief round their hand, as 'fisting' the ball can be painful. The game continues until all but one have been hit and are 'out', and this player is declared 'King'. When the contestants are skilled (and boys of fifteen and sixteen readily play the game), the ball gets thrown with considerable force: it shoots back and forth across the street or playground, and the game can be as exciting to watch as a tennis match.

As befits a sport in which so much energy is expended, the preliminaries are sometimes wonderfully ritualistic. At Bishop Auckland, for instance, one person shouts 'King' to start the proceedings, and two others follow up by crying 'Sidey'. The players then form a circle round the King, with the two who shouted 'Sidey' standing on either side of him like heirs-apparent. The players making the circle stand with legs apart, each foot touching the foot of their neighbour on either side. The King picks up the ball and bounces it — or, as they say in Bishop Auckland, 'stounces' it — three times in the ring, and then lets it roll. Everyone watches to see whose legs it will go through. If it does not roll through anybody's legs the King picks it up and bounces it again, and if his second turn fails he has a third try. If the ball still has not passed between anyone's legs, he hands it to the first sidey (the 'foggy-sidey') who, as necessary, repeats the performance — for the moment the ball does pass between someone's legs that person is 'on', and everyone runs. At the end of the game whoever becomes King takes the place in the centre of the ring to start the next game, and the first two people to shout 'Sidey' stand beside him.

In Grimsby, where they also start with the circle, they select the person who is first to bounce the ball in the centre by counting round the players with the words:

> Double circle's not complete
> Till it goes through someone's feet.

The person pointed to at 'feet' goes into the centre. In some places, however, it is the person who provides the ball who first goes in the centre.

In Scarborough, especially among younger children, the circle-start to the game becomes virtually a game in itself. If the ball is about to roll between a person's legs he can shout 'Knick-knock', which entitles him to use his knees to prevent the ball going through; or he can shout 'Kicks' which means he may kick the ball away, provided others have not already shouted 'No knick-knocks' or 'No kicks'. Likewise, should the ball touch someone else's foot before passing through his legs the player can shout 'Rebounds', and the ball has to be picked up and dropped in the centre anew. Or again, should somebody say 'Tricks' before anyone has declared 'No tricks', the one in the middle may aim the ball through whose legs he chooses, and that person straightaway becomes 'it'.

This selection of the chaser by the fortuitous rolling of the ball is customary throughout England and Wales, and much care is taken to see that the ground is flat, so that nobody will be at a disadvantage. In some places, particularly in Wales, there is the difference that the players stand in a tight circle, sometimes having their arms round each other's shoulders, and each puts his right foot forward. It is enough then that the ball touches someone's foot for that person to be 'it'. In Aberystwyth if the ball is dropped in the ring three times and does not touch anybody's right foot, the player who has been dropping the ball becomes the chaser. In Welshpool, however, he hands the ball to the person called 'Second King', who was second last out in the previous game, and he himself 'goes for a walk', which ensures that he will not be touched by the ball and become the new chaser.

In the Walworth district of London the boys sit on the kerb with their feet apart. One boy rolls the ball towards them from across the road, and the one whose legs it goes between is He. In Wandsworth, in much the same way, the players line up facing a wall with their legs apart. And in Cleethorpes, Lincolnshire, they stand in a row but with their heels together and toes apart. The ball is rolled towards them and the person whose feet the ball touches is 'it'.

Throughout most of Scotland, although not in Edinburgh, the players form a circle and hold out their clenched fists in front of them. The player in the middle throws the ball to somebody and he catches it between his fists and throws it to someone else in the circle, who throws it to someone else, all with closed fists. When somebody drops the ball that person is 'hit' or 'het'. Sometimes the person throwing the ball is allowed to pretend to throw it to one person and in fact throw it to another. In Forfar this is known as 'jinkies', and can be prevented by the cry 'No jinkies'.

The Rules. Although the ways of choosing the chaser are numerous, the game itself is played with little variation. Reports from more than fifty places have been so similar, it is as if a mimeographed sheet of rules was carried in every grubby trouser pocket. Such a set of rules would read as follows:

1. The number of players shall be not less than six or more than twenty: the best number is about twelve.
2. The boundaries of the game shall be agreed on before the game begins. A flat area of 20 × 20 yards, or a length of street of about 20–30 yards, depending on the number of players, is ample.
3. One person shall be chosen chaser, and the game shall start immediately he is chosen. The chaser shall, however, bounce the ball ten times before he throws it at anyone, to give the players time to scatter.
4. The chaser may not run with the ball; but while he is the sole chaser he may bounce the ball on the ground as he runs.
5. A player shall be 'out' when the ball hits him on the body between his neck and knees (or, as may be agreed, between his waist and ankles). It shall be determined beforehand whether a hit shall count if the ball has first bounced on the ground or ricocheted off a wall; or whether only a direct hit shall count.
6. As soon as a player is 'out' he shall assist the chaser in getting the other players out.
7. When there are two or more chasers they may not run with the ball, but may manœuvre as they wish by passing it to each other.
8. Players being chased may take what action they like to avoid being hit by the ball, including 'fisting' it, i.e. punching it away with their fist. They may also pick up the ball between their fists and chuck it away.
9. Should a chaser catch the ball when it has been 'fisted', or touch a player while he is holding the ball in his fists, the player shall be 'out'.
10. Should a player kick the ball, or handle it other than with his fists, he shall be 'out'.
11. Should a player run out of bounds when trying to avoid being hit by the ball he shall be 'out'.

12. The last player left in shall be 'King', and shall officiate at the selection of the next chaser.

A few local practices may be noted. In parts of West Ham they do not make the chaser bounce the ball ten times before he begins throwing, but appoint a 'bunger' whose duty it is to seize the ball when it has passed through someone's legs, and throw it out of the chaser's reach. In West Ham, too, if a player is hit on the head or foot, the chaser, says an 11-year-old, 'has a free bung, and everyone that's not "he" shouts "Miss him, miss him, miss him" '.

At Rosneath in Dumbartonshire, if the ball is being thrown too hard, and somebody does not want to be hurt, he may shout 'No trade marking', and the ball must not then be thrown so fiercely.

In St Andrews, Fife, if somebody thinks he is not out, and the others disagree, he must submit to 'Blind Shot'. He has to stand against a wall with his arms spread out. One of the throwing side takes aim about six yards away, has his eyes covered, and then throws. If the person is hit he is 'out'; if he is not hit he is not 'out'. A similar rule known as 'Free Shot' is observed in Orkney.

It remains to say that while 'Kingy' is the usual name in England, and 'King Ball' in Scotland, the game is sometimes known in the midlands as 'Hot Rice' (occasionally corrupted to 'Horace'), and in Lincolnshire as 'Dustbin', due to the players being allowed to fend off the ball with bats, pieces of wood, or dustbin lids. There are also the local names 'Buzz' (Enfield and Croydon), 'Fudge' (Basildon), 'Cheesy' (Exmouth), 'Peasy' (Cleethorpes), 'Punch' (South Elmsall), and 'Fisty' (the usual name in the Orkney Islands). The game is occasionally known as 'Ball Tig' or 'Dodge Ball' which are generally taken to be other games. In Scotland girls sometimes call the game 'Queen Ball', and the girl who stays in longest is 'Queen'.

Suspense starts

In some games part of the sport is that the players do not know when the chaser is going to begin chasing. Yet they may have to remain close to him, suffer his jokes and clowning while they wait, and even have their suspense pricked with false starts. It is natural that in these games the start becomes the dominant feature.

Poison

In 'Poison' or 'Bottle of Poison', which is immensely popular with boys of 10 or 11, all players are actually touching the chaser when he begins chasing. He holds out his hands, sometimes with arms crossed, and each player takes hold of a finger and stretches as far away from him as he can, preparing to run. The chaser says 'I went to a shop and I bought a bottle of *vinegar*' (or any other substance). 'I went to a shop and I bought a bottle of *p-p-p-Pepsi*. I went to a shop and I bought a bottle of POISON!' The word 'poison' is the signal for everyone to run. In Wolstanton the players first ask the one they are holding on to 'What's in the bottle when the cork goes pop?' and he replies as he chooses '*tea*', or '*powder*', or 'POISON'. Should anybody run before he says 'poison', for instance, when he says the 'p' of 'powder', that person has to take the place of the chaser, or even be out of the game if he does it twice.

Sometimes this start so overshadows the subsequent chasing that well-known games acquire entirely new names. For example, in Bristol and Kilburn 'Release Touch' is called 'Bingo' (the chaser saying, per-haps, 'B for Bat, B for Ball' and nobody may run until he says 'B for BINGO!'). In Alton the game is called 'Jumbo' (the chaser recites the names of the players in turn, suddenly naming one of them 'Jumbo'); in Langholm it is 'Peapod Poison' ('My mother went down the street to buy some *peel*, to buy some *peat*, to buy some PEAPOD POISON!'); and in Inverness 'Sticky Glue' (Sticky *jam*, sticky *gloves*, sticky GLUE!'). In York 'Chain He' becomes 'Black Jack' ('Black *hat*, black *cat*, black JACK!'); in Fulham 'Black Magic'; and in Northampton 'Black Man's Chimney'. In Accrington 'Help Chase' becomes 'Jimmy Jack Fly'; and in Liss, where 'Help Chase' is called 'Apple Plum Pudding', a young boy describes how they take hold of any part of the chaser they can:

> 'We all say someone's he and we all take hold of them. We hold their trousers or pullover. Sometimes they say "No flesh or hair" so that means we are not allowed to hold flesh or hair. Sometimes they say "No shoe laces" so we are not allowed shoe laces. Then they say "Apple, Plum, *something*" and if they say banana or pie or anything like that and someone leaves go they're he. If he says "Apple Plum Pudding" we all run.'

Crusts and crumbs

In 'Crusts and Crumbs' the players do not even know whether they are going to be runners or chasers. They divide into two sides, 'Crusts' and 'Crumbs', and face each other a few feet apart on the crown of the road. One person, who is not in the game, calls out either 'Crusts' or 'Crumbs'. If he calls 'Crusts', the Crusts chase the Crumbs to the pavement behind them; if he calls 'Crumbs', the Crumbs chase the Crusts to their pavement. Those who are caught before they reach the pavement join the other side. Sometimes the caller hangs on to the 'Crrr' of 'Crusts' or 'Crumbs' for as long as his breath will hold, keeping the players in suspense about the direction they will have to run; and sometimes he causes chaos by calling 'Crrr-umpets'.

This game is often adult-organized, and it is certainly improved by having a good caller. Several children describe it being played in the street in modified forms, for instance an 11-year-old girl in Fulham:

> 'About eight people play the game. It is a very catchy
> game. You have an outer, who stands on one side of the
> road. On the other side the children stand. The pavement
> is crusts and the road is crumbs. The outer shouts out
> either crusts or crumbs. If he calls out crusts you jump onto
> crusts. If he calls out crumbs you immediately jump onto
> crumbs. If you are not quick enough you are out.'

In Stoke-on-Trent the game becomes a kind of race. All the children are on one side of the road, and when the call is 'Crusts' they run across the road and back again; but when the cry is 'Crumbs' anyone who moves is out.

Other names: 'Rats and Rabbits', 'Soldiers and Sailors'.

§ 'Crusts and Crumbs' often appears in the games manuals, e.g. Barclay's *Book of Cub Games*, 1919, and Knight's *Brownie Games*, 1936. In Smith's *Games and Games Leadership*, published New York, 1932, pp. 215–18, it is described under the names 'Black and Blue', 'Crows and Cranes', 'Rats and Rabbits', 'Heads and Tails', 'Wet and Dry', and 'Black and White'. In Bancroft's *Games for the Playground*, New York, 1909, pp. 52–3, only the name 'Black and White' is given. The leader was provided with a flat disc hanging on a string which was white on one side and black on the other. He twirled the disc, and if it

stopped with the white side visible the 'Whites' tried to tag the 'Blacks';
if the black side was shown the 'Blacks' tried to tag the 'Whites'.
Although neither Bancroft nor Smith seems to have been aware of it,
the game they describe is more than 2,000 years old. Pollux, under
'Ostrakinda' (The Game of the Shell), tells how boys in Greece took a
shell, and smeared one side with pitch, calling that side 'Night', while
the other side, which remained white, was 'Day'. They drew a line,
picked up sides, and decided which side should be Night and which
Day. The shell was twirled, and the side whose colour came uppermost
chased the other party; anyone caught was denominated 'ass', which
meant (as is known from other references) that the boy had to carry his
catcher on his back (*Onomasticon* ix. 111). Pollux himself alludes to the
curious passage in Plato where the philosopher remarks how a lover and
a loved one often change roles. 'The shell being turned again', the lover
or pursuer, as he was, becomes the pursued and strives to flee, while the
object of his love tries to catch him (*Phaedrus* 40, written *c*. 365 B.C.).
Plato again refers to the game, or so it seems, in his *Republic* (vii. 521);
and it appears that the game was so well known, anyway by the second
century A.D., that it was proverbial for something to change 'at the turn
of a shell'. It is interesting that the game continues to be played in Italy,
and to be called 'Giorno e notte' (Day and Night), although no longer
played with a shell; that in France it is 'Le jour et la nuit'; that in Austria
it is 'Schwarz-Weiss'; and that it is an old game in Germany, 'Tag und
Nacht' being fully described by Gutsmuths, *Spiele für die Jugend*, 1796
(1802, pp. 266–8), the leader tossing a disc or coin.

How well the game was known in England in the past is uncertain. John
Higins in his *Nomenclator*, 1585, described 'Ostrakinda' as a play 'not in
use with us' in England. Yet it seems to have seeped through the centuries
at gutter level. In *London Street Games*, 1916, p. 47, Norman Douglas
mentions a lowly game played by girls called 'Rolling Pin' in which two
parties 'decide which of them has to chase the other by the red or blue
colour marked on a rolling pin which is rolled between them'.

Little black man

To the younger children, naturally enough, a chasing game is immeasur-
ably more exciting if the chaser is not thought of as a playfellow but as
someone strange and fearsome; and the thrill is even greater if the strange

character exchanges pleasantries with them before he gives chase. Half a century ago it was not uncommon for the start of a chasing game to be delayed while the players joined in a song or took part in a set dialogue. This still occurs in the neighbourhood of Welshpool in the game called 'Little Black Man'. When a girl has been selected chaser, the players make a circle round her, and she asks 'Where have you been?'

'Down the lane', they reply.

'What did you see?'

'A little white house.'

'Who is in it?'

'A little black man.'

'What did he say?'

'Catch me if you can!' they shout, and speed off in all directions, with the chaser after them.

§ Such a beginning to a game is a 'delayed start' rather than a 'suspense start'. The dialogue is of a set length, and the runners themselves give the signal for the chase to begin. In general today in games of this type the preliminary dialogue not only sets the scene and delays the start, it intensifies the suspense, for the player who decides when the chase shall start is the chaser. Thus, as can be seen in the games which follow, the players who have to converse with the chaser, and remain near him while they converse, become increasingly apprehensive the longer the dialogue continues.

What's the time, Mr. Wolf?

This game is extraordinarily popular. One child is Mr Wolf and walks along the road rather haughtily, while the rest follow in a group as close behind as they dare. They call after him, 'What's the time, Mr Wolf?' Mr Wolf does not turn round. He replies in a gruff voice 'Eight o'clock', or any other time, and keeps walking. The children follow along a little further and call again, 'What's the time, Mr Wolf?' The wolf replies, perhaps, 'Five o'clock'. The children continue to follow the wolf, and begin to pester him to know the time. Suddenly he cries it is 'Dinner time!', turns round, and chases them. The children rush back to the safety of the starting-place (usually screaming as they do so), and if Mr Wolf catches one of them before they reach home that person is wolf next time.

Names: 'Mr Wolf' or 'What's the time, Mr Wolf?' (many places),

'Mr Fox' or 'What's the time, Mr Fox?' (Coulsdon, Cruden Bay, Thame, Stoke-on-Trent), 'Foxy' (Stenness in Orkney). Amongst Brownies, 'What's the time, Mr Bear?'

§ Correspondents recall playing 'What's the time, Mr Wolf?' at Midgley, near Halifax, *c.* 1895; Ilminster, *c.* 1920; and Abergavenny, *c.* 1930. The game appears to stem from versions of 'Fox and Chickens' ('Chickamy, Chickamy, Chany Trow', 'Old Dame', etc., see Vol. 2 p. 164) in which the players used to ask the predator the time, although in those days a set dialogue was normal, which gave the chase a delayed start rather than a suspense start. However, the connection between the two games is apparent in *The Home Book*, 1867, p. 16, where Mrs Valentine gives a game called 'Twelve o'clock at Night'. In this one player, a hen, with other children, her chicks, clinging behind her, approaches a fox in his lair and asks the time. When the fox replies 'Twelve o'clock at night' he tries to seize one of them.

Similar games in which a wolf is asked questions are current in France, Italy, Germany, Spain, and South America; and this type of game is probably universal. In Cairo children make a circle round one player, addressing him 'O wolf, O wolf, what are you doing?' and the wolf replies that he is washing, that he is brushing his hair, and such-like innocuous occupations. Finally he replies '*Chasing you*', and does so. It is possible that the wolf's replies in 'Little Red Ridinghood' belong to the same tradition.

In Banbury children play a game called 'Weird Wolf' (Werewolf) in which one person pretends to be an old man. An 11-year-old girl writes:

> 'The rest have to be children and go up to the old man and ask if he will tell them a story. So he tells them a story which is, One day a long time ago I had to go in the forest and kill a weird wolf but the weird wolf escaped and scratched my arm, and the man shows the children the scratch on his arm. He then says, Every full moon I change into a weird wolf. But the children don't believe him. Then he says, There's a full moon now, and he changes into a weird wolf. The children run away and the wolf chases them. When he has caught one of them that child helps him to chase the rest.'

I'll follow my mother to market

In this trivial drama the mother tells her children she is going to market, and gives them jobs to do about the house while she is away. As soon as she has gone, the children stop doing their jobs, band together, and cautiously follow their mother to market. In Somerset they sing as they do so, not altogether logically:

> I'll follow my mother to market
> To buy a ha'penny basket;
> When she comes home, she'll break my
> bones,
> For falling over the cherry stones.

The mother goes into a shop, and the children creep up as close as they dare to hear what she is buying. She asks the shopkeeper for household goods, such as a dustpan and brush, a mop, and some washing-powder. Then she asks the shopkeeper for 'a cane to beat the children with'. The children turn and run for home with the mother chasing after them. In Langholm the game is called 'The Cane'.

Several similar games are played, all of them apparently traditional. In the village school at Chawton, opposite Jane Austen's house, one of the children pretends to be 'Old Mother Hubbard', and the rest of the children shout 'What have you got in your cupboard, Mrs Hubbard?' At first she says she has butter in her cupboard. When asked again she says, perhaps, 'Rice'. When she says that her cupboard contains 'BONES' the children flee, as if for their lives. At Roe, Shetland, one girl is selected to be 'Lucy Anna' and is sent off on her own. The rest follow her a little way behind roaring without restraint, 'Lucy Anna, Lucy Anna', and they keep up the cry (which is part of the fun) until she pretends to be provoked into chasing them. In Golspie, and elsewhere, the player they taunt is 'Black Peter'. He stands with his back to the others and calls out 'Who's afraid of Black Peter?' The others shout back 'Not I' and edge forward a little to prove it. He calls out again 'Who's afraid of Black Peter?' The children respond 'Not I' and creep forward yet further. When Black Peter thinks they are close enough he turns and chases them. (In Aberdeen the game is 'Who's Afraid of the Big Black Beetle?') Similarly, in a number of places, there is a game called 'Big A, Little a' or 'The Cat's in the Cupboard'. One child is a cat and goes to the far side

of the road, turning away and closing her eyes. The other children gradually advance across the road 'making faces', says a Helston girl, and
pointing at the person by the opposite wall. As they do so they chant:

> Big A, little a, bouncing B,
> The cat's in the cupboard and can't see
> me.

'Either during or just after the chant the catcher *suddenly turns* and tries
to catch you.'

§ Previous recordings: *Folk-Lore Record*, vol. v, 1882, p. 84, 'Going to
Market' (Hersham); *Folk-Lore Journal*, vol. vii, 1889, p. 231, 'Basket'
(Dorset); *English Folk-Rhymes*, 1892, pp. 392–3 (Warwickshire);
Gomme, vol. i, 1894, p. 24; *Rhythmic Games*, 1914, p. 19, 'Follow my
Mother to Market' and 'Old Daddy Wiggin'; *London Street Games*,
1916, p. 45, 'Who's Afraid of Black Peter?'; Macmillan MSS., 1922,
'Big A, Little a' (Somerset); correspondent, 'Daddy Mick has lost his
stick' (Staffordshire, *c.* 1915).

In the United States: *Games of American Children*, 1883, pp. 143–5,
'Old Mother Tipsy-toe' and 'Old Mother Cripsy-crops'; Howard MSS.,
1947, 'Grandmammy Tippytoe, lost her needle and couldn't sew'
(Maryland).

John Brown

An intensely dramatic start to a chase occurs when the person who is
'on' feigns that he is dead, or asleep, or an inert object. In Scarborough
the game is called 'John Brown'. One person has the part of John Brown
and lies dead on the ground. The others walk about near him, intoning
'This is the body of John Brown'. John Brown then kicks someone, and
the person who is kicked pushes whoever is nearest him, saying 'Stop
kicking'. 'I didn't kick', says the other. 'You must have kicked', says
the first, 'no one else was near me except the body of John Brown.' John
Brown then kicks another person, and starts a second argument, and
perhaps kicks a third person so that there is a further argument. When
a number of the children are having mock arguments John Brown leaps
up, the children scream, and John Brown tries to tig one of them.

At Ruthin in Denbighshire the Welsh-speaking children have a similar game called 'Nain Gogo' (Grandmother Gogo). In this, Grandmother sleeps on the ground and the children come to her several at a time and tickle her face with grass until she jumps up and tries to catch them. In Swansea they play 'Spider in the Corner'. One player crouches in a corner, and at first takes no notice when she is touched or even prodded, but suddenly jumps up and tries to catch as many players as possible. And at Roe, in the Shetland Islands, the one who slumbers is a giant, and when he catches someone he puts them in his den, and 'the game of "The Giant" goes on until the whole of us is caught' (Girl, 8).

§ A version of this game called 'Only a Stump of a Tree' was described by Mrs Craik (Dinah Maria Mulock) in *Our Year*, 1860, pp. 290–1:

> 'Somebody sits in a corner, while all the rest make believe to be taking a walk, come up to him and touch him and shake him and pull him about saying, "Oh, this is only a stump of a tree", — till suddenly the Stump comes alive — catches anybody he can, and runs after the rest, and there is such screaming and laughing! The grand object is to keep a sharp watch when the Stump is about to rise up — a good Stump will be very cunning and let himself be pulled about for a long time before he offers to stir.'

For continental equivalents see under 'Dead Man Arise'.

Dead man arise

'Dead Man Arise' or 'Green Man Arise', played in the Manchester area, is the most sepulchral of the games in which a prostrate figure becomes the chaser. One player lies on the ground and is entirely covered with a blanket or cloth, preferably green, or with a pile of coats, or, as available, with grass or hay, or with sand if the game is played on the beach. The children process round the heap calling solemnly, 'Dead man, arise ... Dead man, arise.' But they do not touch the heap, and they pretend not to look at it. Then, when least expected, the 'dead' man answers their call. He rushes after those who have resurrected him, trying to touch one of them, and make him the dead man in his place. In St Helier, Jersey, the game is known as 'Green Man Rise-O'.

§ This game was much played in the first quarter of the century, especially it seems, in the poorer districts of London (Bermondsey, Islington, and Bethnal Green), in Glasgow, and in the mining villages around Durham. During the Second World War a yet more ritualistic version was played in Manchester. Young girls joined hands and skipped round the recumbent figure chanting, 'Green lady, green lady, your breakfast is ready.' (No reaction.) 'Green lady, green lady, your dinner is ready.' (No reaction.) 'Green lady, green lady, your supper is ready.' (No reaction.) 'Green lady, green lady, your house is on fire!' — at which the recumbent figure leapt up and pursued the other players, trying to touch one of them.

This game seems to be an example, and not the only one, of a children's diversion being the enactment of an ancient horror story. In the repertory of English folk-tales is one (recorded in the *Journal of the Folk-Song Society*, vol. vi, 1919, p. 83 n.) in which a little girl takes service with a 'Green Lady'. The first morning, after preparing breakfast for her mistress, the girl calls up the stair (and in telling this story the words are chanted rhythmically):

'Green lady, green lady, come down to your break-fast!'

But the green lady does not come down. After preparing dinner for the green lady the maid calls up the stairs again, but the green lady does not come down; and she calls a third time after the preparation of supper, but still the green lady does not appear. At last the little servant girl goes upstairs to the chamber door and, urged by curiosity, looks through the key-hole. Inside the room she sees the green lady *dancing in a basin of blood.*[38]

Analogous to 'Green Man Arise' is the well-known game in Germany and Austria 'Nix in der Grube'. One child (the Water-sprite) crouches on the ground, and the other children form a ring, and sing as they circle round him:

> Water-sprite in the ditch,
> You are a bad lad;
> Wash your bones
> With precious stones,
> Water-sprite make a grab!

At this the water-sprite leaps up, and tries to catch one of them, who in his or her turn becomes the water-sprite. Similar, too, is the old game of 'The Tortoise' played in Greece; and the game of the snail 'Butta-butta corni' played in Italy. In Sicily an even more similar game was 'A Morsi Sanzuni'. One child lay down pretending to be dead while his companions sang a dirge, occasionally going up to the body and lifting an arm or a leg to make sure the player was dead, and nearly stifling the child with parting kisses. Suddenly he would jump up, chase his mourners, and try to mount the back of one of them (Pitrè, *Giuochi fanciulleschi siciliani*, 1883, pp. 265–6). In Czechoslovakia children played games called 'Schämpelän Dît' or 'Prinzessin erlösen'. In these the recumbent player was covered with leaves, or had her frock held over her face. The players then made a circle and counted the chimes of the clock, but each time 'Death' replied 'I must still sleep'. This continued until the clock struck twelve when, as in some other European games, the sleeping player sprung to life, and tried to catch someone. (See Böhme, *Deutsches Kinderspiel*, 1897, pp. 565 and 576–8; Kampmüller, *Oberösterreichische Kinderspiele*, 1965, p. 139; Lumbroso, *Conte, cantilene e filastrocche*, 1965, p. 23.)

A related game in England, now played only rarely (a single account) but popular at the beginning of the century, was the guessing game 'Dead Men, Dark Scenery' or 'Who is the Green-Eyed Man?' In this a member of one side is covered with coats or a blanket by his companions who then disappear, summoning the other side. The newcomers have to guess who is the green-eyed man, and if they guess correctly he jumps up and tries to catch the one who named him.

Bogey

In 'Bogey', which is one of the classic examples of children enjoying being scared (provided that the situation is of their own arranging), the suspense is accentuated by the fact that the game is played in the dark; and that the children who are going to be chased do not even know the whereabouts of the chaser until he jumps out at them. Traditionally the game is played on winter evenings, while walking home from school. The child who is to be 'bogey' goes on ahead and hides in a dark place, as he thinks best, in a doorway, on top of a wall, or behind a pillarbox. The others, after counting perhaps 'five hundred in tens', follow along with an air of unconcern, but in reality successfully scaring themselves by singing out loud:

> Moonlight, starlight,
> The bogey man's not out tonight.
> *Or,*
> Tonight's the night, a very fine night,
> I hope there'll be no ghosts tonight.

When, without realizing it, they come to the bogey's hiding-place, he jumps out at them. Everybody screams to frighten everybody else; and whoever is caught becomes next bogey. Sometimes there is a den or safe place that they can run back to, and sometimes, as in the game 'Ghost Train' in Liverpool, the bogey or ghost takes captives and makes them into 'ghost's assistants'.

Other names: 'Bogey Won't Come Out Tonight', 'Ghostie', 'Moonlight, Starlight', and 'Stealing Witch's Geese' (Accrington).

§ Infantile as this entertainment may be, it has been performed on dark nights in country places for the best part of a century. Numerous correspondents have recalled it, with scarcely any variation on the poetical side. Flora Thompson, who was born in north Oxfordshire in 1877, was one who played it *(Lark Rise,* 1939, p. 26), and since gipsies then seemed as alarming as any hobgoblin, the children sang:

> I hope we shan't meet any gipsies tonight!
> I hope we shan't meet any gipsies tonight!

'Bogey' has also long been played in Germany under such names as 'Das böse Ding', 'Der böse Mann', and 'Der böse Geist'. According to Meier, *Deutsche Kinder-Spiele aus Schwaben,* 1851, pp. 102–3, after the evil spirit had gone off and hidden around a corner, the rest followed, reassuring themselves, as in England, by singing:

> Wir wollen in den Garten gehn,
> Wenn nur der böse Geist nicht war!

And when 'der böse Geist' sprang out they had to run back to their *Bodde* or sanctuary; and whoever was caught had to be the next evil spirit.

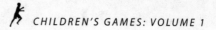

Players being chased assist each other

In the chasing games described so far each of the free runners has thought only of saving himself. In the following games, which tend to be more exasperating for the chaser, the runners are able to assist or rescue each other.

Cross touch

The game starts as ordinary 'Touch', but when the chaser is running after somebody his pursuit can be diverted simply by another player running between him and his quarry. The chaser is now bound to follow the person who crossed in front of him; and as soon as there is a wide enough gap another player is likely to dart between them so that the chaser is again obliged to set off after a fresh runner. 'Cross Touch' is thus a more lively game than ordinary 'Touch'; and it is not always as disheartening for the chaser as it might seem, for in practice the player who runs across is often over-confident, and finds to his surprise that he has been touched.

§ This form of 'Touch' is described in *Juvenile Games for the Four Seasons, c.* 1820, pp. 20–1, where it is called 'Puss', but there is no other authority for the name which has here probably been taken from the French 'Le chat coupé'. At Sedgley Park, about 1803–10, the game was called 'Cross-tag' (Husenbeth, *The History of Sedgley Park School,* 1856, p. 107); in *The Playground,* 1858, p. 13, and in many other juvenile books of the period, it is 'Cross Touch'; in *Games of Argyleshire,* 1901, it is 'Tig and Relieve'. Presumably 'Cross-dadder' in Hardy's *Under the Greenwood Tree,* 1872, ch. ix, is this game. In the United States it is 'Cross Tag' or 'Turn Tag' (Brewster). In Rome it is 'Taglia-salame', the players calling out 'I cut the salame' as they run between chased and chaser (Lumbroso).

Stuck in the mud

If the touch of the chaser in 'French Touch' appears to have a morbid effect on the part of the anatomy touched, the touch in 'Stuck in the Mud' paralyses the player altogether, except, that is, his vocal chords. ('It's a game that makes you sweat sometimes', comments a 9-year-old.) Once a player has been touched he must stand upright where he is, with his arms outstretched, and he has to keep like this, shouting to the others for help — 'Releaso! Releaso!' or 'S.O.S.!' — until one of the free players manages to touch and release him. Meanwhile the chaser attempts to touch and transfix the rest of the players. Thus there is a second element in the game; for the chaser is not only chasing the others, but having to guard the person or persons he has already immobilized. The game ends, or rather, begins again, if the chaser manages 'to get all the players with their arms outstretched', or if one of the players has been twice caught and released, and is then caught for a third time. It may be remarked that the game is not successful if there are a large number of players and only one chaser.

It is a measure of the game's popularity that it is known by a variety of names, of which 'Stuck in the Mud' or 'Stick in the Mud' is the most widespread.[39] Other descriptive names are: 'Aeroplane Tig' (popular in Scotland), 'Wingbird' (Great Ellingham, Norfolk), 'Scarecrow Tig', 'Posts', and 'Lamp-posts' (many places), 'Standstill Tick' (Welshpool), 'Statues' (Manchester), 'Stone Tag' (Gloucester), 'Stooky Tig' (New Cumnock), 'Tick Frozen' (Plympton St Mary), 'Freeze Tag' (Bristol), 'Frozen Tig' (Aberystwyth), 'Jack Frost' (Bristol and St Andrews), 'Frost and Snow' (Sleaford), 'Coolee' (Wootton Bassett), 'Petrified' (Ipswich), 'Stop and Go' (Newbridge), 'Sticky Buds' (Moreton-in-Marsh), and 'Sticky Glue' (a number of places). Names which reflect the rescue element are: 'Release', 'Releaster', 'Reliev-i-o', 'Tig and Relevo', 'Tiggy Release', 'Stick and Release', 'Free Me' (Whalsay, Shetland), and 'S.O.S.' In Aberdeen the game is called 'Stone and Relieve' (often corrupted to 'Stone a Leaf'), the touching by the chaser being known as 'stoning', and in Perth it is 'Stoney Free'. Sometimes the game is played with a suspense start, and the names are the same as for 'French Touch', e.g. 'Poison', 'Poisonous Tick', and 'Sticky Touch' (common). There is sometimes a feeling of sorcery about the game. At Etton on the Yorkshire Wolds it is known as 'Stone Fairy'; in the Avon Valley it is 'Witch'; in Belfast 'Witches' Tag'; in Blaenavon 'Fairies and Witches'; in Spalding 'Cats and Witches', and in Westmorland 'Witches and Trees'. At Knighton in Radnorshire, where much ancient lore mixes with the new, the game is known as 'Will o' the Wisp', and once a player has been touched there is no releasing him. A 14-year-old girl writes: 'For this game you need not less than six boys and girls of which two are picked to be wizards. The others are given one minute in which to get away, then the wizards chase them and must touch them on the *shoulder*. Then they immediately become stuck in the position and stay there until everyone is caught. Then the first and last caught become the wizards and so it goes on.' A further dramatized version, called 'Sun and Frost', is played at Stornoway in the Isle of Lewis, and embodies a peculiar method of choosing the chaser:

> 'You all stand in a row and one person picks the nicest face
> for the sun, and the rest thats left they all put on ugly faces
> and pick the ugliest one. The people thats left all go out
> and the frost goes after them and if they're caught they
> have to stand still till the sun tips them and they will get
> free. Thats how you play the Sun and the Frost.'
>
> *Girl, 11*

§ British children are not alone in finding the game uncanny. In Berlin, where it is known as 'Hexe geh — Hexe steh', three witches do the chasing (Peesch, *Das Berliner Kinderspiel*, 1957, p. 39). In Austria, where the game is variously called 'Versteinern', 'Steinerne Hex', or 'Erlösen', the chaser is also a witch, and is said to turn the children into stone (Kampmüller, *Oberösterreichische Kinderspiele*, 1965, p. 137). And in Italy, too, there are witches, wizards, and enchantments, the names for the game being 'Strega che impala', 'Mago libero', and 'Incantesimo' (Lumbroso, *Giochi*, 1967, pp. 310–12).

Underground tig

This is like 'Stuck in the Mud' (and is sometimes so called) but it is more difficult to release a person who has been touched. 'The rule of the game is there's one person on and if he tick you, you have to stand still with your legs open and somebody has to go under your legs and then you are free' (Boy, 9, Wilmslow). 'It is rather dangerous', adds another 9-year-old, 'because it is easy to knock the person over when one is scrambling through in a hurry.'

Confusingly, the game is often called 'Sticky Glue' or 'Releaso', but special names include: 'Bunny in the Hole' (Fulham), 'Crawly Tig' (St Andrews), 'Ice Block' (Liverpool), 'Jam Tarts' (Chelsea), 'London Bridge' (Bristol), 'Policeman Tig' or 'Stick a Policeman' (Accrington),

'Stride Tag' (Stornoway), 'Ticky Underlegs' (Wigan), 'Underground Tig' or 'Underground Tick' (Aberdeen, Liverpool, Welshpool), and 'Underleg Release-i-o' (Fulham).

Tunnel touch

'Tunnel Touch' is similar to 'Underground Tig' but when a player is touched he has to stand with one arm against a wall, or, occasionally, with one leg lifted up against a wall, and he can only be released if a free player manages to run underneath. Release is thus more difficult to effect than in 'Stuck in the Mud', but easier than in 'Underground Tig' since the players waiting for release are in a line along the wall, and sometimes several can be released at once. The game is not infrequently played with two chasers, one of whom guards the 'tunnel'.

Names: 'Arch Tig' (Oxford), 'Bridge Tick' (Welshpool), 'French Release' (Euston), 'Frenchman's Tuck' (Camden Town), 'Ticky Under Arm' (Wigan), 'Tunnel Touch', 'Tunnel Tig', etc. (many places), 'Under Arm Tick' (Perth), and 'Wall Tig' (Castel, Guernsey).

Ticky leapfrog

'Another variation of the ticky game is "Ticky Leapfrog" ', writes a Manchester boy. 'On being tuck a player has to crouch down in the leap-frog position to await the person to jump over to free him. If he is tuck three times he is on.' In Peckham, somewhat similarly, they play what they call 'Chinese Touch'. 'When a person has you,' says an informant, 'you have to stand still, and to be released a person has to jump on your back.' In both these games it is necessary that the chaser be fairly busy elsewhere before a player can be released; and this is even more neces-sary in 'Circular Touch', played by girls in Swansea, where a girl does not become free unless another girl runs round her three times.

Gluepots

In this game, played mostly by girls, the chaser has to have a place where she can put her 'captives', as she calls them. In versions of the game known as 'Tick Corner' (Welshpool), 'He in the Box' (Peckham), 'Release' (Norwich), and 'Ghostie' (Greenwich), she chooses a convenient recess in a building, or a grating, or the worn ground in front of a gate. In the form of the game known as 'Gluepots' or 'Stewpot' (Accrington, West Ham, St Leonards-on-Sea, and elsewhere), the chaser, who is thought of as a witch, marks out circles on the ground with a chalk or a stick, one circle for each person who is to be chased, and designates these places her 'pots'. The chasing takes place in the neighbourhood of the pots, and when the witch touches someone she leads her to a pot where the person has to stand with her arms outstretched hoping to be rescued. The rescuers, however, have to be careful, for should they accidentally step in one of the pots they must remain in it. In Wigan, as also in West Ham and North Acton, the young children who play 'Witch's Glue' or 'Witches in the Gluepots' feel that the witch, living in a gluepot, must be sticky, and that when she puts a person in a gluepot that person becomes sticky too. As a result, the captive cannot be rescued. On the contrary, the captives lean out of their gluepots and attempt to touch anyone who passes by, becoming an additional hazard to those who are still free. Further, as an 8-year-old states, 'When all are caught they have a punishment. Then the last one who is caught is the witch.'

§ When watching young children play 'Gluepots' or 'Witches in the Gluepots' it is easy to assume that they have made the game up themselves. But more than eighty years ago Newell described American children playing a game called 'Witch in the Jar'. One of the children was selected for a witch. She marked out circles on the ground with a stick, as many circles as there were players, and called these circles 'jars'. A game followed in which those who were caught were put in the jars, and could not escape unless someone else chose to free them by touching (*Games of American Children*, 1883, pp. 163–4). In a note Newell remarked that the children who played this game imagined that it was they who had invented the game; and he pointed out, in his turn, that the game was identical to 'Die Hexe' (The Witch), described by Heinrich Handelmann in *Volks-und Kinder-Spiele aus Schleswig-Holstein*, 1874, p. 65.

Chaser at disadvantage

In some games it is customary for the chaser to be discomfited, or to suffer a form of initiation, before he begins chasing. In 'Bully Horn', as we have seen, he is escorted back, none too delicately, to the starting-line. In the game called 'Dumping', at Forfar, the new chaser is lifted up by feet and arms and dumped around a corner, or in a ditch, and while he picks himself up the others run away. And in 'Ticky Leapfrog' at Sale, he has to bend down and allow all the other players to jump over him, before he can take on his new role. In other games, already described, the chaser may be set at a perpetual, but usually minor, disadvantage while he chases, being obliged to run with his hands clasped (in 'Bull'), or with one hand covering some part of his body ('French Touch'). In the following games the chaser is at so great disadvantage that the players have little fear of him, and tend to gather round and goad him, rather than run from him. Thus the initiative passes in large measure to those being 'chased', as it sometimes does in catching games where the catcher's field of action is restricted (see Chapter 3). It is interesting that the games that follow are all old; and that none of them are played as often today or with as much verve as they used to be. It seems that games in which one player remains vulnerable and at a disadvantage for some length of time, are not now felt as amusing as formerly. But whether this niceness is due to compassion for the luckless player or to fear of having to take his place is an open question.

Cat and mouse

One player is chosen 'cat' and one 'mouse', the rest form a circle 'holding hands tightly'. The game begins with the cat on the outside of the circle, the mouse within. At Windermere the cat asks: 'Is the mouse at home?'

> Mouse: 'Who wants to know?'
> Cat: 'The cat wants to know.'
> Mouse: 'Yes, the mouse is at home.'
> Cat: 'What o'clock is it?'
> Mouse: 'Time the mouse was gone!'

The cat then attempts to catch the mouse, but the players forming the ring are on the mouse's side, they do not want the cat to get into the ring, and wherever the cat attempts to break through they 'push against each other' to prevent him. If the cat does get through they let the mouse out, and, says a player joyfully, 'the cat gets stuck in the ring'. The chaser is thus continually obstructed. Only if the children are small is the cat likely to get in and out of the ring without difficulty, and the chase speeds up. Indeed, small children in their excitement are liable to let the cat through and bar the way to the mouse. But if the children are older, the mouse may feel so secure on his side of the ring, he will dance about just in front of the cat; while the cat becomes more and more weary trying to break through, and sometimes never catches the mouse. 'If the cat fails to catch the mouse after a long time, the mouse has won,' explained a West Ham girl, 'but if he catches the mouse the cat has won because he pretends to eat the mouse up.' In this game the players making the circle have almost as active a part as the runners.

In Shetland the game is called 'A Mouse in the Meal Barn' or 'Moose in da Meal Barrel'.

§ Strutt in his *Sports and Pastimes*, 1801, p. 285, gives the name 'Cat after Mouse', but the game he describes is a form of 'Kiss in the Ring' in which a player, striking one of the circle on the back, is chased in and out of the ring, without either of them being deliberately hindered. This is the French 'Le chat et le rat', the Spanish 'El gato y el ratón', the Italian 'Topo e gatto'. But when children in Germany play 'Katze und Maus', the cat starts outside the circle and the mouse within. The cat calls out 'Mouse, mouse, come here or I will scratch your eyes out'. The mouse comes out, and when the cat gives chase the mouse can take refuge within the circle and the other children prevent the cat from entering (Peesch, *Berliner Kinderspiel*, 1957, p. 22). In Moscow, according to a Russian correspondent, the name of the game is 'Cats and Mice', and the children help the mouse and stop the cat exactly as in England, lifting their arms to let the mouse through, and lowering them to block the way for the cat. Tolstoy refers to the amusement in *Anna Karenina* (v. 28). In Yugoslavia, according to Brewster, the sport is 'Mácka in Mís', and in Rumania 'De-a Pisica si Scaracele', and in both these countries the players show their sympathy for the mouse by hindering the cat (1953, p. 63). In the United States children sometimes play one form of the game and sometimes another; but as long ago as 1832 Mrs Child in *The Girl's Own Book* said that the players favoured the mouse. However, since, according to Mrs Child, the circle was 'obliged to keep dancing round all the time' the cat soon found a weak link to break through.

A further form of 'Cat and Mouse' is a gymnasium game. The players are formed up in about six lines of six players. Each line joins hands, and the cat and mouse run up and down between the lines, neither of them being allowed to break through. There is a caller who periodically commands 'Turn'; and when he does so each child in the lines makes a right turn, and links hands with the players who were formerly in front and behind him, which usually means that extra distance is put between the mouse and the cat. This procedure gives much satisfaction to the caller, and to those children who are geometrically minded.

Fox and chickens

In this game the fox or chaser is at considerable disadvantage since, to quote a 9-year-old Widecombe boy, 'the fox has to hop on one leg and the chickens can run with two'. In consequence there is an amount of acting as well as activity: the fox has a 'hole', he comes out of his hole, and also takes refuge in his hole; and the chickens behave as foolishly as chickens do, so that sometimes the fox is able to catch one of them. When he does he takes the chicken back to his hole and that person obtains the doubtful privilege of becoming the new fox.

§ In the 1960s this game has been found only among the children of Widecombe-in-the-Moor, the Devonshire village renowned in song. Gomme, in 1894, did not hear of the game in England, only in Cork, under its old name 'Fox in the Hole', the players striking at the fox with handkerchiefs, while the fox, who had to keep hopping, attempted to strike one of them back to make him his victim. Norman Douglas, however, seems to have found it in London in the twentieth century. 'Fox Come Out of Your Den', which he lists as a game with caps, is almost certainly this sport. (The caps would have been used for hitting the fox.)

In the sixteenth and seventeenth centuries the game seems to have been well known. 'Fox in the Hole' or 'Fox in thy Hole' was mentioned by Florio in 1611; by Herrick twice, in *Hesperides*, 1648; and by the author of *The Tragedye of Solyman and Perseda, c.* 1592. Surviving descriptions leave no doubt that the Elizabethan pastime is the ancestor of the game played at Widecombe. Indeed it can be traced back to antiquity. Classical scholars have long remarked a similarity between 'Fox in the Hole' (the game they knew), and the 'Empusae ludus' of the Romans and the 'Ascoliasmos' of the Greeks, where one boy who hopped had to catch others who had the use of both feet (Pollux, ix. 121). John Higins noted it in his *Nomenclator of Adrianus Junius*, 1585, p. 298 ('A kinde of playe wherein boyes lift vp one leg, and hop on the other: it is called fox in thy hole'); and so did Francis Gouldman in his *Dictionarium*, 1664 ('*Ascoliasmus, Empusae ludus*: a kind of play wherein boys lift up one leg and hop with the other, where they beat one another with bladders tied to the end of strings. Fox, to thy hole'). The Rev J. G. Wood, who was a pupil at Ashbourne Grammar School in Derbyshire, 1838–43, states that the game of 'Fox' was extensively played in his day, the players being armed with twisted handkerchiefs, 'one end to be tied in knots of almost incredible hardness', and the fox had a den from which he must hop (*Every Boy's Book*, 1856, p. 7). J. O. Halliwell, whose account of the game (*Popular Rhymes*, 1849, pp. 131–2) most closely corresponds with present-day practice, says that only the fox has a knotted handkerchief, he must always hop when he leaves his home, and the other children are geese. 'Whoever he can touch is Fox instead, but the geese run on two legs, and if the Fox puts his other leg down, he is hunted back to his home.'

The game is also exactly described in *School Boys' Diversions*, 1820, pp. 12–13, but under the name 'Devil in the Bush'. It seems probable that the description and name are here taken from a French source (as are some other parts of the book), for the game has long been played in identical manner in Europe, being known in France under such names as 'Le diable boîteux' and 'La vieille mère Garuche', in Hungary as 'Sánta Róka', and in Germany, as in England, as 'Fuchs ins Loch'. Gutsmuths in his *Spiele für die Jugend*, 1796 (1802, pp. 268–70), described 'Fuchs zu Loche' as 'fairly common with us'; and Böhme, who gives several nineteenth-century names (*Deutsches Kinderspiel*, 1897) suggests that Fischart listed the game in his *Geschichtklitterung von Gargantua*, 1590, under the name 'Wolf, beiß mich nicht'. In support of this attribution Böhme quotes a song in Hainhofer's *Lautenbuch*, 1603, which may have been the game-rhyme in Fischart's day:

> Fuchs, beiß mich nicht, Fuchs, beiß mich
> nicht!
> Du hast ein g'hörig großes Maul.

> Du hätt'st ein guten Schuster g'geb'n,
> Du hast die Borst im Maul.

A friend has rendered this:

> Fox, bite me not, fox, bite me not!
> You have a proper great gob.
> You'd have made a good shoemaker,
> You have the bristle in your mouth.

The bristle referred to would be the one the shoemaker uses as a needle.

Blind man's buff

'Blind Man's Buff' is one game that needs little description, not because of the frequency with which it is played but because of its general renown. Even an 11-year-old, telling us that 'Blind Man's Buff' was her favourite game, added (correctly): 'People in the fourteenth century used to play it.' Indeed the thought of a chaser being at such a disadvantage that he is unable to see those he chases is, in itself, highly agreeable to the juvenile imagination. Thus great care is taken over the blindfolding, which is usually done with a scarf. It is tied tightly over the person's eyes, and he is repeatedly asked if he can see, and is tested with questions, 'What colour is my coat?' 'Who is the tallest here?' To ensure his confusion, willing hands turn him round three times, or spin, or twirl him, or in Norwich 'twistle' him, until he is 'quite dizzy'. Then the blind man stumbles off, stretching his arms out in front of him, and hoping that they will come into contact with someone. The rest of the players amuse themselves by dodging under his arms, making noises behind his back, and pushing each other towards him. If the game is being played outside, whoever he touches usually becomes the new blind man without further formalities. But indoors, at a party, or family gathering (the game is best played in the confined space of a crowded room), the blind man invariably has to guess whom he has caught. He feels the person's hair, his face, his clothes, to help him guess correctly; and if his guess is wrong he has to let the player go and try to catch someone else. Sometimes (even in the playground) the players change clothes to confuse the blind man, and deliberately let themselves be caught, trusting to their disguise to deceive him and keep them from having to take his place.

§ Under its various names 'Blind Man's Buff' is probably more often mentioned in English literature than any other informal game. In 1565 Thomas Cooper referred to 'a childish play called hoodman blind' in his *Thesaurus* (s.v. *Mya*). In 1573 John Baret listed 'the Hoodwinke play, or hoodmanblind, in some places called blindm buf' in his informative *Dictionarie* (H. 566). About 1602 the anonymous author of *The Second Part of the Return from Parnassus* described his play as 'a Christmas toy indeed, as good a conceite as stanging hot cockles, or blinde-man buffe'. And Hamlet, it will be remembered, demanded of his mother: 'What Diuell thus hath cosoned you at hob-man blinde?' (printed 'hoodman-blinde' in the Folio, III. iv).

In the seventeenth century writer after writer names the game, for example Robert Armin in 1609 ('Hud-man blind'); Cotgrave in 1611 ('Hodman blind, Harrie-racket'); and Florio in the same year ('Blind-hob, or blind-man's buffe, or hood-man-blind'); as also Drayton, John Taylor, Heywood, Bramhall, and Randle Holme. Pepys, on 26 December 1664, records that he went to bed leaving his wife and household 'to their sport and blindman's buff', which they did not leave off until four in the morning. William Hawkins, in 1627, shows it was already the custom to turn the blind man round three times: 'You are tyed, now I must turne you about thrice'; and Davenant, in 1669, suggested it should be 'Twice for the maids, once for the men' — perhaps reckoning three turns in all.

It may be asked how it has come about that a game that was so popular, and for so long, is now played only occasionally, and only by small boys and girls. In the eighteenth century, it is clear, adults and children alike continued to make merry with 'Blind Man's Buff', as Gay shows in *The Shepherd's Week*, 1714; Goldsmith in *The Vicar of Wakefield*, 1766; and Blake in his *Poetical Sketches*, 1783. In the nineteenth century, too, Mr Pickwick went 'through all the mysteries of blind-man's buff'; and during the Christmas gambols at Farringford in 1855, even Palgrave, Jowett, and the Poet Laureate diverted themselves with the game, and did so *after* the children had been put to bed (Emily Tennyson writing to Lear).

The fact that the game was popular throughout Britain is attested by the number of regional names it has had: 'Biggly' in Cumberland,

'Blind-Bucky-Davy' in the west country, 'Blind Hob' in Suffolk, 'Blind-Merry-Mopsey' in the North Riding, 'Blind Sim' in East Anglia, 'Blindy-Buff' in the West Riding, 'Willy Blindy' in Durham, 'Hoodle-cum-blind' in Northamptonshire, and 'Blufty' in the midlands. In Scotland: 'Belly Blind', 'Billy Blind',[40] 'Blind Harry' (also in northern counties of England), 'Blind Palmie', 'Glim Glam', 'Jockie Blind Man' (anciently 'Chacke-Blynd-Man'), and 'Jockie Blindie', a name still known in Angus today.

The reason for the game's obsolescence is not hard to find: 'Blind Man's Buff' has progressively softened (Blake pleaded that too much advantage should not be taken of the chaser's blindness); it has lost the buffeting referred to in its name, and consequently its *modus operandi*. In the 600-year-old 'Romance of Alexander' (MS. Bodley 264, fols. 70^v, 130^r and ^{v}) three marginal pictures not only show that the chaser was blinded by having his hood reversed on his head (hence the names 'the Hoodwinke playe' and 'Hoodman Blind'), but that the rest of the players, men, women, and boys, swarmed about him for the sweet pleasure of giving him a buffet with their own well-knotted hoods. Thus the blind man had a chance of seizing one of them; and although the game was violent it was viable. It had in fact already been played like this for a thousand years. In classical times, according to Pollux (ix. 123), it was called 'Chalke muia' (The Brazen Fly). One boy's eyes were covered with a bandage. He shouted out 'I shall chase the brazen fly'. The others retorted, 'You may chase him, but you won't catch him', and they hit him with whips made from papyrus husks until one of them was caught.

In one form or another the sport seems to be part of the social history of the world: in Italy the game continues to be known as 'Mosca cieca' (Blind Fly), in Germany and Austria it is 'Blinde Kuh', in Sweden 'Blind bock', in Denmark 'Blinde-buk', in France 'Colin-maillard'; and it is also played in, for instance, Finland, Russia, China, Korea, Japan, India, and Ethiopia. However, two forms of the game are traditional. In one, as we have seen, the players buzz about the blind man so that they can hit him; in the other they do not hit him but remain close to him because they cannot get away. When Master Picquet played 'à la mousque' in the judicial chamber, and was himself the fly (Rabelais, III. xl), he laughed at the way the gentlemen were spoiling their caps 'in swindging of his Shoulders', so the game they were playing was clearly a version of 'The Brazen Fly'. But Pollux also described a game called 'Muinda', in which the chaser could not see and yet, apparently, was not hit. In *Il Pentamerone*, 1634, one of the games played by the royal household while waiting for dinner on the second day was 'Gatta cecata' (Blind Cat). Although 'Mosca cieca' is the usual game and name in Italy, 'Gatta cecata' survives in the Neapolitan dialect, and in this game there is no hitting of the blind cat. The players hold hands in a ring around her (this is a girls' game), and are wholly occupied in dancing out of her way when she moves first in one direction and then another. Not that it altogether matters when one of them is touched. The blind cat has also to guess the player's identity if she is to be relieved of her bandage, and take the other's place. This graceful game (as Goya depicted it) is popular today in countries such as Greece, Spain, and Uruguay. And had it come to Britain instead of the pugnacious variety of 'Blind Man's Buff', it would probably still be popular here. In fact, amongst guessing games there is one called 'How Far to London?' (Vol.2 p. 165) that is a game of this type, apparently related to 'Muinda', and it is still in vogue in the north.

Jingling

In 'Jingling', known as 'Jingle Chase' in Edinburgh, and 'Bell Man' in Inverness, all the players but one are chasers, and the chasers are all blinded. A semblance of fairness is achieved by making the one who is chased carry a bell or rattle which he has to keep sounding; and the game is played in a confined space so that the jingler cannot move far away, sometimes not outside a circle chalked on the ground. He must thus dodge about amongst his pursuers, continually ringing his bell, and this is a laughable game to watch: the sightless chasers bumping into each other, falling over each other, involuntarily embracing each other, and frequently grabbing each other with the cry 'I've caught you', under the impression that they have secured the jingler, only to hear the bell ring again at a distance from them. Should a blind man succeed in catching the jingler he changes roles with him; but an agile jingler can sometimes elude capture for a long time, and after a period he may be rewarded by being made a spectator, while another takes his place.

§ 'Jingling Matches' were a popular diversion at fairs and country wakes in the eighteenth and early nineteenth centuries, the jingler receiving a prize if he could remain free a certain length of time, 'commonly about twenty minutes'. Accounts of the entertainment appear in Strutt's *Sports and Pastimes*, 1801, p. 277; *The Sporting Magazine*, May 1810, p. 63; Pierce Egan's *Book of Sports*, 1832, p. 265; and in Thomas Hughes's *Tom Brown's School Days*, 1857, pp. 35–6, and *The Scouring of the White Horse*, 1858, pp. 110 and 149–50, where Hughes quotes a hand-bill of 1780 announcing that one of the attractions at a Scouring was to be:

> 'A jingling match by eleven blindfolded men, and one unmasked and hung with bells, for a pair of buckskin breeches.'

The informal game is referred to by William Hawkins in *Apollo Shrouing*, 1627, p. 51: 'You must have this Morice-bell tied to your point, that I may heare where you goe. Else you will haue too much oddes of me'; by Jamieson in his *Scottish Dictionary*, 1825, under 'Blind Bell'; in *The Boy's Own Book*, 1855, pp. 43–4; in Dean's *Alphabet of Sports*, 1866, under 'Rat and Bell'; and in *The Modern Playmate*, 1870, pp. 7–8. Games on the same principle, but in which there are only two players, are 'Cat and Mouse' in *The Boy's Own Book*, 1829, p. 28; 'Jacob! Where are You?' in *The Girl's Own Book*, 1832, p. 50 (called 'Jacob and Rachel' in *London Street Games*, 1916, p. 47); and 'Baiting the Badger' in *The Book of Cub Games*, 1919 (1958, p. 53).

Frog in the middle

Few chasers can be at greater disadvantage than the 'Frog' in this game, who is not permitted to move about or even rise from the ground, but must sit or squat where he is while the others dance round in a circle singing:

> Hey, hey, hi! Hey, hey, hi!
> Frog in the middle and there shall he lie.
> He can't get out, he can't get in,
> Hey, hey, hi! Hey, hey, hi!

'Then,' says a 13-year-old girl in Bristol, 'the frog has to try and touch the people who come and poke him or her, but the frog is not allowed to get on his feet. When he has touched somebody, then that person is the frog.'

§ The song 'Hey, hey, hi!' is almost identical to one given by Gomme, vol. i, 1894, p. 146, which may indicate a literary rather than oral continuity. On the other hand, the game itself had already been played for 1,700 years before Gomme found it, so it can well have survived for a few more decades. In the sport called 'Chytrinda', described by Pollux (ix. 113), one boy, termed the *chytra* or 'pot', sat on the ground while the others ran round in a circle, plucking him, or pinching him, or striking him, as they went. But if the *chytra* succeeded in catching one of them, the person caught took his place. As Strutt remarked in 1801: 'I scarcely need to add that "The Frog in the Middle", as it is played in the present day, does not admit of any material variation.' 'Frog in the Middle' is also described in *The Girl's Book of Diversions*, 1835, p. 19, and in *Games and Sports for Young Boys*, 1859, p. 75, the players baiting and hitting the frog, and calling 'Frog in the middle, you can't catch me'. The game appears to be depicted in the medieval manuscript, 'The Romance of Alexander' (fol. 97^v), which was completed in 1344. And in the sixteenth century the names for the game may have been 'Selling of Peares' and 'How many plums for a penie', since these are the English names John Higins supplies for 'Chytrinda' in *The Nomenclator of Adrianus Junius*, 1585, p. 298.

Many related games were formerly common, both in Britain and on the Continent: notably 'Brunnenfrau' or 'Frau Holle' in which the lady of the well, seated on a stool, had to catch one of the players who were teasing and tugging at her (Böhme, *Deutsches Kinderspiel*, 1897, p. 579); 'Sling the Monkey', in which a boy suspended by the waist from the branch of a tree tried to touch one of the players who were hitting him with their knotted handkerchiefs ('the best of the basting games', said *The Boy's Own Paper*, 12 November 1887); and the well-known game of 'Baste the Bear', 'Badger the Bear', or 'Badger the Bull', described in most books of boys' games in the nineteenth century, from *Youthful Sports*, 1801, onwards.

In 'Baste the Bear', played in the United States under the name 'Watchdog' (Brewster, 1953, p. 183), and still current in Britain in the 1920s, a keeper holds the bear, who is on all fours, either with a rope or by the back of his coat, and tries to catch one of the players whose sport it is to lash at the bear with their caps or knotted handkerchiefs whenever they can get near. This game is international. It is depicted in *Les Jeux et plaisirs de l'enfance*, 1657, under the name 'La Poire', which may relate it to the Elizabethan 'Selling of Peares' above; it appears to have been well known in classical times, being shown in wall-paintings of both Pompeii and Herculaneum; and, as a correspondent reported in *The Athenaeum*, 29 December 1883, it was still being played in the Greek island of Samos in the nineteenth century.

> 'Nothing I ever saw played can equal in roughness *glyko krasi* "sweet wine", as they euphoniously name it. A boy sits in the middle with one end of a long rope in his hand; another boy takes the rope after the fashion of a whip. The object is for the boys around to belabour the boy in the middle without getting hit with the rope. Whilst playing this game I have seen many ugly blows given and received, but, I am bound to say, with the greatest good nature.'

Since this game is ancient, and is here called 'Sweet Wine', it seems possible that it is as much a descendant of Pollux's 'Game of the Pot' as is 'Frog in the Middle'.

3. Catching Games

'If he is cot you have to lift him up or drag him to the side.
He is aloud to kik or punch. It is rather a ruf game but most
people like it.'

Boy, 9, Edinburgh

Catching games differ from chasing games in that the runners' chief object is usually to reach a designated place, or accomplish a particular mission, rather than keep out of the chaser's reach. Thus the catcher does not so much run after the other players as intercept them. Very often, too, he has considerable control over their movements. He is able to order when they shall run, is allowed to place himself in position before he gives the order, and sometimes has the power to name individual players (usually poor runners) who must attempt the run on their own. On the other hand, the catcher often has to do more than touch a runner to make him a captive. He may have to keep hold of him for a prescribed length of time, or perform some ritual action on his body, or even force him to the ground; and the runner's response, needless to say, is unlikely to be passive. In consequence some of the catching games take on the appearance of a series of dog-fights, and it is remarkable that they ever manage to remain games. Indeed, when it is remembered that the majority of catching games consist of no more than the crossing and recrossing of one small piece of ground (the basic pavement-to-pavement street game), and that they are played without equipment or preparation, or the approval of other road-users, it may be felt that the number there are of these games, and the gusto with which they are played, is no small testimonial to a people compelled to be city-dwellers.

Running across

'Running Across' is one of those games, they say, that 'requires a great deal of energy'. The players split into two groups, one group going to one side of the road or playground and one to the other, with the catcher midway between them. When the catcher shouts 'Change' (or in Spennymoor, for some reason, 'Lamp oil'), the two sides rush across the ground to change places, getting in each other's way when they meet and giving the player in the middle an opportunity to catch at least one of them, sometimes more. Whoever is caught joins the catcher in the middle, and the running back and forth continues with an ever-thickening line of catchers until everyone is caught. Then the first person who was caught stays in the middle, and the game recommences: all the players running back and forth again at command 'until you are very tired and need a rest'. It is, in consequence, an inviolable rule that a player may not drop out at the end of one game when he is due to be the catcher in the next game.

Other names: 'Foxes' (Lydeard St Lawrence), 'German Bulldog' (St Leonards), 'Hunter and his Dogs' (Bristol), 'Lamp Oil' or 'Lamb Boys' (Spennymoor), and 'Running Across He' (Brightlingsea).

§ The game has also, in the past, been known as 'Katie on the Landing' (Halifax, *c.* 1925), and 'Getting Across' (Melbourne, Australia, *c.* 1916); and there is some evidence that the game has an unusual history.

In North Carolina a game called 'Molly Bright' is played in virtually the same way, except that the player in the middle is held to be a witch. The game starts with a player on one side calling to the other side: 'How many miles to Molly Bright?'

The opposite side replies: 'Three score and ten.'

The first player asks: 'Can I get there by candlelight?'

The other side replies: 'Yes, if your legs are long and light, but watch out for the old witch on the way!'

Both sides then rush across the open space, trying to avoid the witch and reach the other's base (Brewster, *American Nonsinging Games*, 1953, p. 52). This form of the game seems to be traditional in the United States, being given under the name 'How many miles to Babylon' in Eliza Leslie's *Girl's Book of Diversions*, 1835, pp. 6–7, where the catcher is also a witch. The verse 'How many miles to Babylon' (alternatively 'How many miles to Bethlehem', 'Burslem', 'Banbury', 'Barney Bridge', 'Barley-Bridge', and 'Marley Bright') has long been known in Britain where it has added wonder to various children's amusements, including this very game (Somerset, 1922). Further, Mactaggart in his *Gallovidian Encyclopedia*, 1824, p. 300, described a game called 'King and Queen o' Cantelon' (a 'chief school game' in Galloway), which also turns out to be a version of 'Running Across'. Two boys, he says, stood between two 'doons' or places of safety, and had to try and catch the rest of the players when they ran from one doon to the other, after being addressed with the rhyme:

> King and Queen o' Cantelon,
> How mony mile to Babylon;
> Six or seven, or a lang eight,
> Try to win there wi' candle-light.

Likewise a game known as 'King Caesar' or 'Cock and Chickens' was played in Cheltenham in the nineteenth century with the chant:

> Warning once, warning twice,
> A bushel of wheat and a bushel of rye,
> When the cock crows, out jump I.

Here, too, the 'cock' or chaser who repeated these words stood between two sets of players ranged at opposite bases; but there was this difference that the cock had to hold his hands clasped together while he chased, and not loosen his clasp until he caught someone, when he joined hands with that person, and remained linked to him while chasing the rest (Bodley MS. Eng. misc. e 39–40). This *modus operandi* seems not unlike that in the celebrated Tudor game 'Barley-break', where the players also came from opposite ends of the ground, and two chasers in the middle had, in similar fashion, to keep their hands linked while chasing (see under 'Stag' p. 176). Thus there may be linguistic connection between 'How many miles to Babylon' or 'How many miles to Barley-Bridge', and the name 'Barley-break' of 400 years ago.

Chinese wall

Two parallel lines are drawn across the middle of the playground about a yard apart. This is said to be the 'Chinese wall', and one player or sometimes two stand between the lines, and may not go beyond them. The others have to run across the wall without being touched. If they are touched while crossing they join the catchers on the wall. This is often an organized game, the instructor on the side-line taking upon himself the not over-fatiguing task of commanding when the children shall rush one way across the wall, and then the other way, and so on until all have been caught.

Additional names: 'Giant on the Wall' (Thirsk); 'Over the Wall' (Market Rasen).

Wall to wall

'Wall to Wall' is often played in the school yards of junior schools, or at home in the evening across a road. One player stands mid-way between the two walls and the rest ('there need to be more than twenty children for a decent game') line up at one wall and have to run across to the other, keeping within agreed boundaries. Anyone touched while running from one wall to the other joins the catcher in the middle, as in the previous games, so that the balance gradually changes in the favour of the catchers, and the last two or three players are hard put to it to get from one wall to the other without being caught. Nevertheless the runners are not allowed to remain at either wall for more than the count of ten, nor may they turn back once they have left a wall, but must keep running to the opposite side even if they are bound to be caught.

Other names for this much-played game include 'Den to Den' (Bristol), 'Wall to Wall Tig' (Bacup), 'Brixers Last Up' (Cruden Bay, Aberdeenshire), 'Charlie' (Knighton), 'Cross Channel' or 'Dicky Birds and Breadcrumbs' (Croydon), 'Fox and Hounds' (Widecombe-in-the-Moor), 'King Alely' (Ponders End), 'Lollipop' (Glastonbury), 'Old Grannie Witchie' (Edinburgh), 'Poison' (Knighton), 'Running Across' (Retford), 'Touch Road Must Go Over' (Enfield), 'Onefootoveryoumustgo' (Norwich).

At Market Rasen the game is sometimes played between the two semi-circles of a netball court and then called 'Top and Bottom'. At Meir, Stoke-on-Trent, where the name is 'Press Button', the catcher stands by a 'clod of grass' placed in the middle of the road, and everyone has to run when he puts his foot on it. At Wilmslow the players run across when the one in the middle shouts 'Tally-ho', and the game is thus called 'Tally-ho'. In Ipswich and Troutbeck, near Windermere, it is called 'Boiler's Bust'. Everyone must run across when the catcher or caller says 'Boiler's bust', which may come as part of a story (perhaps a Brownie version). In New Cumnock the name and cry is 'Peas and Beans', and an old-style ending to the game is maintained: 'When the last person is caught he tries to tig somebody before they get to the starting-place. If he tigs one they start off the next game [i.e. become the catcher], but if he does not he starts the next game himself.'

Sometimes the game is played with everybody hopping, and it is then called: 'Half Loaf' (Eassie), 'Hauf the Loaf' (Cumnock), 'Hop and a Stag' (Leicester), 'Hopping Red Rover' (Enfield), and 'Yorkshire Pudding' (Knighton). Compare 'Cockarusha' p. 186f.

§ Children seem to have been running back and forth across the road playing this game ever since Georgian days. Jamieson, in 1825, described a game called 'Rin-'im-O'er', played by children in Roxburghshire, 'in which one stands in the middle of a street, road, or lane, while others run across it, within a certain given distance from the person so placed; and whose business it is to catch one in passing'. The only difference from the present-day game seems to have been that when someone was caught 'the captive takes his place', which is now rare. Jamieson says that the game was also known as 'King's Covenanter'. Other names have been: 'Bristol' (*Yorkshire Folk Lore*, vol. i, 1886, p. 46); 'Cock-a-Reedle' in Nottinghamshire (*EDD*, vol. i, 1898); 'Dyke King' in Tyrie, 'Rax' or 'Raxie-boxie, King of Scotland' in Ballindalloch, Banffshire; and 'Red Rover' in Liverpool (*Traditional Games*, vol. ii, 1898, pp. 106–7); 'Rex' in Perthshire, and 'Kinga be Low' (*Games of Argyleshire*, 1901, pp. 209–10); 'Pirates' (*Folk-Lore*, vol. xvii, 1906, p. 95); 'Lockit' (Bristol, *c*. 1920); 'Middlers' (Crewkerne, 1922).

In both the United States and Canada, where the game is often played on the ice, the common name is 'Pom Pom Pull Away', the one in the middle crying:

> Pom pom pull away,
> If you don't come I'll pull you away.

In Missouri it is 'Wolf Over the Ridge' (Brewster, 1953, pp. 53 and 76); and a similar game is, or was, 'Black Tom' played in Brooklyn, and known in the South as 'Ham, Ham, Chicken, Ham, Bacon' (Bancroft, *Games for the Playground*, 1909, pp. 54–5).

Stag

This game is played like 'Wall to Wall' with the difference that when the player in the middle has shouted 'Cross', and succeeded in catching someone who was crossing, he links hands with him. The pair then shout 'Cross' together, and have to remain attached to each other while they catch someone else crossing. The next person caught links up between the first two catchers, so that the first two continue on the outside (this is felt to be important), and anyone else caught joins, similarly, in the middle of the line. The two end players remain the only two with the power to catch, no matter how long the line becomes. If there are a large number of players the last few remaining free will find themselves faced by a great chain of catchers spreading out in both directions; but since only the player at each end can catch them, and even these two only when the chain is unbroken, the last few players usually charge at the middle of the line, hoping to tear their way through before the ends can curl round and reach them.

'Stag' is particularly popular in Montgomeryshire and Radnorshire, where it is also known as 'Stag Tick'; but elsewhere it is not played as frequently as it was before the war. In West Ham, where it is called 'Sheep Dogs', the game starts with two catchers in the middle holding hands. The first person they catch joins hands with them to make a threesome; but when a further person is caught and there are four catchers, they split into pairs, and the crossing thus becomes considerably more difficult for the free players. Compare 'Chain He' which is similar, but the free players are at liberty to run when and where they like within the boundary of the game.

§ It appears that an ancestor of 'Stag' is the renowned game of 'Barley-break' or 'Last Couple in Hell'. Unfortunately, despite Barley-break's great popularity in Shakespeare's day, no precise account exists of how it was played; and subsequent expositions by scholarly but unathletic commentators (notably William Gifford) have tended to obscure rather than clarify the rules of the game. Yet, by ignoring the rules of more recent games that happen to have similar-sounding names, and compounding the poetical descriptions in Sidney's *Arcadia* (written in the early 1580s), Nicholas Breton's *Barley-Breake, or a Warning to Wantons*, 1607, and Suckling's allegorical piece 'Love, Reason, Hate' in *Fragmenta Aurea*, 1646, it is clear that Barley-break was a game for six players, three of whom were boys and three girls, who divided into pairs of boy and girl; one pair going to one end of the ground, one pair to the other, and the third pair taking the middle position known as 'Hell'. It appears that the two pairs on the outside had to 'break', and attempt to change partners with each other, while the pair in hell, coupled together, tried to intercept them. If the two players in the middle succeeded in catching someone, that person, together with the player he or she should have linked with (i.e. the member of the opposite sex who started at the far end of the ground), took their place in hell for the next round. But the catchers could not catch if they were not joined together; and the outside players were safe once they had linked with their new partners. Each game seems to have consisted of a series of two to three 'breaks' or 'barley-breaks', and whichever two players ended up in the middle were said to be 'Last couple in hell'. The basic operation of the game was thus not unlike 'Sheep Dogs', and also some versions of the game 'Befana' played in Italy. This concept of the game is reinforced by hints from Cotgrave (1611) — although he compared the game with 'Tiers'; by Florio (1611), who compared it with 'Pome'; and by Randle Holme's bald description in *The Academie of Armoury*, 1688:

> 'Barla Brakes, is a play of 6: runing, of which two that stands in
> the midle are to take and hold any of the other lott, and so to put
> them in their place of catching.'

Further allusions to the game occur in Henry Machyn's *Diary*, 1557 (1848, p. 132); Fletcher and Shakespeare's *The Two Noble Kinsmen*, iv. iii; and Ben Jonson's *The Sad Shepherd*, i. iv. It is also mentioned in the writings of Armin, William Browne, Burton, Chettle, Dekker, Holiday, Massinger, Rowlands, Shadwell, and Shirley. It is apparent from Beaumont and Fletcher's *The Scornful Lady*, v. iv and *The Captain*, v. iv; and from Brome's *The Queen and the Concubine*, iv. iv, that the term 'last couple in hell' was so well known it was proverbial.

See also under 'Running Across'.

Black Peter

In this game, too, the catcher, here named 'Black Peter', stands out in front, and the rest have to dodge past him to the safety of the other side. Black Peter calls out: 'Who's afraid of big Black Peter?'

The rest shout back, 'Not I.'

The player out in front calls again, 'Who's afraid of big Black Peter?' The rest reply, 'Not I.'

Black Peter calls out a third time, 'Who's afraid of big Black Peter?' and the rest chorus 'I', and rush across to the other side of the street or playground. The first person caught then becomes Black Peter, or sometimes helps Black Peter to catch the others.

Descriptions from Aberystwyth, Knighton, Langholm, and Lerwick.

§ The game's present-day distribution suggests that it has long been played in Britain, but no account has been found earlier than 1922, in Somerset, when it was called 'Black Tom' (Macmillan MSS.). It has, however, a well-documented history in Austria, Germany, and Switzerland, where it continues to be popular, the catcher generally being known as the Black Man. Kampmüller (1965, p. 138) reports that in Upper Austria the catcher starts the game by demanding: 'Fürchtet ihr den schwarzen Mann?'

> Children: 'Nein!'
> Black Man: 'Wenn er aber kommt?'
> Children: 'Dann laufen wir davon!'

Peesch (1957, p. 36) reports that in Berlin 11– and 12-year-olds have three names for it, 'Wer fürchtet sich vorm schwarzen Mann', 'Wer hat Angst vorm schwarzen Mann', and 'Schwarzer Mann', the dialogue often being:

> 'Who's afraid of the Black Man?'
> 'Nobody!'
> 'And if he comes?'
> 'Then we'll go to America!'
> Black Man: 'America is all burnt up!'
> Children: 'Then we'll come over', and they
> rush across the street, hoping to get past
> the Black Man.

'Der schwarze Mann' certainly goes back to the eighteenth century, when it was fully described by J. C. F. Gutsmuths in *Spiele für die Jugend*, 1796 [1802, pp. 261–3]; and it may even be the game 'Der schwarze Knab' listed by Fischart in 1590. The possible antiquity of the game, the foreboding colour of the chaser, and the fact that in Switzerland players sometimes made a ring round the Black Man while they defied him (Rochholz, *Kinderspiel aus der Schweiz*, 1857, p. 376) has given some nineteenth- and twentieth-century scholars sufficient grounds for suggesting that the game is a relic of the death dances notorious in the Middle Ages. However this may be, in Italy the game is not so morbid, being known as 'Avete paura della Befana?' (M. M. Lumbroso, *Giochi*, 1967, p. 328).

Sheep, sheep, come home

The situation in 'Sheep, Sheep, Come Home' is even more dramatic than
in 'Black Peter', and the game is a favourite with younger children. All
the players are sheep except two, one of whom is a shepherd and the
other a wolf. The shepherd leaves the sheep and goes to the far end of the
field or playground while the wolf hides (or pretends to hide) somewhere
between sheep and shepherd.

> The shepherd calls: 'Sheep, sheep, come
>   home.'
> The sheep reply: 'We are afraid.'
> Shepherd: 'What of?'
> Sheep: 'The wolf.'
> Shepherd: 'The wolf has gone to
> Devonshire,
> Won't be back for seven year;
> Sheep, sheep, come home.'

The sheep then run towards the shepherd. The wolf waits until they are
near him and springs out, and tries to catch one of them. Any sheep who
is caught either helps the wolf or takes the wolf's place, or sometimes
has to wait in a den. The shepherd goes to the opposite end of the playground, and the drama recommences.

In Stoke-on-Trent they play the game without a shepherd. One player
volunteers to be wolf ('to save dipping') and stands in the middle of the
road, the rest are the sheep, and stand on the kerb.

> Wolf: 'Sheep, sheep, come over.'
> Sheep: 'We are afraid.'
> Wolf: 'What of?'
> Sheep: 'The wolf.'
> Wolf: 'The wolf has gone to Lancashire to
>   buy a penny hankershire.'
> Sheep: 'How deep is the sea?'
> Wolf: 'Try it and see.'
> Sheep: 'It's too deep. How many days will
>   it take us to cross by boat?'

The wolf then says a certain number of days. 'If the wolf says "Two days",' explains a 13-year-old, 'the sheep will cross the road to the other kerb and back, that is one day, so they will do the same to make two days. After they have walked the two days they have to run across the road before the wolf can touch them. If he touches them they have to help the wolf to catch the others and so on. The first one caught is the wolf in the next game. This game is played in our street.'

Other names: 'Who's Afraid of the Wolf' (Langholm); 'Mr Wolf and the Sheep' (Norwich).

§ This is another game that is exactly paralleled in Austria, the shepherd saying: Alle meine Schäflein, kommt nach Haus'!

> Sheep: Wir können nicht.
> Shepherd: Warum denn nicht?
> Sheep: Der Wolf ist da.
> Shepherd: Was tut er denn?
> Sheep: Uns fangen.
> *Oberösterreichische Kinderspiele, 1965, p. 139*

It is also traditional in Germany, 'Schäflein, Schäflein kommt nach Haus!' being described in, for instance, Meier's *Deutsche Kinder-Reime aus Schwaben*, 1851, p. 370, and Böhme's *Kinderspiel*, 1897, pp. 572–3. In Italy, at Maniago near the Yugoslav border, children play a biblical version, 'Sette Secella', in which the Lord calls his angels to run to him, but they are reluctant to come because the Devil is waiting to chase them (Lumbroso, *Giochi*, 1967, p. 220).

The game was much played in Britain in the nineteenth century, the usual name being 'Sheep, Sheep, come home' (another name was 'Wolf'), while sometimes the players were 'Fox and Geese', as at Eckington in Derbyshire where the dialogue was as follows:

> Fox: 'Geese, Geese, gannio.'
> Geese: 'Fox, Fox, fannio.'
> Fox: 'How many geese have you today?'
> Geese: 'More than you can catch and
> carry away.'
> *Traditional Games, 1894, pp. 140–1*

In Arkansas the game is called 'Fox in the Wall', and the fox has to tap a goose on the shoulder three times to make a capture (Brewster, 1953, pp. 78–9). In *North Carolina Folklore*, 1952, p. 78, it is called 'Fox in the wall'. O. Henry, born in North Carolina in 1862, describes 'Fox-in-the-Morning' in *Cabbages and Kings*, 1904, ch. I.

Other forms of the game in England have been 'Old King Dick', played in Berkshire, *c*. 1920; and 'Blackthorn' which was still being played in the Yorkshire dales in 1930:

> Geese: 'Blackthorn, Blackthorn, Buttermilk and barley corn.'
> Blackthorn: 'How many geese have you today?'
> Geese: 'More than you can catch and carry away.'

'Blackthorn' is named as early as 1837 in William Thornber's *Account of Blackpool*, p. 90 (*EDD*); and further descriptions occur in *Notes and Queries*, 3rd ser., vol. vii, 1865, p. 285 (recalling a Lancashire childhood), and in the *Almondbury and Huddersfield Glossary*, 1883.

Farmer, farmer, may we cross your golden river?

This is probably the most popular game in the streets of Britain today (descriptions from 127 places), being fascinating to little girls, partly, it seems, because of the way it draws attention to item after item of their clothing. One child is named the farmer and stands in the middle of the road while the rest line up on the edge of the pavement. The children on the pavement call out 'Farmer, Farmer, may we cross your golden river?' and the farmer replies, choosing a colour, 'You mayn't cross my river unless you have *blue*'. The children who have this colour on them, even if only on part of a garment, or on a handkerchief or a brooch, are allowed free passage across the river (that is to say the road), and take pleasure in walking sedately across unmolested (this is why, according to one informant, mothers get asked to knit multi-coloured jerseys); but those who are not wearing the colour have to dash across the road and risk being caught by the farmer. When the children ask if they may cross the river from the other side the farmer chooses another colour ('He may choose purple because he knows none of us wears that colour'), and the rush across the road is repeated. In some places when a person is caught he takes the place of the farmer; but more often he is out of the game until everyone has been caught, or he has to help the farmer catch the rest, so 'it is harder to cross as the game goes on'.

If ever there was a game which showed children's love of blending fancy with strenuous activity this is it, for the game, in its multiplicity of forms, has the weirdness of a fairy-tale.

In Liss the players on the pavement ask: 'Farmer, Farmer, may we cross your golden river in our silver boat?'

At Wilmslow: 'Farmer, Farmer, may we cross your golden bridge on our golden horse?'

At Cleethorpes:

> Farmer, Farmer, may we pass
> Over the hills and over the grass?

On Tyneside: 'Farmer, Farmer, may we cross your stinking dirty clarty water?'

The player in the middle may variously be known as 'Jack' (particularly in the south-west and in Wales), 'Boatman', 'Policeman', 'Mr Duck', 'Mr Fish', 'Mr Jellyfish', 'Mr Fisherman', 'Mr Frog', 'Mr Piggie', 'Mr Crocodile', 'Charlie' (north-east England), 'Charlie Chaplin' (parts of Scotland), and 'Charlie Chapman' (Cumnock).

In Headington the players plead: 'Boatman, Boatman, ferry me across the water.'

In Rossendale: 'Old Mother Witch may we cross your ditch?'

In Ipswich: 'Please Mr Frog may we cross your Chinese Channel?'

In Offham, Kent: 'Please Mr Crocodile may we cross the water in a cup and saucer?'

In some places it is customary to give an excuse for crossing. 'Farmer, Farmer, may we cross your golden river to fetch our father's dinner?' (Featherstone). 'Please Mr Crocodile, may we cross the river to take the Queen's dinner?' (York). 'Charlie, can I be over the water to take my father's bait?' (Spennymoor). In Sheffield they chant:

> Farmer, farmer, may we cross your waters today?
> Because we go to school this way
> To learn our A.B.C.

In Plympton St Mary:

> Please Jack, may I cross the water
> To see the Queen's daughter?
> My mother's gone, my father's gone,
> And I want to go too.

In Walworth, where the catcher is Mr Porter, the girls ask politely:

> Please Mr Porter
> May we cross your golden water
> To see your fairy daughter
> And have a cup of water?

But the boys say:

> Please Mr Porter
> May we cross your water
> To see your ugly daughter
> Swimming in the water?

And in Swansea they ask:

> Please Mr Froggie may we cross the water
> To see the King's daughter
> To chuck her in the water
> To see if she can swim?

'It is an exciting game to play when you are bored with other games', comments a 10-year-old.

Names and variations: The names of the game are as various as the formulas, e.g. 'Boatman, Boatman', 'Mr Fisherman', 'Please Mr Crocodile', and 'May I Cross the River?' Sometimes two or three names may be current in the same locality, one of which may be 'Colours' or 'The Golden River', and in Scotland, from Orkney to the English border, the game is often known as 'You Can't Cross the River' or 'Ye Canna Cross the Golden Stream', because the person in the middle of the road is the 'king' or 'keeper' and starts the game by issuing a challenge. In some places the guardian of the river or field tries to dissuade the players from crossing, asserting: 'the river is too deep', 'there is a bull in the field', 'the corn is being reaped'. In Somerset 'Jack' first answers with a blunt 'No, you can't cross my river', and traditionally makes this refusal three times before he names a colour. And in Monmouth and south Wales Jack at first procrastinates, saying 'No today and yes tomorrow', and in so doing he repeats words that have been customary in Glamorgan since the beginning of the century.

§ Little is known of the history of this game other than that our correspondents played forms of it when they were young, e.g. 'Jack Across the Water' (Glamorgan, *c.* 1900); 'Charlie, Charlie, Let Me Over the Water' (Lanarkshire, *c.* 1902); 'Farmer, Farmer, Can We Cross Your River?' (Forfar, *c.* 1910). Peesch reports that children in West Berlin play it, asking 'Fischer, welche Fahne weht?' (*Berliner Kinderspiel*, 1957, p. 37); and Kampmüller describes the game, somewhat defectively, in Austria, 'Wassermann, mit welcher Farbe dürfen wir hinüber?' (*Oberösterreichische Kinderspiele*, 1965, p. 138). The game's currency in Germany and Austria may, however, be due to British occupation following the war.

Bar the door

The children say this is an 'interesting game' probably because it is in part a spectator game. The catcher who is in the middle of the road or open space starts by choosing one player to run across on his own. The rest of the players on the pavement or touch-line watch while he attempts to dodge the catcher, for if he succeeds in getting across he cries 'Bar the door!' (or in Forfar 'Schoolie!', in New Cumnock 'Squatter!') and they rush after him in a body, hoping not to be caught themselves. But if he is caught he joins the catcher in the middle and challenges a further player to make the crossing, who has now to run the gauntlet of two catchers. Thus an increasing number of catchers face the runners as the game proceeds ('Always the person who is last tug shouts out the next name'), and the winner, naturally, is the player who remains free longest, while he who was caught first has the unenvied duty of staying in the middle to be catcher in the next game.

Names: 'All Over' (Langholm), 'Bar the Door' or 'Barley Door' (Dunoon, Forfar, Kingarth, Liverpool), 'Bloaters' (Pontypool), 'Bolter' (Newbridge, Monmouthshire), 'Burning Bar' (Cumnock), 'Cross Tig' (Flotta), 'Cross and Across Tig' (one boy, Forfar), 'Levi-hi-hoe' (Pontefract), 'Run Across' (Acocks Green), 'Running Across' (Broadbridge

Heath), 'Semi' (Hayes, Middlesex), 'Tally-ho' (Brightlingsea).

§ 'Bar the Door' was being played in Argyllshire at the end of the nineteenth century (Maclagan, 1901, p. 210), also in Forfar, c. 1910, and in Dunedin, New Zealand, in 1870, where the catcher had to tap a runner three times on the back to make him captive. In Aberdeenshire the game was known as 'Burrie' (*EDD*, 1897). Another name in Argyllshire was 'Cock-a-Rosy' (*Folk-Lore*, vol. xvii, 1906, p. 96). And on the Scottish border, c. 1925, it was called 'Joukie', the players having to jouk or dodge past the one in the middle (*Southern Annual*, 1957, p. 28).

Cockarusha

'Cockarusha' is basically the same game as 'Bar the Door', but everybody hops, and this limitation considerably affects the character of the game. The player who is 'cocker' or 'he' goes into the middle of the road (the usual site for the game) and stands on one foot with arms folded. He challenges any player he likes (or dislikes) to cross the road, and this person, with arms similarly folded, hops forward and tries to get past him. If he does not manage to dodge him it does not matter. What counts in this game is a player's ability to stay on one leg. Only 'if the cocker barges you so that you fall over or put your other foot down have you to stay and help the cocker'. And should the cocker put his own second foot on the ground the player can continue across without further hindrance, whereon he shouts 'Cockarusha', and the rest of the one-legged players attempt the crossing. However, the cocker can now start hopping again, and he weighs into them, unbalancing whom he can; so that the next time a player is challenged to cross over, the cocker may have more than one ally beside him. Thus the game is one of charging, barging, and 'dunting', until only one player remains to batter his way through the rest, who if he succeeds is highly regarded; and if he succeeds a second time is acclaimed a 'double winner'. In fact in some places the game is more a tourney than a catching game. For instance, in Helensburgh the boy who has been challenged is not permitted to dodge, but must withstand being barged three times by his challenger. 'If after three bumps the victim has escaped unhurt he may hop across to the other side and the others may follow him.' In Forfar whoever wins the duel automatically joins the others on the pavement, so that there is only ever one person in the middle, and 'the game carries on like that until you are fed up with it'. In all variations of the game that have been noted, players are not allowed to change legs while hopping, not allowed to turn back once they have started crossing, and not allowed to hold their opponent, or push him, or trip him up. In 'Cockarusha' the power of the shoulder is paramount.

Names: 'Cockarusha' (Southwark, Walworth, Offham in Kent), 'Cockeroosher' (Camberwell), 'Cock-a-Rooster' (Swansea), 'Cock of Roosters' (Spennymoor), 'Cockeroustie' (St Andrews, Fife), 'Cockay Duntie' (Ballingry), 'Cock Heaving' (Perth), 'Cripple Dick' (Kirkcaldy), 'Hop-a-Kicky', 'Hop Charge', and 'Hopping Bulldog' (St Peter Port), 'Hop All Over' (Helensburgh), 'Hopping Barge' (Camberwell), 'Hop and Dodge', 'Hoppie Diggie', 'Hoppin' and Diggin'', and 'Hoppie Dick' (Forfar), 'Hoppie Bowfie' (Aberdeen), 'Hopping Caesar' (Enfield), 'Hopping Charlie' (Cumnock), 'Hopping Jinny' (Birmingham), 'Hopping Johnny' (Manchester), 'Hopping Tommy' (Welwyn), 'Knock 'em Down' (Barrow-in-Furness), and 'Tally-ho' (Chelmsford).

§ Previous recordings: 'Cock Dunt' (Clackmannanshire, *c.* 1920), 'Dunty' (Belfast, *c.* 1910), 'Hippy Joukie' (Scottish Border, *c.* 1925), 'Hop-o-Cock-Rusty' (Nottingham, *c.* 1920), 'Hopping Johnny' (Newton-le-Willows, Lancashire, 1930s). In Melbourne, Australia, 'Hoppo Bumpo' for two generations; in Denniston, New Zealand, 'Humpty Dumpty' formerly 'Dunk and Davey' (Sutton-Smith, *Games of New Zealand Children*, 1959, p. 136).

Cigarettes

It will be appreciated that in the games 'Bar the Door' and 'Cockarusha' the catcher, having his own interests well in mind, is not inclined to choose out the swiftest runner or craftiest fighter to be his opponent: he prefers someone he is confident he can overcome. In 'Cigarettes', here described by an 11-year-old girl in Edinburgh, this luxury is denied him:

> 'Cigarettes is a game where you all stand on the pavement and one person stand in the middle of the road. The people pick the name of a cigarette and tell each other what they have picked but they do not tell the person in the middle of the road. Here are some of the cigarettes

> you could pick: Black Cat, Camel, Compass, Three Threes,
> Prize Crop, Churchman 1 and 2, Bar One, Airman, Player's
> Weights, Codgent, Dunhill, Four Square, Piccadilly, and
> Kensitas. Then the person in the middle thinks of all the
> different cigarettes and if she says your one you try to run
> across to the other side of the road without her or him
> tigging you.'

In some places the names of film stars, football players, tennis players, animals, makes of cars, or numbers, are adopted. 'The person who is by himself does not know who has which number but he knows what the numbers are.' Sometimes the game is played with everybody hopping; and sometimes the person who has been caught instead of helping the catcher either takes his place or is out of the game, so that there is ever only one challenger in the middle.

Names: 'Animals' (Norwich), 'Barging' (Peterborough: players choose numbers and hop), 'Bulldog Says' (Spennymoor: players run or hop according to bulldog's instructions), 'Cigarettes' (Aberdeen, Edinburgh, Forfar, Spennymoor), 'Jungle's on Fire' (Glasgow: players choose names of animals, the one who gets across on his own shouts 'Jungle's on fire' and the rest stampede across), 'Long Lamp' (Pontypool: players choose numbers), 'Tally-ho' (Yarmouth: players choose animals).

British Bulldog (1)

'British Bulldog' is the toughest, and the most popular, of the games in which players are waylaid while crossing a street or open space. The players line up on a pavement, within agreed bounds, and usually somebody strong, sometimes two people, face them in the middle of the road. At a signal the players rush across the road to the sanctuary of the other pavement, and the 'bulldog' tries to stop one of them, but it is not enough for him just to seize the runner. As a 10-year-old put it:

> 'If he tigs you but you get away you are all right. The
> bulldog has to catch hold of you and lift you up, and
> say "One, two, three, British Bulldog". You can, however,
> struggle and if you get free before he has shouted all the
> words you are all right.'

Only if the bulldog holds the person so that both his feet are off the ground while he says 'British Bulldog, one, two, three', or counts to five, or to ten, or whatever is the prescribed number, must the player submit and join the catcher. ('It is bad luck if you catch a fat person.') Alternatively, in some places, 'When you catch somebody you have to make him fall down, and hold him down for the count of ten.' In Street, Somerset, he has to be held until he gives in, or until 'everybody who is "on it" touches him'. At Whalsay, in Shetland, the capture is made by tapping the player three times on the back, and a fight usually develops as the boy strives to avoid being tapped. In Edinburgh the runner has to be lifted up, or be 'head 'n tailed', or be dragged to one of the boundaries, and the player is allowed to kick and struggle to prevent this. At Netley, 'You have to hold him up in the air and bump him three times.' In Liverpool, where 'nearly all the street plays the game except the babies and those over fourteen', the catcher or catchers lift the captive off the ground, but do not say 'British Bulldog' themselves, 'they squeeze him until their victim cries out "British Bulldog" '. Thus the game proceeds, with the number of catchers steadily increasing, so that a game which started with one boy against twelve, will end with twelve boys lifting up or piling on to one. 'The bigger boys are usually left to last,' observes a Twickenham lad. 'It is when trying to catch these that the roughness begins. You have only half finished when you have got them down because they kick and punch at everybody in sight.' 'Sometimes,' says a 13-year-old Liverpool boy, 'when about half the boys are caught the game becomes a free-for-all, with no side gaining. In the end everyone stops fighting to lick their wounds.' But then, he says, the game starts again where it left off. 'In one game an ambulance had to be called to take a boy to hospital with a broken leg. Others go home with black eyes and torn clothes, but we really enjoy the game.' As a 9-year-old commented, 'When you've finished playing and go home your mother says you're in a "terrible state".'

This game, which more than one Londoner has declared 'the most commonest game that my friends and I play', is known as 'British Bulldog' almost everywhere. The paucity of regional names is probably due to the Boy Scout and Wolf Cub movement, although a senior Scoutmaster told us they tried to dissuade cubs from playing the game, since the younger boys were likely to get hurt. Alternative names are: 'Across the Middle' and 'One, Two, Three' (Croydon), 'Cannonball' (Fulham), 'Fox and Hounds' (Llandrinio and Welshpool), 'King Come-a-lay' (Whalsay, Shetland), 'Lolly' (Street), 'Pigwash' (Stoke-on-Trent), and 'Stampede' (Bristol). In Liverpool, if too many players are taking part to run across at once, they play a variation called 'Vicious Bulldog', in which they divide into two groups, and the parties rush alternately from opposite sides of the ground.

§ 'British Bulldog' seems to be little different, except in name, from the Victorian schoolboys' excuse for a rough-house called 'King Caesar' or 'Rushing Bases'. In this the player who stood between the two bases was termed 'King', and (according to *The Boy's Own Book*, 1855) when he succeeded in intercepting a player 'he claps him on the head with his hand three times, and each time repeats the words "I crown thee, King Caesar" '. The apprehended player was, however, under no obligation to stay in the middle unless he was 'properly crowned'; and it was during the perform-ance, or attempted performance, of the coronation rites that bruises were liable to be acquired. The actual formula, however, varied at different schools. At King's School, Sherborne, about 1840, where the game was known as 'King Sealing', a boy did not have to submit unless the king suc-ceeded in holding him long enough to utter the words:

> One, two, three, four, five, six, seven,
>   eight, nine, ten,
> You are one of the king-sealer's men.

At Foyle College, Londonderry, about 1905, where the game was known as 'Rush', the formula to complete the capture was:

> One, two, three, a man for me,
> Lock him tight, Amen.

At 'King's School, Tercanbury', in *Of Human Bondage*, where the game was called 'Pig in the Middle', the words that mystically turned a boy into a prisoner and caused him to change sides were:

> One, two, three,
> And a pig for me.

And in the town of Marlborough, where the game was known as 'Click' (*Traditional Games*, 1894, pp. 69–70), the catcher had to retain his hold long enough to say:

> One, two, three, I catch thee,
> Help me catch another.

Here, if the last player succeeded in getting across three times after all the others had been caught he was allowed to choose who should be catcher, or 'go click', in the next game; and it may be remarked that several children have reported this rule today when playing 'British Bulldog'.

Other names: 'Cock' at Nairn, where the captor had to 'croon' his captive (i.e. put his hand on his head), and 'Rexa-boxa-King' at Duthil in Inverness-shire (*Traditional Games*, 1894, pp. 72–3); 'Cosolary' at Cross Fell, *c.* 1885, where the captor had similarly to clap his captive on the head (*Journal Lakeland Dialect Society*, no. 7, 1945, p. 6); 'Fox a' Dowdy' in Warwickshire, where the captor had to cry 'Fox a' dowdy — catch a candle' while holding his captive (*EDD*); 'Lamplighter' at Chard, *c.* 1922, where the captive's head had to be patted three times; 'Pirates' in Hull, *c.* 1895, where the captive had to be 'tailed' (i.e. have both hams pinched); and 'Run-Across' at Ackworth School, Yorkshire, *c.* 1805, where the captor had to detain his prisoner for the count of ten (William Howitt, *Boy's Country Book*, 1839, pp. 219–20).

British Bulldog (2)

'British Bulldog' is also, but rather less often, played in the manner of 'Bar the Door', with the catcher in the middle of the road first challenging some player by name to cross on his own. This makes the game initially somewhat easier for the one in the middle; but rather less pleasant for the weaker players, since however strong the boy in the middle he is unlikely to call out someone of his own size to oppose him. It is not to his advantage that the person he challenges should succeed in getting past him, for that player then shouts 'Bulldog', and the rest can swamp him in an overwhelming wave. To avoid discrimination, they sometimes give the players numbers or the names of colours, so that the one in the middle does not know whom he is calling out (cf. 'Cigarettes' above); and sometimes, says an 11-year-old, the game is played at night when it is 'difficult to see the running person, and therefore makes the game more exciting'. Yet the game, however played, is a tough one. As it progresses the opposition in the middle grows more formidable; and a player who is called out in the latter part of the game knows he must charge full tilt at the barrier of boys on the road if he is to break through and avoid being piled upon. Indeed, as a Barrow-in-Furness boy commented, 'It's hard luck for the last boy to be caught because he gets quite a hammering.' It was a young lady (age 11) who commented: 'Very often the game ends in a fight *and it is a very interesting game to watch.'*

Names: 'British Bulldog' is the usual name, but this version of the game is also known as 'Cruso' (Kilburn), 'Cock a Rusha' (Southwark), 'Cocky Rusty' or 'All Across' (Wigan), 'Cock a Rooster' (Swansea), 'Cocker' or 'Cockeroustie' (St Andrews, Fife), 'Long Range' (Coventry), and 'Ten a Foxy' (Forfar). In each of these places the player caught usually has to be held for the count of ten; or in Wigan for the count of 'Cocky Rusty, two, four, six, eight, ten, twelve'. Sometimes for a joke the game is called not 'British Bulldog' but 'French Poodles'; while in the land of the Outback, perhaps predictably, it is 'Australian Dingo'.

§ For an antecedent see under 'Red Rover'.

Walk the plank or join the crew

This game, which can be as rough as 'British Bulldog' if the contestants are so minded, is played mostly in the north-east of Scotland, very often by girls. One player goes into the middle of the road, while the rest stand on the edge of the pavement. The one in the road calls someone's name, and asks 'Walk the plank or join the crew?' If the person addressed agrees to 'join the crew', he or she peaceably joins the one in the middle, and another player is asked his choice. But if the player is bold, or thinks himself a fast enough runner, he replies 'Walk the plank', and has to try and reach the other side of the road without being caught. If he succeeds he shouts 'Schoolie' or 'Overboard', and all the others rush over in a body. But if he is caught the one in the middle 'tortures him' until he agrees to join the crew. There are then two in the middle, and the game continues until everybody has, in one manner or another, been persuaded to join the crew. 'If they catch you before you reach the other side of the road, they pull off your socks and shoes and tickle your feet, and twist your ears, and pull your hair, until you join the crew' (Girl, 12, Aberdeen). 'You are allowed to do anything but bite, kick, or scratch' (Boy, 14, Forfar). 'I like best when the others walk the plank because

I like making them take off something' (Girl, 13, Aberdeen). 'You can play this for hours because there is plenty of fighting and you are never cold' (Boy, 14, Forfar).

§ Compare 'Pressgang' in *School Boys' Diversions*, 1820, pp. 32–3:

> 'One of the boys represents an officer, and four or six others the gang. They catch their companions, one at a time, and, on catching one, say to him,
>
> > "High ship or low ship;
> > King's ship, or no ship?"
>
> If he chooses either of the ships, they send him as a prisoner, in the custody of two of their gang, to any place they may agree upon, where he must stop a prisoner; but if he say "No ship", they must all take him by force, by his hands, legs, and arms, to their rendezvous for pressed men. When they are all pressed, the pressed-men and volunteers, by turns become Press-gang and officer.'

Kings, Queens, and Jacks

'Kings, Queens, and Jacks' has only been reported from Edinburgh. The catcher stands in the middle of the playground and calls out 'Kings', 'Queens', or 'Jacks'. If he calls 'Kings' the players have to run across to the other side of the playground without being seized by the catcher and dragged to the place where they started. If he shouts 'Queens', the players have to hop across without being knocked over by the catcher, who is also hopping. And if the cry is 'Jack', anybody who puts a leg forward or even moves, has to join the catcher in the middle, just as if the catcher had seized him or had knocked him over. 'The last man left is the winner.'

Prisoners' base

'Prisoners' Base', which for centuries was the most renowned of catching or capturing games, needs some organization, and is not now much played by children when on their own: its place, particularly in the south, being taken by Relievo (p. 225). Nevertheless the principle of Prisoners' Base is ingenious, and it is certainly one of the most exciting of organized games. Two bases or camps are chalked out on the same side of the playground, or marked in a field with sticks or cricket stumps: six stumps are enough since the bases can adjoin each other. At the other end of the playground, or about twenty yards away, two prisons are marked out. Two captains pick up sides (it is best if there are some twenty players), and each side takes possession of a base, but the prison in which they hope to place their captives is the one diagonally opposite, not the one nearest them. The captain of one side sends one of his players into the middle to taunt the others and start the game. The captain of the other side sends one of his players out to catch him, and the first player has to try and get back to his own base. He is helped by the fact that as soon as someone has been sent to catch him, his own captain will send someone in pursuit of his pursuer, whereon the other captain will send someone to pursue that pursuer, and the first captain will send someone after him. Thus each player, other than the first, will be both chasing and being chased, and as soon as a player gets back to his base, he can be sent in pursuit of someone else. But a player may only chase the one person he has been sent after. If he succeeds in catching him he cannot be caught himself, but takes his captive to the prison and returns to base ready to be sent out again. Once a prisoner has been taken and put in the far corner, the captain of his side will send someone running to attempt his release, and the captain of the side who has the prisoner will send someone chasing after to prevent him, whereon the captain of the first side may send someone after him, and it will be noticed that the player attempting a rescue, although he starts first, will have to run further than the player who is sent after him to frustrate the rescue. However, should a rescue be effected both rescuer and rescued can return to their own side unmolested. This active game, which also needs some skill and concentration on the part of the leaders, continues until all the players on one side have been made prisoner, or until an agreed time has elapsed (the side with the most prisoners being counted the winner), or, not infrequently, until the players are in such confusion about who is chasing whom, that the game has to stop. For orderliness it is helpful if the sides wear distinguishing marks, but it is not essential.

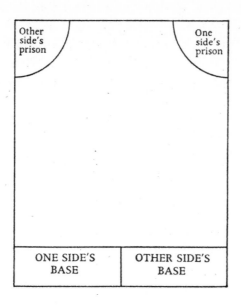

Other side's prison		One side's prison
ONE SIDE'S BASE	OTHER SIDE'S BASE	

Playground markings for 'Prisoners' Base'

§ Up to the twentieth century 'Prisoners' Base', also known as 'Chevy Chase' or 'Chivy', was one of the most-played of schoolboy games: a favourite sport at Sedgley Park about 1805; and played alike by Southey at his Bristol school and George Sturt a lifetime later at Farnham in Surrey. It was one of the games Tom Brown played with the village boys in the Vale of the White Horse even before his real schooldays began; which Tom Newcome played at Grey Friars, along with cricket, hockey, and football, 'according to the season' (*The Newcomes*, ch. ii); and which was played daily and was 'in a great measure compulsory' at Dr Grimstone's establishment, as the unhappy Mr Bultitude was to discover (*Vice Versâ*, ch. v).

For generations, too, the game was more than a juvenile diversion. Strutt recalls going, *c.* 1770, to the fields behind Montague House (now the site of the British Museum) to see a grand match of 'Base' played by twelve gentlemen of Cheshire against twelve of Derbyshire 'for a considerable sum of money' (*Sports and Pastimes*, 1801, p. 62). Charlotte Burne records that men-servants in the eighteenth century 'were wont to ask a day's holiday to join or witness a game of prison-bars, arranged beforehand as a cricket-match might be' (*Shropshire Folk-Lore*, 1883, p. 524). Gomme reprints a ballad describing a match played at Ellesmere in Shropshire, 8 August 1764, between a team of bachelors and a team of married men, eleven a side, in which the bachelors (huzza'd by the fair maids amongst the spectators) seem to have had the best of the contest. And it will be recalled that Samuel Povey in *The Old Wives' Tale*, who had never played cricket, could yet boast of 'the Titanic sport of prison-bars' played in the Five Towns, where the teams went forth preceded by a drum-and-fife band, and the game was such that 'in the heat of the chase, a man might jump into the canal to escape his pursuer'.

Even in the eighteenth century the game was an old one. In 1598 Drayton could describe a place as one 'where light-foot Fayries sport at Prison-Base' (*Heroicall Epistles*, xxi. 200). In 1611 Cotgrave in his French-English *Dictionarie* defined *Barres* as 'the play at Bace; or, Prison Bars'. And Bace, Base, or Bars was frequently alluded to at this time, notably in *Cymbeline* (v. iii) where the youths Guiderius and Arviragus are described as —

> two striplings (Lads more like to run
> The Country base, than to commit such slaughter);

and in *The Faerie Queene* (v. viii. 5) where two knights pursuing a damsel fleeing on horseback are in turn pursued by another knight and are said to run —

> as they had bene at bace,
> They being chased that did others chase.

Indeed the game was so well known to the Elizabethans that when a person provoked someone to come after him, it was customary to say he 'bid the base'.[41]

This notoriety in the sixteenth century is not surprising, for the game seems already to have been popular for 200 or 300 years. In the preamble to the Parliamentary Statutes of 16 March 1332 the playing 'à barres' was explicitly prohibited in the precincts of the king's palace while Parliament was sitting. The game was named in Jean de Garlande's glossary of the early fourteenth century. Froissart played 'aux bares' in his boyhood at Valenciennes, about 1345 ('L'Espinette amoureuse', l. 221).

And D'Allemagne in his *Sports et Jeux*, 1904, p. 56, suggests that on the Continent, at least, barres was the chief communal competitive game of the Middle Ages.

French and English

The great object of the players in 'French and English' is to run off with the property of the opposing party, and it is this that gives the game its spice. Two leaders pick up sides, agree upon a line that shall divide their territories (preferably a natural feature, such as a ridge or stream), and each player deposits some possession, as cap, coat, or handkerchief made into a flag, a certain distance back within his side's territory. The members of each side then attempt to make away with the other side's possessions, the game being one of forays into enemy territory. Sometimes a single player darts off on his own when he sees an opportunity; at other times three or four players make a concerted sortie, hoping by so doing to divert attention from one another. But even if a player finds himself to be momentarily unopposed he may take only one object at a time. Once a player has crossed the dividing line he can be caught, and is kept prisoner in the enemy's camp along with their possessions. A member of his own side must then rescue him before any more booty can be taken. In this way the fortunes of the two sides can alter dramatically in less than a minute. Four people may sally out from one side and perhaps all be captured, or perhaps all four return with treasure. It is a 'busy game', as one child put it, a game in which every player is important; and the sport continues until one side or the other has acquired every article of property that the other side has laid out, or until (what amounts to the same thing) one side has made every member of the opposing side a prisoner.

For some reason the game is not as popular as it used to be, even in the north; and it seems possible that the briefer and more impersonal versions of the game which are currently organized for children in the shelter of gymnasiums have taken the edge off the traditional game. In organized versions of the game each side usually has to capture only a single flag or trophy.

Names: 'French and English', 'Scotch and English', 'Germans and English'. Organized versions: 'Flag Raiding', 'Capturing the Flag'.

§ In the eighteenth and nineteenth centuries this game, made romantic by reference to the marauding raids of the Borderers, was much played in the northern half of Britain, the sport being enriched by taunts and feigned enmity: 'Here's a leap into thy land, dry-bellied Scot'; 'Here's a leg in thy land, thieving Sassenach'. In those days, it is said, a well-contested match might last 'nearly a whole day', the young players on the losing side replacing lost property with further of their garments until each of them was approaching the state of nature. The game was indeed a 'heroic contention, imbued with all the nationality of still older days'; and those who describe it often seem to feel that they are recalling some of the happiest hours of boyhood.

As might be expected the game has been played under a great number of names, amongst the earliest being: 'Scotch and English' (W. Hutton, *History of the Roman Wall*, 1802, p. 105); 'Wadds', 'Steal-Wads', 'Rigs', and 'Tak-Bannets' (Jamieson, *Scottish Dictionary*, 1808–25); 'England and Scotland' (Cromek, *Remains of Nithsdale and Galloway Song*, 1810, p. 251); 'Scotch-and-English', 'Stealy-Clothes', and 'Watch-Webs' (Brockett, *North Country Words*, 1829); 'Set-a-Foot' on Tweedside, *c.* 1820, and 'Stone Heaps' in London (*Notes and Queries*, 4th ser., vol. ii, 1868, pp. 97, 165). In more recent times: 'French and English' at Bitterne in Hampshire, 'Range the Bus' in Aberdeen and 'Bonnet Ridgie' at Dyke in Morayshire (Gomme, 1894–8); 'Beggarly Scots' and 'Watch Webb' in Wigton, late nineteenth century (*Journal Lakeland Dialect Society*, 1951, pp. 38–9); 'Lands' in Argyllshire (Maclagan, 1901, pp. 218–19); 'Herdie Pans' in Orkney, and 'Regibus' in Banffshire (*Folk-Lore*, vol. xvii, 1906, pp. 104–5); 'Seizing Sticks' (*London Street Games*, 1916, p. 17); 'Japs and Russians' (Chard, 1922); 'Prisoners' (Taunton, 1922, also New Norfolk, Tasmania, *c.* 1910).

In the United States, somewhat restricted versions: 'Stealing Sticks' (*Games of American Children*, 1883, p. 168), 'Stealing Sticks' or 'War' (*North Carolina Folklore*, 1952, p. 80), 'Capture the Flag' (*Saturday Evening Post*, 19 December 1964, p. 18).

In the Philippines 'Kawat-Kawat' (Brewster, p. 70). In Italy 'Guerra francese'.

4. Seeking Games

'At night is the best time to play. My friends and I went to hide.
We hid in a man's cabidges. John walked by us about six times
and he never saw us.'

Boy, 12, Luncarty

Few people can feel more tense than the young player as he sets out
alone to search for his companions, seeing no one, where a minute
before was a mob, yet knowing that every bush and tree may be a
mask for a pair of eyes. Seeking games have this peculiarity, that
for much of the game the players are out of sight of each other,
uncertain of what is happening, yet are all the while within hailing
distance. In consequence there is much calling, and the calls, being
traditional, are often curious and even poetical.

At the outset of a game, when the seeker has finished counting to a
hundred, or whatever number has been agreed, he announces his search
by calling into the emptiness: 'Coming, ready or not', or 'Here I come,
ready or not, if ye're spied it's no my fau't' (Perth and Falkirk), or
'Look out, look out, the fox is about, and he is coming to find you'
(Swansea). In Wickenby, Lincolnshire, he shouts 'Tins' because, says
a 12-year-old, 'this means coming'. In Norwich, before he starts, he
shouts,

> Whether you run or not
> I will catch you hot,

and, as if to force meaning into the words, when he catches somebody he
shouts 'Hot'. In Leicestershire he, or more likely she, calls:

> I hold my little finger,
> I thought it was my thumb,
> I give you all a warning,
> And here I come.

And amongst children in Somerset, where poetry seems to come as second nature, the traditional call is this:

> The cock doth crow, the wind doth blow,
> I don't care whether you are hidden or no,
> I'm coming!

In the United States:

> Bushel of wheat,
> Bushel of rye,
> All not hid
> Holler I.

> Bushel of wheat,
> Bushel of clover,
> All not hid
> Can't hide over.
>> *Widespread, e.g. Carolina, Maryland, Missouri, Nebraska,*
>> *and Texas*

In France:

> C'est-i-fait,
> Minon, minette.
>> *'Les Amours de Bastien et Bastienne, 1753. Cited Rolland,*
>> *1883, p. 152*

In Germany:

> 1, 2, 3, 4, Eckstein,
> Alles soll versteckt sein,
> Hinter mir und vorder mir
> Das gibt es nicht,
> 1, 2, 3, Nun komme ich.
>> *Current Hamburg, 1956*

There are rhymes, too, which the hiders repeat to alert each other. If a seeker has stolen up quietly on one of the hiders, and put him out of the game, the one who has been discovered instantly sets up a roar for the benefit of his companions:

Keep in, keep in, wherever you are,
The cat's a-coming to find you.
Birmingham

Keep in, keep in, wherever you oor,
The rats and mice are at your door.
Helensburgh, Morpeth, and Newcastle upon Tyne

Jeep in, jeep in, whatever do in,
Da clockin hen is seekin de.
Whalsay, Shetland[42]

If the seeker is becoming discontented with his task, and beginning to imagine that the hiders have vanished in reality as well as from sight, he may make the plaintive appeal or threat:

A whistle or a cry,
Or let the game die.
Luncarty

A whistle or a cry,
Or the game gans by.
Langholm

And if the game is to be brought to an end prematurely, because the players have become tired, or there has been an argument, or, says a 13-year-old, 'because the hunter is going away for his tea', the general cry is 'Alley, alley in', or 'Allee-ins, not playing', or 'All the ends stop play', or 'Olly, olly in', or the wonderful liquid warble of 'All-ee, all-ee, eeeze'. In Scalloway, in Shetland, the call is appropriately nautical, 'All hands ahoy!' In Bishop Auckland: 'All in, all in, spuggy in the tin.' In Plymouth:

All in, all in, wherever you are,
The monkey's in the motor car.

In Bradford and Birmingham:

All up, all up, wherever you are,
If you don't want to play stay where you are.

In South Elmsall:

> All up, the game's up,
> Ready for Sunday morning.

In Manchester and Newcastle:

> Billy, Billy Buck,
> The game's broke up,
> And all through *Tommy Skelly*.

While in Scotland if something has gone wrong with the game, 'the game's a bogie':

> Come oot, come oot, wherever you are,
> The game's a bogie.
> > *Edinburgh, Glasgow, Falkirk, Ballingry, Langholm*

> Come oot, come oot, wherever you be,
> The monkey's up the apple tree.
> > *New Cumnock*

> Lees, lees, whit dae ye please,
> Little boys living on candle-grease.
> Come oot, come oot, where ever ye be,
> Or the gem's a bogie.
> > *Cumnock Academy, 'Those Dusty Bluebells', 1965, p. 26*

Such cries ring out frequently in Scotland, remarks a correspondent, 'because of the Scottish love of litigation and disputation over trivial points arising from rules'.

The names of seeking games

The study of seeking games is complicated by the fact that they have long been played in a diversity of ways, but not under a diversity of names. Even today when a child speaks of 'Hide and Seek' he may be referring to one of four different games; and in the past when a writer mentioned a seeking game he rarely thought it worth describing. It seems best therefore to bring the early references to seeking games together under a general heading, rather than attempt to distinguish which reference is to the forerunner of which particular game of the present day. When Biron felt himself to be playing a part in 'All hid, all hid, an old infant play' (*Love's Labour's Lost*, IV. iii) we know little more about how the game was played in Shakespeare's day than that 'All hid' was the cry to start the game. We receive no help from Dekker when Sir Rees ap Vaughan declares:

> 'Our vnhansome-fac'd Poet does play at bo-peepes with your
> Grace, and cryes all-hidde as boyes doe.' (*Satiro-mastix, 1602, v. ii*)

Nor do we learn anything from William Hawkins when Ludio argues that Phoebus plays

> 'At Bo-peepe, and Hide and seeke. All night is our all hid. But in
> the day We seeke about.' (*Apollo Shrouing, 1627*)

Cotgrave merely confused the issue in 1611 when he defined *Clignemusset* as 'the childish play called Hodman blind, Harrie-racket, or, are you all hid'; and Robert Sherwood was similarly unhelpful in 1632 when he described 'All hidde' as a game 'où vn se cache pour estre trouvé des autres'. (If the cry was 'All hid' would not more than one player have been hiding?)

Possibly Sherwood had in mind a game such as Hamlet's 'Hide Fox, and all after' (IV. ii). Pegge in his *Alphabet of Kenticisms*, 1735, defined 'Hide-and-Fox' as 'Hide-and-Seek'. In 1688 Randle Holme described 'Hide and seech' (his spelling was wild even for the period) as a game in which 'one or more to goe hide themselues, and the rest to seek them out'. And the boys and girls of Lilliput, it will be recollected, played at 'Hide and Seek' in Gulliver's hair (I. iii). Another early name was 'Winck-All-Hid', presumably referring to a player being hoodwinked while the others hid (John Davies, *Humours Heav'n*, 1609, II. iv). But most early names simply echo the dominant call, as 'Whoop' (1798), 'Whoop Oh!' (1828), 'Hoop and Hide' (1711), and 'Hoopers-Hide' (1719) — as it would be 'Cooee' in the present day.[43]

In Scotland one game and cry seems to have been 'Keek-Keek' (' "Te he", quod Jynny, "keik, keik, I se ow".' — *Jok & Jynny, c.* 1568), hence

'Keek-Bogle' or 'Bogle Keik' (1791). In Edinburgh, at the beginning of the nineteenth century, the game and call was sometimes 'Ho spy!' (*Blackwood's Magazine*, August 1821, p. 35), and Gregor told Gomme (vol. i, 1894, p. 212) that in Keith this was abbreviated to 'Hospy'.

Further dialect names that have been recorded include: 'Beans and Butter' (Oxfordshire, 1849), from the cry to commence the search:

> Hot boil'd beans and very good butter,
> If you please to come to supper!

'Bicky' (West Somerset, 1888), 'Boggle-Bush' (Whitby, 1876), 'Cuckoo' (Northamptonshire, 1854), 'Felt' (Scarborough, *c.* 1895), 'Felt and Late' (Sheffield, 1888), 'Halloo' (John Clare, *Village Minstrel*, 1821, i. 5), 'Heddie-ma-Blindie' (Weardale, 1939), 'Heddo' (East Yorkshire, 1889), 'Hiddy' (Leeds, *c.* 1890), 'Hide-a-Bo-Seek' (Berwickshire, 1825), 'Hide an Find' (Suffolk, 1823), 'Hide and Wink' (Leicestershire, 1844), 'Hide-Hoop' (Pembrokeshire, 1888), 'Hiders-Catch-Winkers' (Hampshire, 1871), 'Hie, Spy, Hie' (Newcastle upon Tyne, 1813), 'Hy Spy' (Scott, *Guy Mannering*, 1815, xxxvi), 'Huddin-Peep' (Lancashire, 1895), 'Pee-Koo' and 'Pi-Cow' (Angus, 1887 and 1808), 'Salt Eel' (Suffolk, 1823), 'Shammy Round the Block' (Liverpool, *c.* 1925), 'Spinny Wye' (Newcastle upon Tyne, 1813), 'Spy All' (Bath, *c.* 1890), 'Spy Hole' (York, *c.* 1910), 'Spyo' (Barrie, *Sentimental Tommy*, 1896, xiv), and 'Steik-and-Hide' (Aberdeenshire, 1825).

In France, Froissart played 'à la clignette' and 'aux reponniaus' in his childhood at Valenciennes, *c.* 1345 ('L'Espinette amoureuse', ll. 233 and 226). Gargantua played 'à clinemuzete', 'au responsailles', 'au bourry, bourryzou', and 'à la cutte cache' (Rabelais, i, 1534, xxii). And in Italy, Taddeus played 'a covalèra' and 'a vienela, vienela' (*Il Pentamerone*, 1634, Day II). For hide-and-seek in ancient Greece see below.

Dissimilar Number of Players Hiding and Seeking

Hide-and-seek

The simplest form of 'Hide-and-Seek', the stay-where-you-are-until-found variety, is now played mainly by small children, or when only two are playing, or when the game is played indoors. The first person to be found is the seeker in the next game; the last to be found is the winner. A necessary preliminary is arranging how long the seeker shall contain himself (generally with eyes closed) before he starts his search. He is usually told to count a hundred, or 'ten, ten times', or 'five hundred in fives', or five hundred 'the shortie way' — 'Five, ten, double-ten, five, ten, a hundred' — an abridgment favoured in Scotland. Sometimes the number to be counted is set according to the number of children playing, ten or twenty for each person, and twenty more for the 'den', and twenty more 'for luck'. In Edinburgh they play 'Vehicles' or 'Buses', the child who is 'het' has to wait where he is until a car or van passes by, or — if they are by a main road — until a bus is seen. And in Grimsby, 'very commonly' says a 13-year-old, they make it physically impossible for the seeker to come after them too soon. They tie the boy or girl to a lamp-post, and he has 'to release himself from his bonds' before he can start seeking. (See also under 'I Draw a Snake upon your Back'.)

'Hide-and-Seek' becomes more fun, and is considerably speeded up, when the hiders do not remain in their hiding-places, but try and get back to the starting-place unobserved while the seeker is out looking for them. Even so the game is unsatisfactory. Those who have been found, or who have made their way back safely, often weary of the game before the last person has been discovered (as H. E. Bates has remarked, there is bound to be some clever-dick who has hidden in a coal-hole and refuses to show himself), so that after a while they will be calling in those still in hiding and proposing a different game.

When older children speak of 'Hide-and-Seek' they usually mean a racing-home variety, such as 'Block' (q.v.), which is a faster and more compact game.

Names: 'Hide-and-Seek' is sometimes referred to as 'Hiding Seek' or 'Hidy'; and in Scotland it is often 'Hide and Go Seek' — as also in the United States. When played after dark, as is not unusual, it may have a special name, such as 'Cat's Eyes' (Forest Hill), 'Ghosts' (Inverarity), 'Run by Dark' (Peterborough), 'Toad in the Hole' (Forfar), 'Bug in a Rug' (Accrington), 'Spotlight' (with a torch, Knottingley), and 'Torchlight' (Spennymoor). In Ipswich, when played up trees, it is 'Chip and Chap'. When the seeker has not only to find the others, but has to try and touch them as they run back to the starting-place, the game may be differentiated by a name such as 'Hide and Tick' (Welshpool).

§ The running-home form of hide-and-seek is described in *Every Boy's Book* by J. L. Williams, 1841, under the name 'Whoop!'.

> 'One player takes his station at a spot called the "home", while the others go to seek out various hiding-places in which to ensconce themselves; when all are ready, one of them calls out Whoop! on which the player at the "home", instantly goes in search of the hiders, and endeavours to touch one of them, as they run back to "home"; if he can do so, the one caught takes his post at the home, and he joins the out-players.'

In the sixteenth century players seem actually to have sought the office of seeker: the first to reach the base unimpeded acquired this honour by right, and was known as King. It was thus in the 'old schoole-boyes game' of 'King by your leave' or 'Old shewe', referred to several times by Elizabethans, and described in Huloet's *Dictionarie*, 1572:

> '*Kinge by your leaue*, a playe that children haue, where one sytting blyndefolde in the midle, bydeth so tyll the rest haue hydden them selues, and then he going to seeke them, if any get his place in the meane space, that same is kynge in his roume.'

This procedure was already more than a thousand years old, being the rule in the ancient Greek game 'Apodidraskinda'. Pollux stated (ix. 117) that one player shut his eyes, or had somebody covering them to ensure that he did, while the others ran off. This player then proceeded to look for them, while the object of each of the hiders was to reach the seeker's place and become seeker in his stead.

One man plus

In this game there is initially one seeker, but those whose hiding-places have been discovered, or who have been seen while attempting to reach home, join the seeker in searching for the rest, so that eventually all the players (it is best if there are not more than ten) are looking for the last person. The game is not as common as might be expected, and has no standard name. A Grimsby boy, giving the above name, said, 'We held a special meeting in our gang hut to decide what to call the game'. In all accounts received the game is played around the streets at night. In some parts of Glasgow it is called 'Pea Hot', since this is the hiders' call when they are ready. In other parts of Glasgow it is known as 'Over the Fences', the game being played entirely in other people's gardens, with this rule, that both hiders and seekers must enter each garden by jumping the gate or fence. 'It has to be played in the dark', remarks a keelie, 'so that the neighbours won't know.' In Ballingry the game is called 'Bully Horn': those found may escape, if they can, from their hiding-places, whereon the chasers are rallied with the cry 'Bully horn', for a person is not considered caught until he has been clapped on the back three times. In Glastonbury the game is called 'Multiplication Touch'.

§ According to informants the game was played in the Isle of Dogs, East London, *c.* 1905, under the name 'Point', and in County Kerry, *c.* 1935, as 'Hunts'. Cf. 'Barla-bracks about the Stacks' stated by Jamieson, *Scottish Dictionary*, 1808, to have been played in northern Scotland.

Man hunting

In this version all seek one. Everyone hides their eyes while one person goes off and secretes himself in a place of special difficulty, as 'up a tree or somewhere'. The seekers count to as much as 500 'in ones' to give him plenty of time, and he is also allowed, if he wishes, to move from place to place while they are searching, provided that he is not seen, for to be seen is to be caught. 'If someone sees the hider and he does not come he is out of the game.' At Enfield: 'When we catch him we hit him and then let him go. Then the one who caught him goes and hides.' If he manages to get back to the home without being seen he is safe.

Names: 'Cuckoo' (Alton), 'Exploring' (Bacup), 'Find Her if You Can' (West Ham), 'Hide and Seek' (Market Rasen), 'Man Hunting' (Enfield).

§ This is 'Hide and Seek' as described in *School Boys' Diversions*, 1820, pp. 40–1. 'One boy is appointed to hide wherever he pleases … when he has secreted himself, he is to cry, "Spy all", at which signal, the rest are to search him out; and if discovered, he is to be buffeted with knot-ted handkerchiefs, until he can reach the goal, or starting post.' Much the same game, it appears, was 'Cock's-Odin', played at about the same period in the Scottish Lowlands (*Notes and Queries*, 4th ser., vol. ii, 1868, pp. 97 and 165); also the game of 'Cuckoo', described in Burne's *Shropshire Folk-Lore*, 1883, p. 222, although here the hider, when discovered, 'rushed out and did his best to reach "home" without being captured'.

Sardines

'Sardines', played indoors or out, is the most popular of the games consisting purely of hiding and finding. One person goes off to hide while the others shut their eyes and count to the agreed number. The seekers split up, and search independently of each other. Indeed, if one of the seekers finds the hider he is careful not to let the others know, but slips into the hiding-place when they are not looking. Ideally the hiding-place should be somewhere that will accommodate all the players; but it seldom is, and as further players find it, and crowd in, the silent squeeze becomes tighter and more suffocating, players sometimes having to lie on top of each other. Those who are still searching gradually become aware that their fellow searchers are disappearing, and rush to the places where they were last seen, thinking that they will be near the hidy-hole. When the last person arrives he is sometimes chased back to the starting-place, but more often than not there are just sighs of relief as the sardines extricate themselves from their cramped positions, and complain of their stiffness and the length of time they have been waiting.

The game is usually known as 'Sardines', but also 'Sardines in a Tin', 'Sardines and Tomatoes', 'Squashed Sardines', and 'Squashed Tomatoes'. In Wigan it is 'Mexican Hideout'. The game is sometimes played in couples or with two teams.

I draw a snake upon your back

If 'Hide-and-Seek' is named less frequently than it used to be amongst favourite games, it is because an ingenious method of starting the play has become popular, and given hide-and-seek a new appearance, and new nomenclature. There now need to be at least four players. One of them is chosen to turn his back to the others, and usually leans against a wall or lamp-post, with his face buried in his arm. The others gather round, and the leader chants:

> I draw a snake upon your back.
> Who will put in the eye?

When he has drawn the snake, another player (taking a hint from the leader) stretches forward and pokes the person's back. The person whose back has been poked then turns round and guesses who poked him, but — here lies the sport — he is not told whether his guess is correct. He has first to set a task for the person he has named; and it is only after he has done so that he learns whether or not his guess was correct. If it was, the person who 'put in the eye' has to perform the task he has been set; but if the guess was wrong, the guesser himself has to carry out his own instructions; and whichever of them it is also becomes the seeker, for while the task is being performed the others run off, and the game which follows is, as the children say, 'just like hide-and-seek really'.

This manner of starting the game is not only fun ('It's really really fun'), it is also highly ingenious. It determines, with indisputable fairness, the length of time the hiders shall have to hide in, because he who names the task will not make it too onerous for fear he himself has to undertake it, nor make it too simple since he hopes to be amongst those who hide. Thus he says:

> 'Run round a car five times and count to a hundred in singles.'   *Liss*

> 'Walk five hundred yards shouting "Hot peas and pies".'
> *Hoyland, near Barnsley*

> 'Go to your house and ask for a piece and jam.'
> *Forfar*

> 'Count twenty, then touch a pole, then touch a flower, then come back and count a hundred.'
> *Spennymoor*

In some places (e.g. Bishop Auckland and Pontefract) the player suspected of putting in the eye retorts 'Where are you going to send me?'

and urges the guesser to make the task more difficult, challenging: 'How many times shall I do it?' — 'Hop, skip, or jump?' — 'Drunk or sober?'[44] Indeed versions of the game vary only in their degree of fantasy. At Annesley the leader draws 'numerous squiggle lines' saying, 'I draw ten thousand snakes down your back, who tipped your finger?'; at St Peter Port he says 'I draw a snake on the old man's back, two eyes, a nose, and who puts his tongue in?' In Ipswich:

> Draw a snake on a black man's back,
> Chop off his head and who did *that*?

In Gloucester the snake is drawn on a 'dead man's back', in Sixhills on an 'elephant's back', in Swanpool on a 'unicorn's back'. The game also goes under such names as 'Stroke-a-Bunny' (Liverpool, for past thirty-five years), 'Stroke the Baby' (Welshpool), and 'Smooth the Cat' (Penzance):

> Smooth the cat, smooth the cat.
> Who touches you last?

In Accrington several players engage in the draughtsmanship:

> Stroke a bunny, stroke a bunny,
> Someone's going to wake you in the
>   morning.
> I'll draw the snake (*someone does so*),
> I'll draw the ladder (*someone else draws
>   the ladder*),
> I'll draw the question mark (*a third draws
>   the top part of a question-mark*),
> And someone draws the dot (*a fourth
>   player supplies the dot*).

In St Helier, Jersey, the game is known as 'Crow's Nest'; in Bristol, sometimes, 'Who Put the Egg in the Birdie's Nest?'; and in a number of places it is 'North, South, East, West':

> North, South, East, West,
> Who's the king of the crow's nest;

Draw a snake right down her back,
Who's the one to finish that?
West Ham

North, South, East, West,
Who's the king of the crow's nest;
Draw a ladder, draw a snake,
Would you kindly finish the cake.
Enfield

In Forfar, where they draw a cross on the person's back, the game is called 'I'll Cut the Butter and I'll Cut the Cheese'; in Orkney it is 'Spread the Butter on the Cheese'; in Glasgow, where words are not wasted, it is 'Cheesey'. In Edinburgh the leader chants:

I spread the butter, I spread the cheese,
I spread the jam on your dirty knees.
Guess who tipped.

Here, when someone has been picked, and the task set, he who was named asks, 'How many fish in the barrel?' The guesser, who is still in doubt about the rightness of his guess, gives a number, and the task has to be performed that number of times. The most common task set in Edinburgh is to climb the stairs to the top of a tenement. 'I like this game', remarked an 11-year-old in the Canongate. 'I like the rhyme with its clowny words, and most of all I like the excitement of the child trying to guess who tipped.'

§ This game, or manner of starting a game, is also widespread in the United States under the names 'Tappy', 'Tap-on-the-Back', 'Tappy-Hi-Spy', and 'Tap the Icebox' (Brewster, 1953, pp. 48–50). 'Tap the Icebox' is said to have been played by Chicago children 'for generations' (*Chicago Daily News*, 4 April 1961). 'Poke the Icebox' was played in Canada about 1925. In Melbourne, Australia, it is 'Tip the Finger'. In New Zealand, 'Tip the Finger' or 'Draw the Snake' (Sutton-Smith, 1959, pp. 67–8). And in West Berlin, according to Peesch, *Berliner Kinderspiel*, 1957, p. 42, it is 'English Versteck', the children saying 'Ich mach das Fragezeichen, wer macht den Punkt?' ('I make the question-mark, who makes the point?')

The use, in some versions of the game, of the couplet

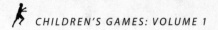

North, South, East, West,
Who's the king of the crow's nest?

shows how the game has evolved. This rhyme has been in juvenile employment for many years, and was formerly attached to the game in which one player, whose eyes were covered, sent each of his fellows to a different starting-place, prior to a race home (see under 'Hot Peas'). It will be appreciated that if the first part of the game is played on its own, and the player whose face is to the wall attempts to guess whose hand touched him, merely to put the other person in his place, the game becomes little different from 'Hot Cockles', popular in the Middle Ages (see Vol. 2 p. 146).

Block

This form of hide-and-seek is both popular and exceedingly energetic: the seeker has not only to locate each player in hiding, but has to race him back to the starting-place. It is often this game that children are referring to when they speak of 'Hide-and-Seek', although local names abound, and the cacophonous 'Block', 'Blocky', or 'Block, One, Two, Three' is common in the south and north-east of England, and in Scotland. The game is usually played at night ('so that the person after you cannot see so good'), and the usual 'block', or starting-place, is a lamp-post, sometimes termed the 'blocking-post'. One person, 'the blocker', hides his eyes and counts to an agreed number while the rest scatter and hide. In Accrington a scarf is tied round his eyes, and when he has finished counting he ties it to the lamp-post to mark which one he started from. The players hide in an area around the block, if possible keeping it in view, for their aim is to reach the lamp-post while the blocker is out searching for them. If they can touch it and shout 'One, two, three, block home', they are free. Sometimes players will sneak up behind the blocker while he is still counting, in the hope of rushing the block the moment he has finished, but generally this is frowned upon. In Scarborough, if the counter hears them approaching, he warns 'No backs, no sides, no front'. In Caerleon he cries 'No behind the cat's tail'.

In this game it is not enough for the seeker to see a person, nor does it mean anything if he catches him. He can only put a player out of the game by racing back to the block, and shouting 'Block, one, two, three, I spy …', giving his name. (In Whalsay, Shetland, 'Block, one, two, three, you are not free'.) Sometimes, to make certain there has been no mistake, the blocker has also to shout the person's hiding-place, as 'Block, one, two, three, I spy *Alan* up a tree'. If his identification proves wrong it is called 'False Alarm' (in Ballingry, 'Burnt Spy'), and the blocker has to hide his eyes and start again. Occasionally the hiders change coats to confuse the blocker; but identification is generally difficult enough, especially if it is dark. Usually the game goes on until everyone has either been 'blocked' or has freed himself, and the first person blocked becomes the new blocker. But in some places, as in Forfar, they have a rule: 'Three free, all free.' If three people manage to reach the block and cry 'Free', those already blocked are at liberty to run off and hide again. In a few places, for example Welshpool, whenever a hider reaches the starting-place unseen he shouts 'Release, one, two, three', and those waiting at the starting-place are released to hide again (compare 'Buzz Off', below). In Fulham, 'If everyone has been spied except one, and that person gets home, he says "Block, one, two, three, saved the lot", and they all go off again'. As a 13-year-old girl commented, 'This game hasn't an ending and goes on until the children are called in to bed'.

'Block' is the basic game in which attention is focused on the starting-place; and there are a score of local names for the lamp-post, or whatever serves as the 'home' or 'den'; for example, 'bay' in Spennymoor, 'billy' in York, 'blobbing place' in Annesley, and 'the bounce' in Jersey and Guernsey. In Wolstanton it is the 'bucking place', in Scarborough the 'carry post', in Bristol, sometimes, the 'cree', and at Welshpool the 'deno'. In Aberdeen and Forfar it is the 'dell' or 'dellie' (pronounced *dael* at Arbroath, as McBain remarked in 1887), and in Cumnock the 'dill' or 'dull' (cf. the *dule* or goal in the old game 'Barla-Breikis' described by Jamieson in 1808). In the southern part of Yorkshire — Pontefract, Barnsley, Ecclesfield — it is the 'dob' or 'dobby' ('the person races back and knocks the dobby three times'), while to the east of the county, and in Lindsey, it is the 'hob'. In Tunstall and Wolstanton it is the 'ducker' (as it also was in 1910), and in Manchester and around Knighton, where a stone usually marks the place, it is called the 'kick-stone', though they do not kick it. It is also known as the 'kig' (Stockton-on-Tees), 'fleaky post' (Leek), 'lurgy post' (Ipswich), 'mobbing post' (south Wales and Monmouthshire), 'relevo place' (Wilmslow), and 'rally' (Coventry). At Crickhowell in Brecon, 'You run to the tally post and tally the person'.

At Holmfirth, 'You try to win the other person to the whipping den'. While at Oldham and Nelson children happily make for the 'whipping post', the game being commonly known in the north-west as 'Whip'.

Other names for the game, which also provide the call as the runner reaches home: 'Acky' or 'I-acky' in Warwickshire and Northamptonshire ('I acky *Freddie*, one, two, three'; 'First person "ackyed off" is "it" next time'), 'Hicky, One, Two, Three' (Chester), 'I-erkey' (Leicester), 'Hi-Lerky' (Newton Abbot), 'Erkie' (Plymouth), 'Urkey' or 'Murkey' (Helston), and 'Ookey' (The Lizard). It is 'Forty Forty' in Ipswich and district, Ramsey in Huntingdonshire, Cranborne in Dorset, and in south-east London generally, although in Walworth 'Fifty-Two Bunker' (seeker counts to fifty-two; shouts 'I see *Janet*, fifty-two bunker'). It is usually 'Mob' or 'Mob Mob' from Aberystwyth to Bristol. At Lydeard St Lawrence in Somerset it is 'Mop Mop'. It is 'Om Pom' or 'Pom Pom' in Norwich, Great Staughton in Huntingdonshire, Hayes in Middlesex, Weymouth, Chichester, Liss, and Fulham, SW6 ('Pom, pom, *Ernie*, one, two, three, i-o-key'). Idiosyncratically, it is known as 'Billy, One, Two, Three' (York), 'Cocoa-Beanie' (Edinburgh), 'False Alarm' (Ponders End), 'Free' (Orkney and Shetland), 'Hidy-bo' or 'Hidy-bo-Seek' (Brinsley and Annesley), 'My Bounce, One, Two, Three' (St Helier, Jersey), 'Tackie' (Letham, Angus), and 'Whip Out' (Windermere).

§ The following names were familiar in the past: 'Billy Rush' (York, *c*. 1910), 'Block Block' (Gainsborough, *c*. 1910), 'One, Two, Three, Block' (Hull, 1890s), 'Bucky Bean' (Glastonbury, 1920s), 'Bunky-Bean Bam-Bye' (presumably this game, North Devon, 1867, see *EDD*), 'Eci' (pronounced *Ekki*, T. Hudson-Williams, *Caernarvonshire*, 1952, p. 65), 'Forty' (London, 1910 and 1916, probably this game), 'Gilty Galty' (Huddersfield, 1810, seeker counted to forty as today, after reciting 'Gilty galty, four and forty, Two tens make twenty' — *Almondbury and Huddersfield Glossary*, 1883), 'Hacky', 'Hi-acky', 'I Hacky' (Midlands, *c*. 1915), 'Ackee' (Somerset, 1920s), 'Jacky' (Warwickshire, *c*. 1890), 'I-erkee' (Oxford, *c*. 1910), 'I-urkey' (Earl Shilton, Leicestershire, *c*. 1910), 'Key Hoy' (Argyll, 1906), 'Lurky' (Nottinghamshire, 1902), 'Lerky' (? this game, D. H. Lawrence, *Sons and Lovers*, 1913, ch. iv), 'Mop-and-Hide-Away' (Cornwall, 1880), 'Mopan-Heedy' (Devon, 1889), 'Moppy-Heedy' (Cornwall, *c*. 1900), 'Point' (*London Street Games*, 1916, p. 20), 'Squat' (Sundon, Bedfordshire, *c*. 1900), 'Whip' (apparently this game, but see below, Lancashire and Potteries, *c*. 1900).

It is hardly necessary to confirm that the game is international. When a child, today, in Canada or the United States speaks of 'Hide and Seek' it is this racing-home game that he ordinarily means. This is also so in Australia, although children there sometimes know the game by one of the English dialect names, e.g. 'I-ackey' in Queensland. In Germany and Austria, likewise, the ordinary game of 'Versteck' is this racing-home variety; and according to Jeanette Hills, *Das Kinderspielbild von Pieter Bruegel*, 1957, p. 36, the game appears in Veit Conrad Schwarz's *Bilderbuch*, 1550, and is there called 'Ekkete Eck'. Brewster (1953) collected Armenian, Greek, Rumanian, and Hungarian analogues, the one from present-day Greece being remarkable in that the seeker commonly counts to forty before starting his search: the same number that custom dictates children should count when playing this game in southeast London.

Buzz off

This game, played mostly in Scotland and the north country, is no more than a variation of 'Block' or 'Hide-and-Seek', but is carefully differentiated by the children, and is never, it appears, referred to as 'Hide-and-Seek'. It has the one additional rule that any hider who succeeds in racing back to the starting-point without being blocked exclaims 'Buzz off' and frees everyone there. Further, on hearing the cry 'Buzz off' the seeker must return to the starting-point, hide his eyes, and count all over again to give those freed time to rehide, a rule that places considerable strain on his patience. As a 13-year-old girl in Aberdeen commented: 'I am not very fond of "Buzz Off", neither are the other people in my area. We think that it is unfair as the "man" [the seeker] may be the "man" for ten times at least.' In a few places the seeker is given the marginal concession that each time he has to count again he counts twenty-five less than he did the time before; and in New Cumnock he only counts to twenty the third time, and announces that this time 'Last in's het', that is to say whoever reaches the den last will be seeker next time, no matter what happens.

Names: 'Buzz Off' (Aberdeen, Forfar, Inverness, New Cumnock, St Andrews, Spennymoor, York, and Knighton), 'Twenty Buzz Off' (Kirkcaldy), 'Bazooka' (Vale and Castel, Guernsey), 'Rescue' (St Helier, Jersey).

Come to Coventry

Here the seeker is at almost greater disadvantage than in 'Buzz Off', for a hider can rescue a prisoner merely by getting in sight of the den. However, the seeker has only to see and recognize a hider to make him a captive. He shouts 'Back to camp' or 'Come to Coventry' and the player's name, and the person must come out of his hiding-place and wait at the den or starting-point. The hiders can release the prisoner by creeping close enough to be seen and waving a hand. When a person at the den sees someone waving he is free to sneak away, provided, of course, that the seeker does not see him and call him back. It is important in this game that a good site is chosen for the den: if it is too exposed the seeker's task becomes very difficult; if it is too hidden-away it may be too easy. On the whole, as an 11-year-old remarked, 'It is tough for the person who is "on it", he or she does a lot of running about'. And there is a further point that is important, as another child commented: 'In this game you must not cheat, and go and hide without somebody waving to you.'

Names: 'Back to Camp' (Edinburgh), 'Coventry' (Ipswich), 'Come to Coventry' (Bristol), 'Go to Coventry' (Bury St Edmunds), 'Flashie' (Forfar, waving torches), 'One, Two, Three, Hide-and-Seek' (Hounslow). 'Wavy Wavy' (Colwyn Bay), 'Wave Hiding' (Triangle near Halifax, c, 1930).

§ In the United States 'Beckon' and 'Sheep in My Pen' (Brewster, 1953, p. 42).

Whip

Girls are the chief players of this curious game, which commences like the previous games with the players hiding while the seeker counts to an agreed number at the home or den. But thereafter the game embraces elements of other games, for when the seeker catches sight of someone, whether in hiding or attempting to reach home (merely to see the person and recognize her is enough), she names the person, and calls 'Stop', 'Whip', or 'Whipit'. The player must immediately stop wherever she is, and wait there until everyone else has either reached home or been similarly stopped. The seeker then estimates the minimum number of special steps, such as 'fairy feet' or 'giant strides', that she thinks each person will need to reach the starting-point ('The seeker is always amazingly fair in this', comments one observer), and if the person can touch the home in the prescribed number of steps she is free; while the first person to fail to reach the home becomes the next seeker. The attraction of this game, which is distinctly slow-moving, is not immediately apparent, but seems to lie in its deliberateness and precision, in the variety of stages, and in the opportunity it gives of watching other players. 'It is great fun to play, we play it nearly every night', a 10-year-old assured us.

Names: 'Whip' (Accrington, Bramford near Ipswich, and Oxford), 'Whipit' (Scarborough), 'Wave Me' or 'Whip' (Doncaster).

§ Alfred Easther, *Almondbury and Huddersfield Glossary*, 1883, giving 'Whip' as the local name for 'Hoop' or 'Hoop Hide' suggests it comes from the local pronunciation, *hooip*.

Tin Can Tommy

'Tin Can Tommy' is probably the game that most commonly disturbs the evening repose of the back streets. Its chief requirement, other than energy, is a good-sized tin can; and sometimes the children's way of determining who shall be the first seeker is to have everyone find an empty tin (there is a scramble through the dustbins), and whoever is last back with one acquires the uncoveted role. The best tin is then chosen, placed in a chalk circle in the road, or on a manhole cover, and one player, perhaps the strongest, kicks it or throws it as far as he can down the street. This is the signal for everyone to run off and hide, while the seeker (also known as the 'canner', 'denner', 'den-keeper', 'hound', or, in Plymouth, the 'slave'), has to retrieve the tin, walk backwards as he returns, replace it in the circle, and has in addition, sometimes, to walk round the tin ten times, or count to 300 'in fives', before he commences his search. When the seeker sees someone he has to race back to the tin, place his foot on it or rattle it on the ground, and shout 'Tin Can Tommy, one, two, three', and call out the name of the person he has seen. This player is then obliged to come out of his hiding-place and stand by the tin; while the other players, hearing the cry, know that someone has been caught.[45] When the seeker continues his search, any hider who thinks he will be unobserved can rush to the tin and free whoever is standing there by kicking the tin out of the circle. The seeker has no power either to hold people captive or to put them out of the game when the tin is not in position. Thus the seeker has two conflicting tasks, for he has to leave the tin to find further hiders, yet repeatedly race back to see that his captives are not being released. Further, should he make a mistake when he sees someone, and call out a wrong name (and sometimes players will change coats or jerseys and deliberately show their backview or just an arm to mislead him), there is, as in 'Block', a jubilant cry of 'False Alarm' (or 'Blin' spy' in Langholm, 'Sly Fox' in Stoke-on-Trent, 'Double D, double D-motion' in Bristol), and 'everybody comes out of their hiding-places, and the person who was "on it" has to be on again'. In New Cumnock they jeer:

> Hard up, kick the can,
> *Archie Gibson's* goat a man
> If ye want tae ken his name
> His name is *Ian Scott.*

Indeed the seeker's role is not an enviable one, and as the game progresses, and he has perhaps acquired a number of captives, he becomes increasingly unwilling to move far from the tin, while the impatience of the captives and those still in hiding grows in proportion. In Scotland the captives taunt 'Go oot, go oot, ye lazy hen', urging him to give them a chance to be rescued:

> Leave the den, ye dirty hen
> An' look for a' yer chickens.

If there are many players (and the more players the longer the game), the seeker's task is nearly impossible, and they sometimes make it a rule that if the captives have been released three times the next person 'caught' shall become seeker, and the game start again. Yet juvenile enthusiasm for the game is unflagging. Even a 14-year-old boy said, 'I spend hours playing this game. I love it, and so do all my pals'. There are, nevertheless, clearly two opinions about its virtues. 'This is a game which the people where I live don't like us playing very much', admitted a 13-year-old girl. 'They say it is too noisy, and the mothers say it wears out our shoes.' 'The truth is, it is a perfectly evil game guaranteed to put me in a bad temper', commented a headmistress. And a 15-year-old, attempting to defend it, remarked innocently, 'The only inconvenience it causes is that when the tin is being kicked about it has a tendency to wake up the neighbours' babies'.

Names: 'Tin Can Tommy', which is the basic name in London, is widely distributed, e.g. Glastonbury, Ipswich, Wolstanton. 'Kick the Can', the usual name in Scotland and the Isles, is also not uncommon in Dublin, Liverpool, Manchester, and much of Wales. Other names: 'Bobby, Kick the Tin' (Swansea), 'Can Can' (Tetchill), 'I-erky Kick the Can' (Lydney), 'I-o-kay' (Welshpool), 'Kick Can Copper' (Camberwell), 'Kick Out Can' (Featherstone near Pontefract), 'Kick the Bucket' (Hexham and Plymouth), 'Kick the Cog' (Spennymoor),[46] 'Kick the Tin' (occasional but widespread, e.g. Bishop Auckland, Rhondda, and Guernsey), 'Kicky-Off-Choff-Choff' (Spennymoor, alternative name), 'Kit Can and Hop It' (occasional, Wigan), 'Kit the Can' (Crickhowell, Breconshire, and Meifod, Montgomeryshire), 'Maggie, Kick the Can' (occasional, Spennymoor), 'Om Pom Rattle Tin' (Liss), 'Pom Pom' (Berry Hill, Gloucestershire), 'Rin Tin Tin' (usual name Norwich, not uncommon Ipswich, Bristol, Swansea), 'Tap the Tin' (Glastonbury), 'Throw Out Can' (usual name, Wigan), 'Tick Tock Tony' (Stornoway, Isle of Lewis, alternative name to the usual 'Kick the Can'), 'Tin-a-Lerky' (Annesley, Nottinghamshire), 'Tin Can Alley' (Croydon and St Ives, Cornwall), 'Tin Can Annie' (Knighton), 'Tin Can Bosher' (Laverstock), 'Tin Can Copper' (Clapham and Millwall), 'Tin Can Leaky' (Caistor and Lincoln), 'Tin Can Lizzie' (Four Crosses, Montgomeryshire), 'Tin Can Lurky' (Leicester and Windermere), 'Tin Can Nurky' (Barrow-in-Furness and Wolverhampton), 'Tin Can Squash' (Holmfirth), 'Tin Can Topper' (Stoke Newington), 'Tin Can Whippet' (Stoke-on-Trent), 'Tin in t'Ring' (Burnley and Rossendale), 'Tin Leaky' (Lincoln), 'Tin Pot Monkey' (St Helier, Jersey), 'Tin Tam Tommy' or 'Tin Tan Tommy' (common Fulham, West Ham, and Camberwell, also Devon and Cornwall), 'Tin Ton Talley' (Henstridge, Somerset), 'Tin Tong Tommy' (Alton), 'Tin Whip' (Workington) 'Tinny' (Accrington, Bacup, and Colne), 'Tip the Copper' (Gower Peninsula), 'Whip the Can' (Liverpool).

'You cannot really play this game at school because it is awkward to get a tin' (Girl, 10), but in some places they regularly use a stick, stone, half-brick, or ball, and the game is known as 'Ball Out' (Kingerby, Lincolnshire), 'Chuck the Stick' (Langholm), 'Kick Ball Fly' (Cleethorpes and Grimsby), 'Kick Ball Kick' (Scarborough), and 'Kick Ball Lurky' (Sleaford).

§ The game seems to have been well known in city streets before the First World War. In districts of London such as Canning Town it was called 'Kick Can Bobby', 'Kick Can Copper', and 'Kick Can Policeman'; in the Clifton district of Swinton 'Kick Can', and in the North Country and across the Border it was 'Kick the Block' (played with stone or block of wood). Other names: 'Ecky' (*Warwickshire Word-Book*, 1896), 'Fly Whip' (Gomme, vol. ii, 1898, p. 438), 'Foot in the Bucket' (Belfast, *c.* 1905), 'I-er-kee' (Lydney, *c.* 1870), 'I Spy, Tin Can' (*Folk-Lore*, vol. xvii, 1906, p. 97, Argyllshire), 'Kick the Bucket' (? this game, *Suffolk Words*, 1823, p. 238), 'Kick the Bucket' or 'Kick the Tinnie' (listed *Notes and Queries*, 5 June 1909, Stromness), 'Kicky Tin Spy-Ho' (Easingwold, *c.* 1930), 'Kickstone' (*Journal of Lakeland Dialect Society*, 1945, p. 7, Cross Fell, *c.* 1885), 'Lerky' (Nottinghamshire, before 1898, *EDD*), 'Mount the Tin' (Gomme, vol. i, 1894, p. 401, Beddgelert, Caernarvonshire), 'New Squat' (Gomme, vol. i, 1894, pp. 412–13, Earls Heaton, Yorkshire), 'Nurky' (Windermere, *c.* 1900), 'Old Tin Can' (Wrecclesham, Surrey, *c.* 1895), 'Releaser' ('played with a block of wood, a ball, or an empty tin', *More Organized Games, c.* 1905, p. 129), 'Squat' (Leeds and Midgley near Halifax, *c.* 1895, with stone), 'Tin Can Squat' (J. B. Priestley, Bradford, *c.* 1905).

In Canada and the United States generally 'Kick the Can' or 'Kick the Tin' (Newell, 1883, p. 160, describes it played in New York with a stick, and called 'Yards Off'; Brewster, 1953, 'Throw the Wicket' in Illinois). In Australia in 1930s, 'Kick the Block' and 'Kick the Tin'; 'I-Acky' in Sydney, *c.* 1890. In *Games of New Zealand Children*, 1959, p. 58, 'Kick the Tin', 'Kick the Boot', 'Kick the Block', and 'Homaiacky'. In Italy it is 'Barattolo'. In France it is 'La boîte', played with a ball. In Berlin it is 'Stäbchenversteck', played with two sticks placed together, and 'Ballversteck' or 'Russisch Versteck', played with a ball (Peesch, *Das Berliner Kinderspiel*, 1957, p. 41). In Antwerp, *c.* 1900, it was 'Buske Stamp' (*Radio Times*, 21 March 1958, p. 54).

Equal Number of Players Hiding and Seeking

Outs

When hide-and-seek is played between two teams, with equal numbers hiding and seeking, it is generally known in the London area as 'Outs', 'Outings', or 'Runouts', the 'outs' or hiders having no home, but keeping hid or moving around until caught. A feature of this game, usually played at night, is the indisputableness with which a person has to be caught. Thus at Blaenavon in Monmouthshire a player who has been caught has to be held while the catcher counts ten. In Aberdeen the catcher has to jump over his captive's back. In Welshpool, where the game is generally known as 'Buckum' (alternative name 'Find Them and Catch Them'), 'when you tick them you have to say "Buckum" '. At Dovenby in Cumberland a person is not considered caught until he has been patted on the head three times, as also at Enfield ('You have him three times on the head'), although at nearby Ponders End the captive submits only when his captor has been able to 'pull his hand off his hair'. (Was he, originally, protecting his head from being tapped?) One reason for emphasizing the capture may be that those caught are out of the game, and have to wait until the rest have been caught and a new game can begin; or because, as at Enfield, they are made to change sides and join the seekers. Indeed, at Ponders End, when a hand has been separated from a head, the captive calls out 'Ripe Bananas', to warn those still in hiding that they should change their hiding-places, for he is now obliged to tell where he last saw them.

Other names: 'Chasey' (Dovenby), 'Night Chase' (Grimsby), 'Ripe Bananas' (Ponders End), 'Scouting' (Golspie), 'Spotlight on Sally' (Cwmbran, the seekers being armed with torches), 'Topsy Turvey' (Aberdeen). At Mousehole, near Penzance, the game is known as 'Coosing' ('One side hides and the other side tries to coose them out'); in Bristol 'Bunk and Chase' ('We tossed to see which team bunked first and which chased'). Also 'Runouts on Bikes' (Herne Hill) and 'Cycle' (Grimsby, 'When you have them you must put your hand on them or the cycle').

§ The two sides in a seeking game were referred to as 'Ins' and 'Outs' by Jamieson in his description of 'Hy Spy' (*Scottish Dictionary*, *Supplement*, 1825). Compare *Folk-Lore Journal*, vol. v, 1887, p. 60, 'Buckey-How' (Cornwall); *Notes and Queries*, 11th ser., vol. i, 1910, p. 483, 'Inners and Outers'; *London Street Games*, 1916, p. 20, 'Inner and Outer'.

Kiss chase

Sometimes the game of 'Outs' becomes a contest between the sexes. 'We play boys versus girls', says a 10-year-old girl in Camberwell. 'The boys get the longest outs because they hide on roofs where the girls

can't get. The girls won't go very far away because they are frightened
of the dark.' In Pontypool, where the game is also known as 'Outs',
those caught 'are either kissed or head and tailed'. But ordinarily, if the
game is to involve kissing, the name gives warning: it is 'Kiss Chase' or
'Kiss Catch', or in Norwich 'Kiss Cats' (according to every child asked),
in Swansea 'Kiss Touch', in Langholm 'Catchie Kissie', in Liverpool
'Catch the Girl, Kiss the Girl', in Langham, Rutland, 'Hide-and-Seek
Kiss', in Croydon 'K.C.'. They play when school is over, sometimes
having a special place for the game, 'in the woods', in a park, or where
there is shrubland, somewhere 'away from the watchful eyes of parents'.
It is played in the street only after dark. 'We go round the backs very
late at night and ask the girls if they want to play', reported a 15-year-
old. 'First you give the girls a chance to get out of sight then the boys
try to catch them, and when you catch one girl you kiss her as a reward.'
In Swansea when a boy has caught and kissed a girl he lets her go and
chases again, and the boys see how many kisses they can get. More
often when the boys have caught the girls, the girls go after the boys.
Sometimes there is more hiding in the game than running, sometimes it
is mostly chasing about. There are also degrees in their acquiescence to
the 'reward' or penalty for being caught. A 10-year-old girl declared that
the boys do not always have their way: 'We struggle and whack … and
run away like wild horses.' But an older girl said: 'According to who's
chasing you, sometimes you run fast, sometimes you hardly run at all.'
Some boys speak of 'having to kiss' the girl they have caught as if it was
a dull duty in an otherwise enjoyable game. In general, however, from
12 upwards, both sexes show a certain willingness for this part of the
game; and it is certainly much played, sometimes in sophisticated forms.
In Monmouthshire, for instance, the game is sometimes 'Kiss, Hug, or
Both' ('We usually say "Both" '), and on the Firth of Clyde, where it is
called 'C.C.K.' (Catch, Cuddle, Kiss), a 12-year-old girl records:

> 'If a girl is caught by a boy, then she has to leave the game
> with that boy and kiss him. Therefore that couple cannot
> resume to play the game that day. Then the game goes on
> until everybody is caught and they all start kissing the girls.'

'Different letters', remarks a 15-year-old boy 'can be added to the C.C.
to describe different variations of the game.'

In some parts of England (chiefly, it seems, in the west and north), a further and less-pleasing choice is offered, and the game becomes 'Kiss Torture', 'Kiss, Cuddle, or Torture', or 'Kiss, Kick, or Torture'. 'Some girls who are tough have kicks and torchers', writes a 12-year-old girl, 'but the older girls seem to enjoy being kissed. It is quite a nice game if you like that sort of thing.' And occasionally, but not often, the gentler alternatives disappear; the game is 'Tiggy Torture' or 'Kick, Prick, or Torture'. 'If the person wants a kick you kick (with the knee) in accordance with their age, i.e. 13 years, 13 kicks. If she wants a prick you prick her in the hand with a pin. If she wants torture you twist her hand or something like that. When all the team have been caught three times their team is on it' (Girl, 13).

§ One ancestor of 'Kiss Chase', and indeed of 'C.C.K.', is the game of 'Stacks' recorded by Gomme (vol. ii, 1898, pp. 211–12) as formerly played in farm rickyards after harvest time in Lanarkshire. At the end of the game each lad tried to catch 'the lass he liked best, and some lads, for the fun of the thing, would try and get a particular girl first, her wishes and will not being considered in the matter; and it seemed to be an unwritten law among them for the lass to "gang wi' the lad that catched her first" '. Indeed in the eighteenth century and earlier, as is well known, the chief pleasure if not purpose of certain roisterous games was the opportunities they afforded adult society for promiscuous, and even selective kissing. The author of *Round about our Coal-Fire*, 1731, for instance, directed that in the game of 'Hoop and Hide':

> 'The Parties have the Liberty of hiding where they will, in any
> Part of the House; and if it should prove to be in Bed, and if they
> even then happen to be caught, the Dispute ends in Kissing, &c.'

Hunts

This is straightforward hide-and-seek between two teams, as in 'Outs', except that the aim of those in hiding is to get back to the starting-place without being caught. Should they succeed in this, or should an agreed number of the hiding side, say three players, be successful in this, the side has the privilege of going out to hide again. The game, which is now little played compared with 'Relievo' below, is known as 'Chasing' (Knighton), 'Hunts' (Helensburgh), and 'Yelly Yelly' (Bacup).

§ In *The Boy's Treasury*, 1844, p. 64, the game is called 'I Spy I', the seekers being declared the winners if they catch a specified number of hiders; in *Games and Sports for Young Boys*, 1859, pp. 2–3, it is 'High Barbaree'; in Gomme, 1898, 'Save All'.

Hunt the keg

This game, which has been reported in the present day only from St Andrews ('Hunt the Keg') and Golspie ('Smooglie Gigglie'), is played in much the same way as 'Hunts', with the hiding side creeping around trying to get back to the starting-place without being caught; but one of the hiders carries 'the keg', and it is on his success in making his way back to the starting-place that the course of the game depends. The keg is a stone or penknife or anything easily held in the hand. The side that hides are smugglers; the side that goes after them are coastguards, and the coastguards do not know which smuggler has the keg. If a smuggler is caught he is ordered to 'Deliver the keg'. If he has not got it he is merely taken into custody at the 'coastguard station' (some hut or den); but if he has the keg he has to hand it over, and the coastguards become the smugglers. The smugglers, however, may muster what ingenuity they possess to outwit the coastguards. Some of them as they approach home may let themselves be seen, and deliberately lure the coastguards after them, and perhaps even allow themselves to be caught, to distract attention from the player with the keg. It is of no account how many smugglers are taken prisoner, provided that the player with the keg is not amongst them. Even if the keg-bearer is the only player to reach home, his side has won and goes out again.

§ 'Smuggle the Geg' (or Keg, Gag, Gage, Gig, or Giggie) seems to have been one of the usual round of boyish games in Scotland in the nineteenth century. In *The Scottish Dictionary, Supplement*, 1825, Jamieson described boys in Glasgow playing it:

> 'The *outs* get the *gegg*, which is anything deposited, as a key,
> a penknife, &c. Having received this, they conceal themselves,
> and raise the cry, "Smugglers". On this they are pursued by the
> *ins*; and if the *gegg*, for the name is transferred to the person who

holds the deposit, be taken, they exchange situations, the *outs* becoming *ins*, and the *ins — outs*.'

Other references: James Ogg, *Willie Waly*, 1873, p. 75 (Aberdeen); W. B. Nicholson, *Golspie*, 1897, p. 121; Gomme, *Traditional Games*, vol. ii, 1898, pp. 205–7; Maclagan, *Games of Argyleshire*, 1901, pp. 89–90; *English Dialect Dictionary*, vol. v, 1904, p. 562; *Notes and Queries*, 10th ser., vol. xi, 1909, p. 445 (Stromness); *Buchan Observer*, 23 April 1929. In *Juvenile Games for the Four Seasons, c.* 1820, pp. 81–2, a game is referred to called 'The Wand' which appears to be identical. In Caputh and Dunkeld in the 1930s the game was called 'Gig or No Gig'.

The name 'Smuggle the Geg' is also sometimes given to a Scots indoor game played on the lines of 'Hunt the Slipper'.

Relievo

In Scotland, Wales, and the northern half of England, 'Relievo' is the principal seeking game with two sides. Leaders are chosen to pick the sides; a den, usually a portion of the pavement, is marked out with chalk, boundaries are agreed on (the greater the number of players the wider the boundaries); and the leaders toss to see which side has first 'outs'. The hiding side run off and scatter ('Favourite places where my pal and I hide are in tool sheds, dog kennels, up trees, behind dustbins, and lying in flower beds'); the seeking side wait until they hear a call, or until they have counted 'five-hunder in fives', and when they set off they leave one person in charge of the den. When a hider is caught he is taken to the den, and it becomes the object of his own side to try and release him. However, when a seeker finds someone he must catch him properly in the prescribed manner, for the hider need not submit until he has been ritually taken. In Annesley he has to be touched on the head or 'bobbed and tailed'. In York, similarly, 'the catchers catch the "off" by putting one hand on the off's head and one on his bottom'. In Spennymoor the hand must be kept on the head long enough to say 'Tally ho!' or 'Fliggy, one, two, three'. In Swansea he must be slapped on the back three times, as also in Penrith where the captor must shout 'One, two, three, rallio!' — 'If the captive manages to tear himself away before this is said he is not caught'.[47] In Forfar, Helensburgh, and Rossendale, the captive has to be held for the count of seven before he can be marched to the den.

At Langholm 'When you are caught you struggle your way out, but if they count ten on you, you are caught'. Similarly in Grimsby a person is 'not properly caught until "Two, four, six, eight, ten, ree-leave-i-o" is shouted'. In Wolstanton the hider will not submit until his captor has kept his grip on him while crying:

> Rallio, Rallio, one, two, three,
> You are the jolly man for me.

And in Liverpool, where the leading of the prisoner to the den is something of a triumphal ceremony, the prisoner is not allowed to try and break away, unless that is, his captor has forgotten, in his excitement, to utter the formula 'Nockey-no-twist-no-breaks'.

The actions necessary for releasing a prisoner are less formal but not easier to perform, since the prisoners are guarded by the den-keeper, who has only to touch the one attempting the rescue to make him also a captive. However, the den-keeper is under certain restrictions. He may have to keep out of the den, or keep more than three yards from it, or keep one foot in it and one foot out. 'If he puts two feet in the den all those caught are free' (Liverpool). Commonly it is enough for the 'releaser' to shout 'Relievo' or 'Rallio' or perhaps 'Bish-bash' as he rushes through the den, although he may also have to touch the person on the head three times, and in Bishop Auckland he 'must spit in the bay [the den] and shout "Tally-ho" '. Very often he may manage to release a prisoner but get caught himself. It is up to the prisoners to keep awake while they are in the den, and sometimes, when there are several of them, they will form a chain from the den to make it easier to be rescued. At Accrington when the last hider is caught the prisoners chant 'Last man, last man', and the last man is allowed to struggle while he is being put in the den, and if he manages to pull one of his captors in with him, all the captives are free to run off and hide again.

Like most other seeking games 'Relievo' is 'best played at night in a dimly lit street where there are plenty of places to hide', and the game is mostly played by boys, or so the boys say, 'because it is a little rough for girls'. Nevertheless there are few games in which some girls will not join, and in several accounts we have been given, the girls make a side to play the boys.

General names: 'Leavo', 'Leavio', 'Rallio', 'Realio', 'Release', 'Releaso', 'Relievo', 'Relievio', 'Rileo', 'Tally-ho'. Local names: 'Bedlam'

(New Cumnock), 'Bish Bash' (Knighton and Langholm), 'Chasies' (Forfar), 'Fliggie' (Spennymoor), 'Free Me' (Cumnock), 'Lallio' (Bootle), 'Le-oh' (Barrow-in-Furness), 'Li-vo' (Stromness), 'Mile a Minute' (Helensburgh), 'Offers and Catchers' (Kirkwall, Orkney), 'Relvo' (Scarborough), 'Rolio' (Tunstall), 'Rowlies' (Lossiemouth), 'Run, Sheepie, Run' (Cumnock), 'Sally-o' (Seaforth and Wrexham), 'Sides' (Penkhull), 'Skiely' (Wigan), 'Tiggin In and Tiggin Out' (Rossendale).

The game is sometimes given a dramatic form as 'Spitfires and Gliders' (York, 1961). In Rossendale, one of the many places where the game develops into 'Cops and Robbers', the den becomes jail, and the seekers dress up as policemen, wearing their caps back to front and their coats cape-wise. Occasionally the catching side is limited to only one or two players, and the game is then called 'Corner Tig' (Langholm), 'Tig and Release' (Knighton), 'Tiggin Out Hide-and-Seek' (Rossendale), 'Stag in Den' (Welshpool), 'Sticker in the Den' (Blaenavon), 'Bully Horn' (yet another game with this name, Ballingry, Fife), 'Daddy Grandshire' (the 'daddy' or seeker has a stick, Newbridge, Monmouthshire), and 'Sun, Moon, and Stars' ('Sun' chases 'stars' and only 'moon' can release them, Aberdeen). At Spennymoor, when played on bikes, it is called 'Bike Tally-ho'.

The game is scarcely known in London and the south, except in a playground or confined-space version, usually known as 'Release', in which the 'runners' or 'releasers' instead of hiding have a base like the seekers, and the emphasis is on the releasing — indeed the catchers may start with a volunteer prisoner. Other names: 'Hide and Seek Releaso' (Alton) and 'One, Two, Three, Post He' (Croydon).

§ The manner of playing the game in the north of England seems to have altered little over the past hundred years. Alfred Easther, headmaster of King James's Grammar School, Almondbury, 1849–c. 1873, who knew the game as 'Stocks', described it fully, adding the detail that a boy's captor had to count ten while he held him (*Almondbury Glossary*, 1883). Clough Robinson, who knew the game as 'Bed-o!' and 'Bed-Stocks', said that the captor had to count 'Two, four, six, eight, ten', and spit over the captive's head (*Dialect of Leeds*, 1862). And S. O. Addy, born 1848, educated Sheffield Collegiate School, confirmed that in 'Bedlams' or 'Relievo', 'the tenter' who had charge of the den had always to 'stand with one foot in the den and the other on the road' (*Sheffield Glossary*, 1888). Other old names: 'Alla-Least' (Cwmavon, Glamorgan, c. 1905), 'Delievo' (Sheffield, 1888 and c. 1934), 'Inamon' (Forfar, c. 1910). With

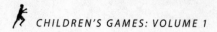

two chasers only: 'Shepherd in the Box' (Bearpark near Durham, *c.* 1925). London version: 'Box Release' (Wandsworth, *c.* 1912).

Gee

This game has been reported only from Meir, Stoke-on-Trent. Two sides are chosen, and having agreed on a starting-place, usually a lamp-post, the hiding side goes off and hides, to be followed in due course by the seekers. When one of the seekers sees one of the hiders he shouts 'Gee!' All the *seekers* then rush to the lamp-post and the hider who was seen chases them. If the seekers get back to the lamp-post without being caught, the hider becomes a captive. But if the hider manages to touch one or more of the seekers before they reach the lamp-post, he frees that number of hiders who have already been caught, and they run off and hide again.

§ 'Gee' is a survival of an old form of 'I Spy' (described in *Every Boy's Book*, 1856, p. 4) and of 'Spy-Ann' as Mactaggart knew it:

> 'A game of hide and seek, with this difference, that when those
> are found who are hid, the finder cries *spyann*; and if the one
> discovered can catch the discoverer, he has a ride upon his back
> to the *dools*.' ('*Gallovidian Encyclopedia*', 1824, p. 435)

Other names for it have been 'Spy for Ridings' and 'I Spy the Devil's Eye' (*Notes and Queries*, 7th ser., vol. x, 1890, pp. 186, 331); and 'I Spy Charlie across the Sea' (*Folk-Lore*, vol. xvii, 1906, p. 98).

Endnotes

1. In her early appeals for assistance in collecting she asked only for singing games; and years later, when she contributed the article on 'Children's Games' to the *Encyclopaedia Britannica*, all games other than singing and dramatic games were disposed of in three lines.

2. 'This mania for playing at cat', commented *Punch*, 23 April 1853, 'is no less absurd than dangerous, for it is a game at which nobody seems to win, and which, apparently, has no other aim than the windows of the houses, and the heads of the passengers.'

3. That this was also the custom in the seventeenth century seems evident from John Suckling's allegorical description of 'Barley-break'. In this game there were three pairs of players, of whom one pair were the catchers and had to stand in mid-field, designated 'Hell' (see below). Suckling's account, printed in *Fragmenta Aurea*, 1646, p. 24, begins:

> Love, Reason, Hate, did once bespeak
> Three mates to play at barley-break;
> Love, Folly took; and Reason, Fancy;
> And Hate consorts with Pride; so dance they:
> Love coupled last, and so it fell
> That Love and Folly were in hell.

4. Cf. Mme de Chabreul, *Jeux des jeunes filles*, 1856, p. 2, n.: 'Souvent, pour indiquer la personne qui dirigera le jeu, ou qui y remplira un certain rôle, on tire au sort, par le *doigt mouillé*.' See also Littré's *Dictionnaire* under *doigt mouillé*, where he explains that the child who picks the damp finger wins or loses what has been agreed upon.

5. Compare a method of testing a boy's truthfulness cited in *The Lore and Language of Schoolchildren*, p. 128.

6. The practice of saying 'dip' before starting the rhyme apparently dates from the nineteenth century. In the *Journal of American Folklore*, vol. x, 1897, p. 319, appears the following rhyme from Penzance, Cornwall:

> Dip!
> Ickery, ahry, oary, ah,
> Biddy, barber, oary, sah,
> Peer, peer, mizter, meer,
> Pit, pat, out one.

Children seem to feel that if the first count is to the ground, the subsequent counting is more magical, or is anyway less under the control of the counter. In France when children start in a similar fashion, they say 'pouce'.

7. Several collections have been made of dipping rhymes, and references to the following

in the next few pages are given with only the editor's name or short-title: Henry Carrington Bolton, *The Counting-out Rhymes of Children*, 1888; W. Gregor, *Counting-out Rhymes of Children*, 1891; Patricia Evans, *Who's It?*, 1956; Jean Baucomont, Roger Pinon, and others, *Les Comptines de langue française*, 1961; Matizia Maroni Lumbroso, *Conte, cantilene e filastrocche*, 1965.

8. Compare:

> Look upon the mantelpiece,
> There you'll find a ball of grease
> Shining like a threepenny piece,
> Out — goes — she.
> *Stratford-le-Bow, 1890s, and 'London Street Games', 1916, p. 56*

9. Dish cloths or clouts (usually old, dirty, or torn in two) have for years been verbally awarded to the player who is counted out. In *The American Boy's Book of Sports and Games*, 1864, p. 32, one of the 'best known' rhymes ends:

> O-U-T — spells out,
> With the old dish-clout —
> Out, boys, out!

10. At the beginning of the century this was, in the slang of the time,

> If you do not want to play
> You can 'sling your hook' away.
> *Rymour Club*, vol. i, 1911, p. 237, and *London Street Games*, 1916, p. 63.

11. In other versions of this encounter the aggrieved party is said to be 'Piggy', 'Peggy', 'Polly', 'Tommy', or 'Teddy'. The rhyme apparently stems from an old Scots ditty 'Pussy at the fireside suppin' up brose'. See our *Puffin Book of Nursery Rhymes*, 1963, p. 140.

12. In Lancashire:

> Ip, dip, pen and ink,
> Who made that great big stink?
> I believe it was you.
> You shall have it for your supper
> On a piece of bread and butter.
> O-U-T spells out.

13. The saying 'Every man who has no hair may lawfully wear a wig' appears in *Peter Prim's Pride, or Proverbs, that will suit the Young or the Old*, 1810.

14. See *Midwest Folklore*, Winter 1951, p. 255. Compare:

> Engine number nine;
> Ring the bell when it's time.

O-U-T spells out goes he,
Into the middle of the dark blue sea.
Pennsylvania, Bolton, 1888, no. 709

Engine, engine, number nine,
Running on Chicago line;
When she's polished, she will shine.
Engine, engine, number nine.
North Carolina Folklore, vol. i, 1952, p. 168, from 1925

15. Compare:

Ra, ra, chuckeree, chuckeree,

Ony, pony,

Ningy, ningy, na,

Addy, caddy, westce,

Anty, poo,

Chutipan, chutipan,

China, chu.
Fraserburgh, Gregor, 1891, p. 30

Rye, chy, chookereye, chookereye,

Choo, choo, ronee, ponee,

Icky, picky, nigh,

Caddy, paddy, vester,

Canlee, poo.

Itty pau, jutty pau,

Chinee Jew.
Pennsylvania, 'Journal of American Folklore', vol. x, 1897, p. 321

16. A reader's contribution to *John O'London's*, 14 April 1950. An almost identical rhyme from New Town, Tasmania, appears in the *Journal of American Folklore*, vol. x, 1897, p. 319; and another similar has been sent us by Dr Ian Turner, emanating from a Tasmanian born 1853.

17. The score was still being used by boys in Yorkshire in the 1940s, when a 12-year-old reported that when he counted out he said: 'Ya, ta, tethera, pethera, pip, slata, lata, covera, dovera, dick' (*Daily Mirror*, 22 May 1948, p. 7).

18. Respectively from A. E. Pease, *Dictionary of North Riding Dialect*, 1928, p. 164 (a particularly eccentric score); Bolton, 1888, p. 121; a correspondent who had it from her Welsh grandmother, who said it was learnt from soldiers disabled in the Napoleonic wars; A. J. Ellis, *Transactions of the Philological Society*, 1878, p. 357, 'a boy's school method of "counting out" '. For further examples and references, see A. L. J. Gosset, *Shepherds of Britain*, 1911 (article by Skeat); Melius de Villiers, *The Numeral Words: Their Origin, Meaning, History and Lesson*, 1923; *Notes and Queries*, vol. clxii, 1932, pp. 332, 373, and 411–12; and Michael V. Barry, *Transactions of the Yorkshire Dialect Society*, 1967, pp. 21–31. Some shepherds' counts appear to belong to a different tradition. The following is quoted in *Word-Lore*, vol. i, 1926, p. 148, as usual

among Sussex shepherds, the sheep being counted in couples: 'Onetherum, twotherum, cocktherum, qutherum, setherum, shatherum, wineberry, wigtail, tarrydiddle, den.' The formula, at Lewes, was said to be 'Egdum, pigdum, fifer, sizer, cockerum, corum, withecum, taddle, teedle, ten.'

19. In these earlier versions there is a word at each line-end giving a natural four beats that has often been dropped in the modern English rhyme, so that the third measure has to be stretched to make two beats by accenting the terminal *ar*. This possibly illustrates the ease with which a numeral can be dropped if a digital score is becoming accommodated to counting-out.

20. The same stipulation is made in Austria, where Carinthian children say:

> Mein Vata geiht ins Wirtshaus,
> Was for House hat er oaun?

The player pointed at, names a colour.

> Hast du eine solche Farbe an dir,
> So zoag s' mir.

If the girl can show she is wearing that colour she is out.

21. This rule keeps being expounded in the playground, as if it had just been invented. Yet the necessity for it has been recognized for generations. In *Games and Sports for Young Boys*, 1859, p. 1, it was laid down: 'When Touch succeeds in touching another, he cries "Feign double-touch!" which signifies that the player so touched must not touch the player who touched him, until he has chased somebody else.' That is to say (in contemporary parlance): 'The one he tiggies tries to tig one of the others but he can't tiggy the one what tug him' (Boy, 14, Dovenby). The same rule holds on the Continent. In France the chaser 'ne peut reprendre son père'. In Berlin children cry 'Widerschlach gildet nich' or 'Widerschlach is Katzendreck!'

22. It is worth noting that the juvenile preterites 'tug' and 'tuck', which are sometimes cited as modern examples of 'lazy' speech are at least as old as their oldest critic. 'Any player "tug" before his return "home" becomes the toucher' was reported from Holderness, Yorkshire, in 1884 (*Notes and Queries*, 6th ser., vol. x, p. 266). 'I was the fust in the gaime to be tuck', was recorded in south Staffordshire in 1905 (*EDD*, vol. vi, p. 134). And the reinforced preterites 'tugged', 'tuggen', and 'tucked', are also of long standing. Robert Chambers describing 'King and Queen of Cantelon' in 1842 said that when a boy was caught 'the runner places his hand upon their heads, when they are said to be *taned*' — not *ta'en*, for taken, as would be expected (*Popular Rhymes of Scotland*, 2nd ed., p. 63).

23. This has long been so in North America. The 'tagger' and the game of 'tag' were reported from Philadelphia in *Notes and Queries*, 1st ser., vol. xi, 1855, p. 113.

24. We kept being struck, when we were in Guernsey, by the affinity the Guernsey lore had with that of Yorkshire and Lancashire. Children not only spoke of 'tigging'

each other, and played 'Tig', 'Ball Tig', 'Chain Tig', 'Four Den Tig', and other games with northern names, they even celebrated Mischief Night on 4 November as do their northern contemporaries (see *The Lore and Language of Schoolchildren*, pp. 276–80). It transpired that when in 1940 about 5,000 children, virtually the whole schoolchild population, were evacuated, it was to the north of England that the majority were sent, and remained for the rest of the war. Afterwards, when they returned home, they naturally played the games and used the language they had become familiar with in Britain. Today, unconsciously, children in Guernsey are bearing witness to the northern hospitality given their predecessors years before they were born.

25. Lurgi came to Britain in reality, on 24 October 1958, in the shape of the Lurgi High-Pressure Coal Gasification Plant at Westfield in Fife. This name had been derived from the middle of the first word of Metallurgische Gesellschaft AG, a company established in 1897, the predecessor of the present-day owner of the Lurgi companies, Metallgesellschaft AG of Frankfurt-am-Main.

26. In recent years, possibly under the influence of this game, children on the way to school have become victims of an absurd game or superstition that they must be 'off-ground' when a car passes. The consequent dodging on to doorsteps and hedgebanks when a car is seen approaching assists neither their own progress nor the serenity of the driver.

27. Compare the fancy names given to the game by those in charge of children: 'Cat and Sparrow', 'Dog and Rabbit', 'Fox and Rabbit'. Children on their own are not so childish.

28. *Causey*, causeway or pavement. Similar games are 'Hopping on my Granny's Causey', *Games of Argyleshire*, 1901, p. 134; 'Mannie on the Pavement' in Aberdeen, *Traditional Games*, vol. ii, 1898, p. 443; and 'Padrone marciapiede' played by children in Rome (*Giochi*, 1967, p. 305).

29. Cf. J. H. Vaux, *Vocabulary of the Flash Language*, 1812, 'Nash, to go away from, or quit, any place or company; speaking of a person who is gone, they say, he is nash'd or Mr Nash is concerned'. See also *Lore and Language of Schoolchildren*, p. 373, and, purely for fun, Ogden Nash, *Everyone but Thee and Me*, 1963, p. 155.

30. Occasionally the last person caught is the chaser in the next game, but this means that the one who has played best in the last game gets the least popular part in the next one, and this is not usually considered fair.

31. This name seems to have been current for some years. A speaker, quoted in *English Dance and Song*, summer 1967, p. 40, knew it in 'barrel organ days'; and Gomme, 1898, gives 'Sticky Toffey' as the name of a game (undescribed) played by schoolchildren in Hoxton, London, N1.

32. F. C. Husenbeth, 1856, p. 107. In Whitland, Carmarthenshire, the name is 'Cocks-a-morning'.

33. The pacifist Joshua Rowntree is on record as saying that when he was a boy at the

Friends' School, Bootham, York, about 1854, 'Stag-a-rag was one of the best playground games' — S. E. Robson, *Joshua Rowntree*, 1916, p. 25. Northall in his *Warwickshire Word-Book*, 1896, has the game 'Stag-alone-y' with the signature verse 'Stag-alone-y, My long pony, Kick the bucket over'.

34. See S. Baring-Gould, *Red Spider*, 1887, ch. xxiv; *Transactions of the Devonshire Association*, vol. lxxxiii, 1951, p. 77; *Folk-Lore*, vol. lxiii, 1952, pp. 102–9.

35. This warning cry recalls the chant of the hideous boy 'Deputy' in *Edwin Drood*, 1870:

> 'Widdy widdy wen!
> I - ket - ches - Im - out - ar - ter - ten,
> Widdy widdy wy!
> Then - E - don't - go - then - I - shy,
> Widdy Widdy Wake - cock warning!'

36. Cf. 'Stag' still played at Rushmere St Andrew, only some five miles from Woodbridge.

37. Children and teachers alike often regard the game as being special to their school, as well they might from the absence of literature on the subject. Norman Douglas in *London Street Games*, 1916, p. 5, mentions a ball game called 'King' which may or may not be this game; and Sutton-Smith in *The Games of New Zealand Children*, 1959, p. 150, gives a brief account of 'Kingy' as played in Wellington South.

38. It is perhaps pertinent that in parts of Glasgow today children initiate a game of hide-and-seek with the cry:

> Green lady, green lady, come doon for thy tea,
> Thy tea is a' ready an' waiting for thee — Coo-ee!

39. The name 'Stick in the Mud' is listed in *London Street Games*, 1916, p. 32.

40. 'Belly Blind' or 'Billy Blind' may originally have been a form of night time buff or 'Blind Tiggy'. Thus in Henryson's *Fabillis of Esope, c.* 1450, 77:

> Thou playes belly blind,
> Wee seeke all night, but nothing can wee finde.

41. Thus Lucetta, in *The Two Gentlemen of Verona* (I. ii), counselling Julia to fall in love, admits 'Indeede I bid the base for Protheus'; and in *Venus and Adonis* (stanza 51) the wonder horse is thought so fleet of foot he would 'bid the wind a base'.

42. In the eighteenth century as well as the nineteenth, the following was apparently often to be heard in the playgrounds of Edinburgh 'addressed to the secreted personage at Hidee':

> Keep in, keep in, wherever you be,
> The greedy gled's seeking ye.

Blackwood's Magazine, August 1821, p. 37

43. Although now so ordinary, the cry 'Cooee' is of recent date in England, coming from Australia where it was a signal used by the aborigines. Peter Cunningham in *Two Years in New South Wales*, vol. ii, 1827, p. 23, recorded: 'In calling to each other at a distance, the natives make use of the word *Coo-ee*, as we do the word *Hollo* ... [It has] become of general use throughout the colony; and a newcomer, in desiring an individual to call another back, soon learns to say "*Coo-ee* to him" instead of Hollo to him' (*OED*). It will be recalled that Sherlock Holmes in 'The Boscombe Valley Mystery' (1891) could presume a man to have come from Australia because he called 'Cooee'.

44. Similarly in Oldham, about 1930, as recalled by a correspondent, the player asked: 'Where do I go?' — 'How many times?' — 'Eyes closed or open?' — 'Stockings up or down?' — 'Running or walking?' whereafter he might say, 'Well go yourself because it wasn't me.'

45. The seeker's cry and actions vary with local custom. In Langholm he places his foot on the tin, screaming 'Bob-e-tee-bob!' In Wolverhampton he raps the tin on the ground, calling out 'Tin can nerky, one, two, three'. In Glastonbury he 'daps' the tin three times, crying 'Dap, dap, dap'. In Dundee he 'dunts' it ten times, but always counting in threes, 'One-two-three, one-two-three, one-two-three, one'.

46. *Cog* is an old northern term for a hollow, wooden vessel for holding milk or other liquid. Thus Aphra Behn, *Widow Ranter*, 1690, 1. i, 'Come, Jack, I'll give thee a cogue of brandy for old acquaintance' (*OED*).

47. Likewise in Texas, when children are playing 'Release', 'the capture is made by touching a player three times on the back' (Paul G. Brewster, *American Nonsinging Games*, 1953, p. 60).

Children's Games in Street and Playground

Volume 2

Hunting, Racing, Duelling, Exerting, Daring,
Guessing, Acting, Pretending.

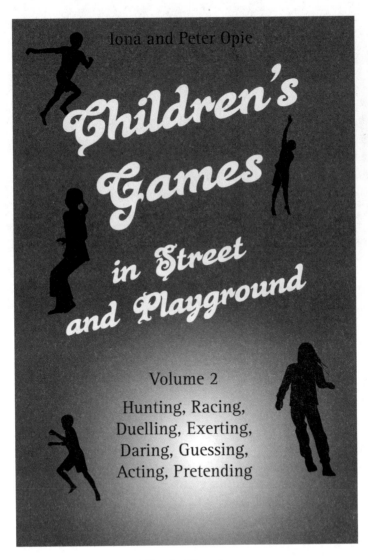

Iona and Peter Opie

Children's Games in Street and Playground

Volume 2

Hunting, Racing,
Duelling, Exerting,
Daring, Guessing,
Acting, Pretending

Floris Books